THE FRENCH NATION

FROM NAPOLEON TO PÉTAIN

1814–1940

Books *by* D. W. BROGAN

GOVERNMENT OF THE PEOPLE

ABRAHAM LINCOLN

FRANCE UNDER THE REPUBLIC

POLITICS AND LAW IN THE UNITED STATES

THE ENGLISH PEOPLE

THE AMERICAN CHARACTER

THE FREE STATE

FRENCH PERSONALITIES AND PROBLEMS

AMERICAN THEMES

THE PRICE OF REVOLUTION

POLITICS IN AMERICA

THE FRENCH NATION

THE FRENCH NATION

FROM NAPOLEON TO PÉTAIN

1814–1940

BY

D. W. BROGAN

denis william

'. . . Incedis per ignis
Suppositos cineri doloso'

HARPER & BROTHERS PUBLISHERS

NEW YORK

FOR
DARSIE
AND
CECILIA GILLIE

CONTENTS

I

THE RESTORATION

I

ON April 20, 1814, Napoleon, so lately 'by the Grace of God and the national will' Emperor of the French, bade farewell in the courtyard of the Palace of Fontainebleau to his Old Guard. Less than two years before, his armies had been in Moscow and in Madrid; Rome, Hamburg, Amsterdam, Ragusa had been cities of the 'French Empire'. Now his domain was 'shrunk to this little measure', the island of Elba. On the French throne, he was replaced by the brother of Louis XVI, the Comte de Provence, who, by taking the title of Louis XVIII, asserted that his nephew, the Dauphin, who had died in the Temple in 1795, had succeeded Louis XVI as 'Louis XVII'. It was a solution to a problem that had perplexed the Allies since they had begun to think it first possible and then desirable to overthrow Napoleon, an idea that the Emperor's intransigence imposed on the Allied sovereigns in the spring of 1814.

It was obvious that no one could replace Napoleon. It was desirable that no one should. But France had to be made reasonably content, the war of more than twenty years ended. Yet if this was the end, there was no agreement on the means. The most obvious solution, the one that least broke legal and emotional continuity, was the recognition of the King of Rome as his father's successor with the Empress Marie Louise as Regent. To that solution loyal Imperialists and, probably, the mass of the exhausted and bewildered French people would have turned with fatalistic relief. But the Emperor of Russia and the King of Prussia were more affected by hostility to a Hapsburg regency than the Emperor of Austria or his Minister, Metternich, was attracted by it. Abandoning Paris by Napoleon's orders, the Empress and her Ministers at Tours were not on the spot when the final decisions were hastily made. 'The absent are always wrong', the French proverb puts it. The way was open for the partisans of the Bourbons: the genuine believers in the Royal cause and the more important body of great Imperial officials who wished to leave the sinking ship but wished to be sure of a welcome on any new bark that might be launched. Chief of these prudent liquidators of the wrecked Empire was Talleyrand, and he had to persuade the Allied Sovereigns that a regency under Marie Louise was impossible or unnecessary, and that a Bourbon restoration was desirable and feasible. The first was made easy when the argument that the Army would never desert Napoleon was proved false by Marshal Marmont's refusal to continue the defence of Paris: the rank-and-file was still loyal; but the Marshals were weary of war. The second was much more difficult for, in a France looking for repose under some estab-lished authority, few sought it in the exiled Bourbons.

Part of the history of France, for the next fifteen years, was an illusory parallel with England, with the restoration of Charles II. But while in 1660 the restoration of the rightful King was the obvious solution, desired by the mass of the English people, there was no such turning to the exiled heir of the House of France in 1814. To millions of Frenchmen and Frenchwomen he was hardly even a name. The gap between the generations, between Royalist fathers and Bona-partist or Republican sons, was marked in families like those of Henri Beyle and Pierre-Jean Béranger. There were Royalist shopkeepers like César Birotteau who remembered how they had risen for the good cause in Vendémiaire to be dispersed by the whiff of grapeshot of young General Bonaparte. But Vendémiaire was nearly twenty years in the past and what twenty years!

In the last years of the Empire, Napoleon had turned more and more to the nobility, returned from exile or obscurity, to provide him with mayors and local councillors. He feared old Jacobins like M. Grandet, Mayor of Saumur, and replaced them where he could. All over France, there were Royalists, by sentiment, serving the Emperor. But except in a few districts like Languedoc and La Vendée there was no widespread Royalist faith, and even there the figures of the exiled Princes were dim indeed. Few young members of Royalist families knew anything of the younger Princes since Napoleon had the Duc d'Enghien shot in 1804. Few knew that the only surviving child of Louis XVI had married her cousin, the Duc d'Angoulême, son of the dead King's youngest brother. Few knew that the royal couple were childless. More was known of brothers of Louis XVI, the Comte de Provence and the Comte d'Artois, but neither was an inspiring figure. There were Royalist secret societies, Royalist conspiracies, but there was, as the advancing Allies noted, no Royalist movement. Bordeaux had, indeed, declared for the Bourbons on March 12: not only had the great port been ruined by the Empire's wars, but its Mayor, Lynch, had been won over by an agent of the secret Royalist society, 'Chevaliers de la Foi', Louis de Gobineau. Yet until it was certain that Napoleon would not return, formal loyalty to the Emperor was observed, and until the Allied Sovereigns decided whom they would recognize, the mass of the people waited.

It was the adroit Talleyrand and great Imperial officials like Pasquier and Chabrol, who gave the Allies the illusion that Paris welcomed the Bourbons and induced the Imperial Senate to depose Napoleon and offer the crown, on conditions, to the Comte de Provence. He was to accept a Constitution, very like the existing Imperial Constitution, and most important of the conditions was the guaranteeing to the Senators of their jobs, safety, and salaries. The venality of the Senators destroyed what bargaining power they had. They were not statesmen with a country, but political profiteers with their skins and their salaries to save. And however mixed the motives of Marshal Marmont, he was now a soldier whose principles and self-interest ran conveniently together. He was not George Monk in 1660; he was, at best, John Churchill in 1688.

The exiled Princes had watched the fall of the Empire with mounting hope. But the failure of all attempts to evoke a spontaneous Royalist movement had disconcerted them. The Comte d'Artois accepted from the Senate the office of 'Lieutenant-General of the Kingdom', rashly promised the abolition of conscription and of the most unpopular Imperial taxes, and set about creating his own Royalist chain of command beside that of the Provisional Government headed by Talleyrand and the Imperial administration. All depended on the decisions to be made by the Comte de Provence, Louis XVIII. The new King was fat, lame, gouty, impotent. He was also lazy, selfish, intelligent, a Voltairian, with belief in the indefeasible rights of the King of France and Navarre as a substitute for religion. He evaded the claim of the Senate to confer the crown on him;

he *was* King and, as King, he freely granted to his subjects a Charter.

The Charter soon acquired an importance that it was not designed to have. It organized a kind of constitutional monarchy on the English model but, more important at the moment, it guaranteed, or professed to guarantee, internal peace. It was, as M. Bertier de Sauvigny has aptly put it, a new Edict of Nantes. There was to be religious freedom; there was to be equality before the law; the sales of property confiscated under the Revolution were not to be questioned. The positive conquests of the Revolution were to be preserved. It was not to be a restoration of the old regime; it was to be something like the Consulate, with a much greater element of political liberty allowed for than had been permitted by General Bonaparte. All initiative in legislation was formally left to the King who appointed all Ministers and exercised all executive power. But the revenue had to be voted annually; all new laws required the assent of the Houses of Peers and Deputies who could petition freely on all subjects. It was a sketch of a system of government which experience would alter and develop in detail. For its successful growth, it needed peace, tact, mutual forbearance, a sense of realities in all groups who would have to work it. It asked too much of the France of 1814.

II

First of all, that France was not converted to Royalism or even away from Bonapartism or Jacobinism or from what was now beginning to be called 'Liberalism'. France was, above all, tired. Tired, not only by the recent catastrophes of defeat and invasion, but tired by the incessant wars of the Revolution and the Empire, by the repeated political convulsions, even by minor earthquakes that showed how thin was the coat of ashes over the fires on which all rulers of France must walk. As Barbier was to put it, France

> 'demanda grace à son cavalier corse
> Mais, bourreau, tu n'écoutas pas'.

She asked the same of her new rulers who should have made it their first duty to ask no awkward questions, to wound no powerful sentiments or interests. The lazy King saw some of this truth; his, unfortunately, more active brother did not. Thus the tricolour, worshipped by the army in defeat as much as in twenty years of victory, was replaced by the white flag with the fleur-de-lis, the banner of those Frenchmen who had fought against their country. The King entered Paris in the same carriage as the old, debilitated and nearly demented Prince de Condé, commander of that army of émigrés against whom the 'Marseillaise' had been written. So they passed under the sullen eyes of the Old Guard. Attempts to win support for the Royal cause, such as the lavish distribution of the emblems of the new 'Order of the Lilies', evoked only scorn from recipients like the intelligent Bonapartist schoolboy, Honoré Balzac, not yet noble or Royalist. With the King came back the most incorrigible of the émigrés, those who had not taken advantage of the various amnesties, who, in consequence, knew least of the strange new world they were entering. They brought with them all the prejudices of the old Court, so ruinous to the crown in 1789; so ruinous in 1814. The slow amalgamation of the old and new ruling classes that Napoleon had aimed at was suddenly stopped. The Baron d'Haussez (not of the oldest nobility himself, it must be admitted) noted how, suddenly, the old, offensive, verbal distinctions of rank were restored, the *real* gentlemen, the men of good family, were marked off again, and social resentments, that had burst into flame in 1789, were rekindled.

The Charter had recognized the Imperial nobility; but the old nobles, intoxicated by the dream of a revival of the old Court, had no more use for the Napoleonic titles than the nobles of Louis XIV had had for the title of 'mamamouchi' conferred on M. Jourdain. The wife of Marshal Ney was the daughter of a Woman of the Bedchamber of Marie Antoinette; but the Duchesse d'Angoulême showed no regard for the child of her mother's devoted servant. For her, the Princesse de la Moskowa was simply Mademoiselle Aiguié. The Marshal-Prince had often to console his weeping wife.

Worse was done. It was most necessary to cut down the Imperial Army, to put thousands of officers on half-pay. It was dangerous, then, to create a new 'King's Household', to revive the old, extravagant companies of guards of the old regime, where every private was an officer, every officer ranking higher than his formal equals in the line. Even the attempts to wed the old order to the new were not happy. Companies were given to Berthier, Prince de Wagram, and to Marmont, Duc de Raguse. But the Paris public christened the 'Compagnie de Wagram' the 'Company of Peter', and the 'Compagnie de Raguse' the 'Company of Judas'.

These mistakes were made when the first relief at the end of the war was turning to disgust at the price of peace. True, the conditions of the Peace of Paris of 1814 were not really onerous. France was hopelessly defeated, yet she was allowed to keep not only the frontiers of 1792, but some favourable modifications of them. She paid no indemnity and even kept the plundered works of art that made the Louvre the delight of the tourists who now poured in again. There was no armed occupation; no control of the new Government. But the shock of the change from the Imperial position of 1812 to the drab realities of 1814 was hard to be borne. Months after Napoleon had abdicated, the garrisons of the great German and Italian fortresses were streaming back, undefeated, into France. So were the officials, judges, tax inspectors, prefects, administrators of the public domains who had ruled for the Emperor the Rhineland, Italy, Dalmatia, the Netherlands. King Joseph had already brought back General Hugo from Spain, and a leader of the French party there, the Conde de Montijo, had been among the last to defend, in arms, the authority of the Empress-Regent Marie Louise whom his unborn daughter was to succeed as Empress of the French.

Many of the victims of the collapse had no claims on the new order. Others (like the Aga of the Mamelouks whom Bonaparte had brought back from Egypt) still drew pensions. Others, like 10,000 officers of the Imperial Army, were put on half-pay. These were necessities of a new and economically minded Government. It was not a necessity, but a natural sense of loyalty that spent much of the money thus saved on the faithful who had supported the Royal cause in exile, often in the armies of the enemies of France. So the sullen soldiers of Napoleon saw the officers they had known sent into retirement and officers whom they had encountered, if at all, as serving the King of Prussia, given high rank. The Old Guard, neither dissolved nor trusted, exiled from Paris, remembered. So did thousands of young serving officers to whom the collapse of 1814 meant the end of quick promotion, the end of dazzling dreams of a bâton, perhaps even a throne.

But these dreams still haunted few. The Army, like the nation, was more sulky than revolutionary or belligerent. No promise of the Royal Government had been more popular than the abolition of conscription, the ending of that 'blood tax' (to use a phrase not yet coined) which, more than anything else, had alienated the French people from the Emperor. He might talk of his annual contingent of conscripts 'to spend'; it had been the more and more detestable luxury of a monarch more extravagant than Louis XIV.

In the last years of the Empire, resistance to the blood tax took the form of widespread desertion and of evasion. In some regions, notably in the Massif Central, sympathy was nearly universally on the side of the recalcitrants. After the open breach between the Pope and the Emperor, the clergy usually sided with the refractory peasants. But even in the towns, it was less and less a discreditable thing to avoid military service. The police system of the Empire was overstrained pursuing the draft-dodgers. Luckily for the future patriotic poet, Béranger, he was prematurely bald and made a point of raising his hat to all officers of the law who thus did not suspect him of being within the dangerous age groups. There was resentment at defeat, at the sudden ending of military careers, at the insult to the Army involved in the change of flags and in the promotion of the émigrés. But there was no burning spirit of revenge, as yet. 'It's a long way to Carcassonne', said the dying soldier on the retreat from Moscow. Few, in 1814, wanted to resume that journey.

The French, so long silenced, now indulged in the joys of controversy and self-exaltation. Chateaubriand could believe that his pamphlet, *De Buonaparte, des Bourbons*, had done more than anything else to restore the rightful King. Under the Imperial censorship, as Albert Thibaudet was to put it, every great writer was exiled or silenced except the Emperor. The Paris salons were now full of constitution- and phrase-makers. The Charter was ambiguous and little was known of the English system on which it was supposed to be modelled. The circle round Madame de Staël professed to know what the English Constitution was and what the French should be.

Her lover, Benjamin Constant, was the 'professor of political science' of the group; her son-in-law, the young Duc de Broglie, was consciously training himself to be a great Whig noble. The dogmatic Royalists were beginning to use and abuse Burke as a weapon against *any* written Constitution. The Press law subjected periodicals of less than twenty sheets to censorship, but this was evaded by irregular publication and by just exceeding the number of pages that distinguished a periodical or a pamphlet from a book. In Paris and in the great provincial cities, the noise of conversation, even of oratory, was almost as loud as in 1788–89.

Not much of this discussion found an echo in the two Houses. The 'Chamber of Deputies' was the old Imperial legislative body, one of the most docile of Parliaments. It had protested against the war-making policy of the Emperor in the last months of the Empire and had, by its sudden dismissal, acquired some of the popularity that accrued, in similar circumstances, to the *Parlements* of the old regime; but its past kept it from having an instructive or influential present. Even the complete control over the budget which it acquired was a royal gift, not the answer to any urgent demands of the Chamber of Deputies.

The 'Chamber of Peers' suffered from two handicaps. The first was temporary, the fact that its nucleus was the venal Imperial Senate. The second was permanent: it was an imitation of the English House of Lords in a country where such an institution was profoundly unnatural. Nothing could have been less in the spirit of Burke than this preposterous institution. There had been a nobility in France; there had never, in the English sense, been a peerage. The nobility had included scores of thousands of Frenchmen, some of whom were Dukes and millionaires; some of whom were mere peasants with few privileges to console them for their poverty. These privileges the Charter specifically refused to restore. But instead, a number of Frenchmen, not notably eminent for virtue, birth, or public favour, were made into an hereditary caste. The Charter had aimed at uniting the old and the new nobility, but the Peers of the Restoration were a Napoleonic institution. They were rigorously ranked not by family, but by title. Every Baron (even a Baron de Charlus) was to rank below every Viscount. At the top were Princes who outranked Dukes (which would have horrified the Duc de Saint-Simon). The Napoleonic nobility had been a 'nobility of service' like the old Russian nobility. Its titles conferred no political power; power was a function of official rank. But the new peers were independent of the King; their heirs were even more so. And this peerage not only had no deep traditional roots (a Duc de Luynes, as was noted, was not a peer); it had not an adequate economic weight. The criteria that were to be laid down for eligibility showed that. A Duke had to be able to settle an income of £1,200 on his son and heir; a Baron £400. This was a long call from the England of the Dukes of Bedford and Devonshire, where the younger Pitt had said that any man who had £10,000 a year was entitled to a peerage. The old French nobility, even the nobility of the Court, had never been rich on this scale. It had a claim on the common property of the higher nobility, the royal bounty. And that was now limited by a civil list, by an annual budget. With all the will in the world, even a less selfish monarch than Louis XVIII could not have satisfied the Royalists. He could only manage to alienate the Imperialists and Republicans.

The nobility, which the King could not satisfy, was not uniformly poor. Some families had not emigrated; the confiscated lands of others were bought in, collusively, by friends. There had been, since the general admission of the émigrés, in 1801, a steady flow of returning exiles. Sons and daughters of great or distinguished families, Montesquiou, Ségur, Caulaincourt, had served the Emperor. Many more had re-established their local position and had become *maires* where they had been *seigneurs*. But there were many genuinely impoverished; others who exaggerated the losses they had suffered. In any case, a great part of the revenues of the nobility had come from their monopoly of great offices in Church and State. There were no great sees or rich abbeys to be given away now. No career like that of Loménie de Brienne, still less no scandalous careers like those of Dillon and Rohan were now possible. Nor was it possible to reserve for the nobility great honorific offices, leaving the hard work and smaller pay to the bourgeois subordinates.

True, the traditions of the old Court died hard. The Duc de Blacas, the King's favourite whose personal position made him the nearest thing to a Prime Minister that the new system had, was genuinely shocked when it was suggested that he, a great household officer, should condescend to be a Minister. (The prejudice died hard. When a La Rochefoucauld, the Duc de Doudeauville, consented to become Minister of Posts, a wit asked, 'Who will now become Duc de Doudeauville?') When all royal favour was allowed for, the nobles had now to live on their private fortunes, that is, on the revenue of their lands. They still owned a great deal. Most landed proprietors were not nobles; that had been true in 1789. Most great proprietors were nobles. But they no longer drew additional income from the Court and they no longer collected the feudal dues, voted away in theory on August 4, 1789, and really abolished by the Convention in 1793. On the other hand, what they owned, they owned more completely than in 1789; there were no legal and few customary restrictions on their naked right as owners.

Yet, in most regions, they had not recovered all that they had lost. Beside them were the bourgeois landlords who had done well out of the Revolution. They were as a rule townsmen, not farming their own lands, hard with their tenants and resented by them for the very fact that their ownership was new. In nearly every parish, there was a new fortune based on skilful investment in 'national properties', confiscated in 1790 from the Church, in 1793 from the nobles. Church property was less a source of discord than family property. France was full of Jack Horners who had pulled out magnificent plums and whose good fortune had not been mellowed by time. But it was in the villages where the old and new owners dwelt side by side, where all the world knew the source of the new wealth, where memories of many a shady affair were living, that the bitterness of the now exultant nobles and the alarm of the new owners were greatest. It was one of Balzac's favourite themes, but he only reported, he did not invent. His Comte de Gondreville had many exemplars. Few there were in Paris who did not know that the vast fortune of Comte Roy had been founded on the liquidation of the Bouillon estates. His daughters played the part allotted by the public opinion of Arcis to Cécile Beauvisage: they married into the old nobility.

It was a natural and healthy fusion, such as had made the fortune of the English nobility and of England; but it was too slow a way of undoing the wrongs of the Revolution for the zealots who, ignoring the King and his Ministers, followed the lead given by the heir-apparent, the Comte d'Artois, from the Pavillon de Marsan in the Tuileries.

Artois, unlike his brother, had kept much of the charm that had made him the Don Juan or at any rate the Almaviva of Versailles. He was an admirable horseman and had an easy charm that concealed, for a short time, the fact that from being a frivolous and dissolute young man, he had become a frivolous and pious old man. He loathed the Charter; he loathed the Revolution. He despised the bourgeois Deputies and Peers, even the soldier Dukes and Princes of the Empire. His timid, graceless, impotent eldest son, the Duc d'Angoulême, shared his father's opinions, and his feeble character, which had its good sides, was dominated by his wife's ('the only man of the family', as Napoleon was to say). She forgave neither the Revolution nor the wicked and perjured people that had murdered her father, mother, and aunt. And the younger son, the Duc de Berry, was ugly, vulgar, coarse and open in his low pleasures which had one advantage: they brought him into touch with part of the people. He had enough sense, as he was to show, to resent the fact that the royal family lived in a kind of ghetto, unlike their more adroit kinsman, the Duc d'Orléans. For Orléans did not forget that he had fought for the Republic under the tricolour and he was not allowed to forget that his father, Philippe Égalité, had been a regicide. Both facts commended him to some of the men who had made the Restoration and who began to doubt its durability. If Louis XVIII was Charles II, too evidently Artois was James II and—the Duc d'Orléans was, would be, William III.

For speculation on the stability of the regime was general. The Allies noted with alarm the absence of any real Government. There was no Cabinet; only Ministers working separately with the King, a system that it would have required an industrious monarch like Louis XIV to make tolerable. Power fell into the hands of formally minor officials, trained under the usurper. The contrast with Bonaparte struck even the most loyal. But the King, the Princes, the Ministers maintained an extraordinary complacency. The ablest of them, Talleyrand, was off in Vienna displaying his diplomatic versatility, getting Louis XVIII secretly accepted by England and Austria as an ally against Russia and Prussia, preventing the transfer of the King's cousin, the King of Saxony, so loyal to Napoleon, to the Rhineland. As a result, instead of a weak, Catholic, Francophile dynasty on the French border, Louis XVIII had the King of Prussia.

But it was not to France that anxious eyes were turned; it was to Italy. There, the winter of 1814–15 was one of suspense. Nowhere, except in Poland, had the French defeat been more bitterly resented. Austrians in Milan, Piedmontese in Genoa, Hapsburgs in Tuscany, the Pope in the Romagna, all the conquests of Bonaparte, all the achievements of the King of Italy were undone. Only in Naples did King Joachim Murat and his Queen, Caroline Bonaparte, cling uneasily to the throne they had saved by betraying Napoleon. All they had was the doubtful loyalty of Metternich to set off against the hostility of England and the hatred of Louis XVIII. King Joachim tried to placate the victors, innocently thinking that, by lavishly entertaining the Princess of Wales, he would endear himself to the Prince Regent! But he also intrigued with the Italian 'Liberals'— and over the water in Elba the Emperor learned every day of the mounting disgust that France felt for the Bourbons. He heard, too, rumours that he was to be taken from his island kingdom and sent to some much more remote spot. He might not be allowed to play the role of a Ulysses retired from the wars. In France, conspiracies grew. A regiment of cavalry in the north mutinied, threw away the white cockades; but there was no general movement. The mutineers surrendered on March 5, and that day the King learned that the Corsican Ogre had landed near Fréjus on March 1.

III

The adventure which a Royalist official was soon to christen 'the Hundred Days' was one of the most reckless and disastrous gambles of modern history. Compared with it, the Forty-Five was almost defensible. In March 1815, the alliance against France was visibly dissolving; the resentment against the Vienna settlements daily increasing, not only in France, but all over Europe. The monarchs assembled in Vienna were busy dissipating the goodwill they had acquired as symbols of nationality. In England, opinion, as usual, was turning away from her recent allies. But the armies of the victorious powers were neither disbanded nor withdrawn; the work of disillusionment was not complete. The enemies of the Bourbons and of the restored old order had everything to gain by waiting. The Emperor alone had, possibly, something to lose, his convenient base in Elba. But his hand was being daily improved, and most certainly it was too soon to put all to the touch.

Yet the first results of the desperate throw seemed, to the short-sighted, to justify the risk. As Napoleon had prophesied, 'the eagle with the national colours' had flown 'from church spire to church spire on to the towers of Notre-Dame'. The 'telegraph', the semaphore system that had kept Carnot and Bonaparte in touch with the eastern border and the armies on the Rhine, did not extend to the Mediterranean, and Bonaparte was at Grenoble before Paris knew that he had landed. Everywhere, the troops refused to fire on their old chief. The Comte d'Artois and Marshal Macdonald had to abandon Lyons; at Lons-le-Saulnier, Ney, so full of Royalist zeal a day or two before, abandoned by his troops, went over to Napoleon. The Duc d'Angoulême raised a futile resistance in the Gard; his partisans were easily defeated by zealous Protestants who triumphed savagely; their triumph was to be remembered. In vain, the King and the Comte d'Artois swore to defend the Charter before the Chamber of Deputies. But there was no hope of resistance; the King set off into exile and on the morning of March 20, the Emperor entered Paris amid delirious enthusiasm. The first round was won.

But the game was already lost. The enthusiasm that had greeted the great adventurer as he moved north came from the poor, from the old Jacobins. There were nearly as many cries of 'Down with the priests' (or nobles) as of 'Vive l'Empereur'. He was no longer the Sovereign, he was the chief of a party and of a party that he had increasingly feared and disliked. He refused, so Benjamin Constant was to report, to be 'the Emperor of a *jacquerie*'. And more than Rouget de Lisle took fright when they heard the mob singing the

'Marseillaise'. For the moment, it seemed like '93 come again.
There were 'Federations', orations, proclamations. But the Jacobin
enthusiasm died, died not only because Napoleon refused to organize
it, but because it was more and more completely realized that
Napoleon's return meant war. In vain he had assured the Allies that
he accepted the treaties of 1814. In vain he announced the speedy
arrival of the Empress and the King of Rome. The Allies promptly
declared him an outlaw, and whatever faint hopes of peace he enter-
tained were wrecked by the folly of Murat who attacked the Austrians in a lunatic attempt to unite Italy. Murat was easily defeated,
and the army that defeated him was freed for the invasion of
France. All over Europe, the armies were on the move, returning on
the tracks of 1814. In vain Carnot was made Minister of the Interior.
In vain Davoût, as Minister of War, showed that he was as great an
administrator as a soldier. The country was not ready for another
'93, and Wellington and Blücher were not York and Coburg. Even
the attempt to raise La Vendée for the King merely diverted some
troops from the decisive battle. Few were ready to fight for King or
Emperor with the old fanatical zeal. Everywhere, the Prefects reported resistance to conscription, to taxation. In vain the Emperor
called for the election of a new Chamber of Deputies and for a
plebiscite to ratify the 'Additional Act to the Constitutions of the
Empire'. The vast majority of the electors stayed away. In vain, in a
curious 'Frankish' ceremony, 'the Field of May' that showed the
influence of romanticism, Napoleon acted the part of a constitutional monarch. It recalled to some the Feast of Federations of 1790
where M. de Talleyrand had celebrated mass, incompetently. To
M. Fouché, Minister of Police, it may have recalled Robespierre's
Feast of the Supreme Being. Fouché had had the head of Robespierre; he was again resolved not to go down with the doomed ship.

The Chamber of Deputies, elected under his inspiration, had few
Jacobins but also few Bonapartists. It was full of 'Liberals' of the
school of Madame de Staël. Its figurehead was Lafayette. Macaulay
described it as the most foolish legislative body that ever sat. There
has been much parliamentary folly since, but Macaulay's dictum
may still be right. All now depended on the campaign. On June 18,
1815, Blücher arrived before darkness and the broken Army streamed

back to Paris. The Emperor was advised to dissolve the Chamber
but he was disillusioned, ill, the shadow of what he had been and
France was what he had made it. As La Bruyère wrote, 'There is no
patriotism under a despotic government; others things take its place,
self-interest, glory, the service of the Prince.' None worked for
Napoleon. He abdicated in favour of the King of Rome who was,
for a moment, Napoleon II. The Chamber debated; the Allies hesitated; but Louis XVIII took the road back to Paris. It was the bitter
end of an adventure in which Napoleon had behaved less like a
condottiere, weighing his chances, than like a Prince of the Blood, a
'Son of France'. The dramatic catastrophe of Waterloo, unfortunately, hid from the French people that the nearest parallel to the
Hundred Days was the Fronde.

IV

The Restoration that matters in the history of France was the second.
The first was the preliminary and excuse for the Hundred Days. It
left nothing behind but the memory of a ludicrous failure. The
second marked France for good. If it was untrue that the Bourbons
returned, in 1814, 'in the baggage waggons of the foreigner', it was
true in 1815. That the invaders did not relish giving the returning
King a lift mattered little. Fictions that were plausible in 1814 were
unbelievable in 1815. Louis XVIII was now not called to the throne
of his ancestors by the Senate or by a loyal and repentant people. He
was, at worst, the head of a discredited party, at best a convenience,
with no deeper roots in the country than had the first Hanoverians
in England. And it was as the head of a humiliated and embittered
party that he began his second reign. He remembered the singing of
the 'Marseillaise'; it alarmed him as it had alarmed Napoleon. He
had learned how rootless was the loyalty of the mass of the French
people. Napoleon had stepped back into his old position as easily as
the bees had replaced the lilies, which had replaced the bees, on the
furniture of the Tuileries, which had now more the air of an hotel,
receiving any plausible visitors, than of the old palace of the most

august of dynasties. Good Royalists like Haussez had calmly taken
the oath of allegiance to Napoleon. The bishops had ordered the
prayer 'Domine salvum fac regem' to be replaced by 'Domine
salvum fac imperatorem' in 1815, as they had reversed the process
in 1814. Many of the country clergy had ignored the change, but
that was more because they could express their dislike of and disbelief in the revived Empire with impunity, than because they were
animated by a passionate devotion to the Bourbons.

Louis XVIII had learned something from his second exile. Mere
courtiers like Blacas were got rid of, a Cabinet was formed and the
second Restoration began under the joint guidance of Talleyrand
and Fouché, 'vice supported on the arm of crime'. It was a painful
necessity; but above all the King needed peace, so he needed to convince the Allies that he was worth backing—something of which,
after the Hundred Days, they were naturally sceptical. This time,
however, there could be no question of leaving France to herself.
The invading armies stayed as armies of occupation. There was
plundering and outrage, and every outrage of the 'Allies of Louis
XVIII' was imputed to the Royal Government. Even the British
troops, whose behaviour, on the whole, was admirable, were a
nuisance, for the rank-and-file (and some officers) did not bother to
conceal their admiration for 'Boney' and their contempt for Louis
XVIII. In vain Talleyrand manœuvred; the crime of the Hundred
Days had to be expiated. The fragments of Savoy and the Saar that
had been left to France were taken away. Prussia had much to
revenge and openly coveted Alsace. Yet further frontier rectifications
were avoided, the indemnity was reduced to £28,000,000, the occupation to five years. It was a bitter commentary on the resented peace
of 1814! Not cured of their illusions, many Frenchmen blamed the
Royal Government for disbanding the Imperial Army; but Waterloo
had decided that France would be what the victors wanted it to be.
That the treaty terms were comparatively light was due to England
and Russia, not to any French power of resistance. Louis XVIII
could give his adherence to the vague religio-political manifesto of
the Holy Alliance but, as Sir Winston Churchill was to put it of Italy
in 1943, France had to work her passage. She had also to secure
internal peace.

The revolutionary spirit revealed during the Hundred Days had awakened a counter-revolutionary spirit. The murder of Marshal Brune at Avignon was only the most dramatic episode of the 'white terror'; his body had to be buried in secret. In Languedoc, where there was both more Royalist and more religious feeling, the spirit of the wars of religion was revived. For the Protestants of the Gard, the name of Trestaillon was, for long after, a source of terror, and Trestaillon claimed to be avenging what the Royalists had suffered during the Hundred Days. There was, indeed, the *fons et origo mali*. Bonaparte on St. Helena was casting himself, with great skill, as a martyr. The real martyrs were in France. Chief of them was Marshal Ney. He was tried before the Chamber of Peers; his formal guilt was undoubted, but what was it beside that of the chief witness against him, Bourmont, who had deserted the cause of the King for that of the First Consul, who had gone over to the King in 1814, then to the Emperor in 1815, and had deserted to the enemy just before Waterloo? He was honoured; Ney was shot. Ney was more of a Homeric hero than a great commander. But his posthumous fame grew, and it was remembered that the only peer to vote against his sentence was the Duc de Broglie. It might have been wiser for the King to have pardoned Ney; but it was necessary, so it was thought, to show firmness in face of the suspicious Allies. It was the price of being taken seriously. It was a high price. Executions continued until 1816, culminating in a preposterous rebellion in Dauphiné, which may have been arranged by the police. It was savagely punished; there was fresh blood between the King and his subjects.

It was necessary to purge the administration, the Académie Française, the Army, and that meant that Frenchmen of great eminence were deprived of their posts, honorific or real, and that there were more jobs for the loyalists of old devotion, or for the numerous converts to the new and savage doctrines of the triumphant party that was to be known as 'the Ultras'. For the King had now to deal, for the first time, with a real Parliament. The Chamber of Deputies of 1814 was dissolved and a new Chamber and a new electoral law were created by mere royal fiat. Deputies need only be twenty-five years old, so there was room for youthful zeal. The electoral body numbered less than 80,000 names and less than 50,000 voted, voted under every kind of pressure. The result was a Chamber over-whelmingly Royalist, a 'windfall Chamber', as Louis XVIII put it; he was soon to doubt the quality of his luck.

It had been the claim of all French governments since Thermidor 1794 to 'close the Revolution'. It was the aim of the most vehement of the orators of the new Chamber to undo it. Everything that seemed to suggest the permanence of the conquests of the Revolution was hateful. If the State proposed to sell forests that had once belonged to the Church to pay off some of its most pressing obligations, that was treason towards God, for it made more remote the day when the Church, from being the mere branch of the civil service to which the Concordat of 1801 had reduced it, would be the first Estate of the realm with its own property to replace the meagre salaries doled out by the Government. The treason of 1815 must not only be punished, it must be bloodily punished as an expiation of a national apostasy. Despite the promises of the Charter, the land settlement of the Revolution was again to be put in doubt and the debts of the usurper's government repudiated for the benefit of the loyal servants of the King. These were alarming claims; they alarmed the King, his Ministers, and, more important, the representatives of the Allies, above all the Duke of Wellington who both commanded the army of occupation and was Ambassador to the Most Christian King. To a realist like Wellington, the bloodthirsty rhodomontades of the Chamber were an intolerable nuisance and a danger to the peace of Europe. To the King and to his Prime Minister, Richelieu, they were an obstacle to the restoration of the Kingdom of France to her rightful position among the great monarchies. The Minister had a view of Europe wider than was popular among the fanatics of the Palais Bourbon—or of the Liberal cafés and salons. The Duc de Richelieu was the grandson of the too famous Marshal but he was very unlike that gallant sponsor of *mayonnaise*. He had spent most of his years in exile as a servant of the Tsar; he had created the great port of Odessa and knew what government was. 'He is the French-man who knows most about the Crimea', said Talleyrand. It was not really a handicap. He was above the battle like a medieval *Podestà*, indifferent to money, to the pride of office or power, horrified by the virulence of French political passions which made him regret the

comparative calm of the Euxine. Richelieu had with him in his
policy Élie Decazes, the new favourite of the King. Decazes had replaced Blacas, but he was not a mere favourite. An important official
of the Empire, he also knew what government was, but he owed his
position to the extraordinary hold he had over the King. Even in
France, even among his most bitter enemies, Decazes was not seen
as a new Epernon, a new Cinq-Mars. To the King, he was his
'darling Élie'; to the Royalists, he was the embodiment of that
policy of compromise with the accursed thing that the Chamber had
set itself to make impossible. 'France prefers twenty mistresses to one
favourite.' No doubt, but the favourite was there; the mistresses
were not.

Deceived by their King, the Royalist leaders were forced to make
the most extravagant claims of parliamentary supremacy. Louis
XVIII was given by them hardly more power than Bagehot allowed
Queen Victoria. They were for the King 'in spite of everything'.
Chateaubriand enunciated the pure Whig doctrine and a squire from
Toulouse who had been a sailor and a planter in the Île Bourbon
(now Réunion), Jean-Baptiste de Villèle, showed in the defence of
extreme Royalist doctrines remarkable talents as a debater. That he
had other, more important, talents was yet to be proved.

As the Royalists strove to reduce the King to the level of a 'Peshwa
of the Mahrattas', the defenders of the conquests of the Revolution
were forced to exalt the royal prerogative as the one secure point of
reference, the one guarantee against a new civil war. Their talents
were almost as great as they thought them. They were indeed 'Doctrinaires'. Their chief was Royer-Collard in whom the probity,
severity, basic pessimism of the Jansenists of the generation of the
Abbé de Saint-Cyran were even more obviously incarnated than in
his disciple, Duvergier d'Hauranne. It was the doctrine of the
Doctrinaires that certain questions, too confidently posed and
answered in the recent and dangerous past, were not to be put. As
important as the orators was the brilliant civil servant and historian,
François Guizot. For him, representation was not a right; it was a
device to organize all the legitimate elements of power. This was not
very clear; perhaps it was not meant to be. But for the moment, the
one, valuable instrument of this organization was not the Chamber,

but the King. Wellington, Pozzo di Borgo (the Corsican Ambassador of the Tsar), above all Decazes worked on the King and on the
Prime Minister. The Chamber was suddenly dissolved, less than a
year after its triumphant election. Louis XVIII and Richelieu had
brought off a new 'day of dupes'.

The dissolution was a necessity, but it was an unfortunate necessity. In Paris it was received with applause by the bourgeoisie who
had seen in the 'Ultra' Chamber a threat to liberty—and to solvency,
and the greater part of the national debt was held by Parisians. It
pleased the occupying powers; it made possible the acceptance, at
Aix-la-Chapelle, in 1818, of France as an equal, and brought about
the ending of the occupation before the five years had run out. But
it put the defenders of liberty in the awkward position of being the
defenders of the royal prerogative and it forced the infuriated
Royalists, cheated of their hopes, back into the too familiar way of
silly conspiracy and Court intrigue. All their hopes were now set on
the succession of the Comte d'Artois, no longer commander of the
National Guard, the not very occult leader of the Ultras, but indubit-
ably the heir. And what stirred hope in Ultra, stirred alarm in
Liberal breasts and turned eyes towards the Duc d'Orléans who,
since the King had no children and the Comte d'Artois no male
grandchildren, was, remotely, the heir presumptive.

Then it was unfortunate that the dissolution and the easy victory
of the ministerial candidates showed that, under the Charter, all
depended on the royal will. Henceforward, elections were called
for, electoral laws altered, elections subjected to all kinds of official
pressure as the current Ministry decided. Nothing was fixed. Even
the rights of the tiny minority who were eligible to be electors were
not secure. Just before an election, notable opponents of the Ministry
like Paul-Louis Courier could find their assessments reduced just
enough to disqualify them. Not until 1828 were the lists of electors
printed in time for claims to be lodged. The 'legal country' was less
a microcosm of the country than a body called on to ratify the royal
will. But there was little doubt that, as far as there was any freedom
of election under this system, 'the country' would, in normal circumstances, be liberal. Even La Vendée returned enemies of the Ultras
and it was no wonder that the Ultras dallied with the idea of a much

wider franchise, believing, or professing to believe, that the peasantry would, as in the days when they were faithful vassals of the *seigneurs*, vote as the big landowners wanted. Some Ultras, like Villèle, dallied with plans of decentralization. For the Ultras were Royalists rather than absolutists. The more intelligent of them could see that among the causes of the Revolution was the royal centralization set up by Richelieu and Louis XIV; for them the model King was not the 'Grand Monarque', but Henri IV.

The temporary conversion of the Ultras to parliamentary government was short-lived. Most of the converts fell back on the belief of the Abbé de Rauzan that 'any constitution is a regicide'. More believed, with Joseph de Maistre, that the King *could* not alienate his historical rights, or saw, with the Vicomte de Bonald, in the doctrines of the Revolution the defiance of the laws of Nature and of Nature's God. For Bonald and his disciples, the Revolution was an aberration; the *real* France had existed before 1789, the twenty-five years of revolution was a breach in the natural and good order of things. No wonder Bonald wished the Government to take over the copyright in the works of Rousseau and Voltaire—and not reprint them. A few years later, an ingenuous priest was to ask that the building of new paper mills and the recruiting of printers' apprentices should be drastically curtailed.

These dreams of an idealized past fitted well with some fashionable literary doctrines. For like the rest of Europe, France was under the spell of the 'Wizard of the North'. French history was seen through the eyes of Sir Walter Scott; fidelity to the Stewarts was identified with fidelity to the Bourbons, and the nobility, real and fictitious, regilded its arms with colours borrowed from the Waverley novels.

This literary version of history was used by the Liberals, too. For, taking over the absurd theory invented by Boulainvilliers under Louis XV to justify noble pretensions, French history was seen by Guizot and many others as the slow emancipation of the Third Estate, the descendants of the Gallo-Romans, from the Gothic and Frankish tyranny which the nobles represented. It was socially flattering to a class where fake pedigrees were almost as common as in England or Ireland, but it was politically important that the claims of the men who had done well out of the Revolution should be given the importance of a great and millennial historical movement. A young Royalist poet might, in the ruins of Montfort l'Amaury,

> 'croit qu'un ombre a froissé la gigantesque armure
> D'Amaury, comte de Montfort',

but the scepticism of Gérard de Nerval was, in the not long run, more popular: he refused to see in modern nobles,

> 'ces preux à fronts de bœuf, à figures dantesques'.

And if *Ivanhoe* was to be taken seriously, the future was with Gurth and Wamba, not with Reginald Front de Bœuf. But henceforward, Royalist politics had a strong dose of mere romance to muddle heads already clouded by resentment and by a refusal to accept the fact that the Revolution had happened. It had not only happened, it had been a good and necessary thing, driven off its true course by civil and foreign war, but profoundly changing France and Europe for the better. So François Mignet wrote in the first *Histoire de la Révolution Française* that could claim to be objective. France could henceforward be governed only if the double need of real political liberty and material progress was met.

To discuss the Revolution in these terms was itself revolutionary. For the Royalists, the Revolution had been a great crime; under the Empire it was as far as possible ignored. But now interest was reviving. Madame de Staël's *Considérations* was the first swallow of a hot summer. A flood of memoirs, many of them bogus, contributed to keep alive the interest of the middle classes in the great liberating movement. And lower down in the social scale, the Royal Government was learning the old lesson taught by the wise friend of Fletcher of Saltoun, the greater importance of ballads than of laws. The balladmongers were busy creating a new epic figure, Napoleon. Agricol Perdiguier read the *Quatre Fils Aymon* and learned the legend of the Emperor in much the same spirit. The mild balladmonger of the Empire, Béranger, with his assertion that

> 'dans un grenier qu'on est bien à vingt ans',

even with his 'Roi d'Yvetot', was changed into the Béranger who pilloried the nobles and the priests and sang of the Emperor and of the old and banned flag. In vain the police harassed the wearers of old buttons with the Imperial eagles or people who talked too loudly of violets (which meant the Emperor) or of dandelions (which meant the King of Rome). In vain, the Royalists tried to popularize their own songs. 'O Richard o mon roi!' might touch the heart of John Quincy Adams, but it had no popular resonance in France.

The breach between the King and the Ultras had social results. The great nobles of the old order had had no possible life away from the Court. Exile, to Chantilly or Chanteloup, meant the end of power, the loss of friends, boredom, disgrace. It was not so any longer. There was no Court in the old sense. The Tuileries, combined with St. Cloud and Rambouillet, did not make up Versailles. The King had little to give and there were other sources of power, in the future if not in the present: the Pavillon de Marsan of the Comte d'Artois, the Palais Royal of the Duc d'Orléans. Already, in the eighteenth century, Paris, the Paris of the great bourgeois *salons*, had created a rival social centre. But now there were a dozen *salons*, there were the private hôtels of the great bankers Lafitte and Rothschild. The 'Maison Nucingen' was more than the house of a Farmer-General was before 1789. There were the newspaper offices, the bureaux of the great reviews; there were the Academies. And there were, what was unthinkable before 1789, great noble houses which were hostile to the crown, like the hôtel of the Duc de Broglie, and great men whose mere presence created a court of a new kind, like Chateaubriand at 'l'Abbaye-au-Bois'. A great noble now had to fight for his social position against fierce competition; power and prestige did not automatically flow to him from the Court. And the higher nobility had become, in many ways, middle class; it could no longer rely on the King to pay its debts. So a diner-out noticed, gloomily, that the Montmorencies used napkin rings. The Court was as exclusive as ever. George Canning was the first commoner with whom Charles X had ever sat down to dinner. It was nearly as extravagant as ever. Although he was an Irishman, the Duke of Wellington was astonished at the number of horses in the royal stables. The Duc de Doudeauville had to fight continually against a relapse into the irresponsible financial habits of the old days. The Duc de Berry might show his sense of the times, not only by his

vulgar amours, but by treating the banker, Greffulhe, as a friend.
But the 'noble faubourg' of Proust was born; the Court, though it
knew it not, was dead.

At Aix-la-Chapelle, Richelieu reaped his reward. France was a
great power again, but the Prime Minister was tired, disillusioned.
He knew that the Ultras were impossible, but he was himself a
Royalist with no liberal sympathies and the vigorous war waged by
Decazes against Richelieu's natural allies so distressed him that he was
often 'ready to hide myself in the depths of some desert'. His growing conservatism forced the King to choose between the great noble
and the new favourite. He chose Decazes. An obscure general,
Dessolles, became Prime Minister, but the real power was Decazes
and the most important new Minister was the Minister of War,
Marshal Gouvion Saint-Cyr.

The King had told the Comte d'Artois that he did not wish to be
the King of two nations and the new Ministry most boldly applied
this maxim in its military policy. After the Hundred Days, the royal
Government could not be expected to trust the old Imperial Army,
the remnants of which Davoût had assembled behind the Loire. The
very names of the old military order were abolished. Regiments
were replaced by departmental 'legions' locally recruited and the
officer corps was rigorously purged. But the new military organization had the great drawback of not providing an effective army, at a
time when France was trying to regain her rank as a great power.
The task of giving her an army adequate for that rank was undertaken by Gouvion Saint-Cyr, and his military law of 1818 was one
of the most important pieces of legislation of the nineteenth century,
in its main lines in force until 1872 and, in its social consequences,
alive much later. What inflamed the Royalist passions of the time
was the open appeal to the veterans of the Imperial Army, who were
no longer the 'brigands of the Loire'. They were to be enrolled in
the reserve for, said the Marshal, in a brilliantly successful speech
which was the first great oratorical effort of his 'ghost writer',
François Guizot, 'The King does not desire that there should be any
national force in France which does not belong to him, a single
generous sentiment which he does not win to him.' 'All that is
national is ours', as a Bourbon Pretender was to put it. If the rank-

and-file were pardoned by being put in the reserve (an unappreciated favour for many of them), officers were pardoned by being given their old rank. Thus Colonel Aupick, who had been wounded at Waterloo, resumed the career that was to lead to distinction as a soldier and a diplomat and notoriety as a stepfather.

More important, in the long run, was the method of recruitment of the new Army. Conscription had been abolished by the Charter, so it was necessary to fall back on compulsory service to fill the gaps which, it was rightly foreseen, voluntary recruitment would leave. Each year, a lottery would decide what Frenchmen of the age of twenty would serve; those with 'good numbers' would escape. So would those with poor physique, and as the 'contingent' called for only 40,000 men, it was possible to insist on high physical standards. This meant that the stunted and otherwise defective youths of the cities were for the most part rejected. (It is to the reports of medical boards that we owe most of our depressing information about the state of public health. Recruits had to be rejected because their teeth were so bad that they could not bite off the ends of cartridges.) The more prosperous classes could buy substitutes and so the peasantry supplied the troops. It also supplied a great part of the officers, for a third of all commissions were reserved for promotions from the ranks and, in fact, there were more than a third of the officers who had begun as privates. Some of these were adventurous youths of good families who, as under the Empire, entered the Army as privates. But most were promoted non-commissioned officers, often barely literate, docile, brave, unideaéd. The great military schools, Polytechnique, Saint-Cyr, by their high fees excluded the sons of the poor; but nearly all high promotions went to the pupils of the great schools. The days of 'a bâton in the knapsack' were over, although one Marshal, Bazaine, did rise from the ranks. The obscurity of origin and, still more, the poverty of the average officer affected the attitude of the ruling classes to the Army. For the higher bourgeoisie it was an eccentricity for a son of a good, that is rich family to become an officer, as Lucien Leuwen found. It was impossible, as Castellane who admired the British system noted, to introduce the army mess into the French Army; the average officer could not afford the expense. The officers were a class by themselves, moving from garrison

to garrison, with their own Masonic lodges and dreary military cafés.
They could not marry without the permission of the Minister of
War, but the minimum *dot* insisted on was only £50 a year, which
showed how modest were the social aspirations of the officer class, a
class that owed everything to its rank, nothing to its own social position. Even the nobility, traditionally trained for military service,
kept out of the Army until late in the nineteenth century, though
there were some traditional military families like the Hautecloque,
de la Tour du Pin, du Paty de Clam.

The Army kept the formal precedence of the 'Decrees of Messi-
dor', but only the rank of Marshal of France was really imposing.
Once that had been attained, as Marshal de Castellane noted with
satisfaction, you had not to make appointments with anybody except
your dentist. But for officers who did not mount so high, military
life was dull, ill-rewarded, ill-considered. Gone were the days when
generals were younger than colonels, when battle and death cleared
the way for promotion. The officers of the Restoration served, as
Alfred de Vigny put it, 'between the echo and the dream of battles'.
But the echo grew faint and the dream remained empty. Success in
the Army was now a matter of pleasing superiors and originality of
mind or character was a fatal handicap. It depended on your superiors
whether you slowly climbed the ladder or stuck; whether, a military
nomad, you moved from one dull garrison to another, or achieved
the goal of Paris. The Army was 'a nation in the nation', to quote
Vigny again. And that nation's chief was the Minister of War, that
nation's religion blind obedience. Though few remarked it, the days
of the military *coup d'état* were over; no Augereau, no Bonaparte
could be bred in the officers trained to the docility of the barracks
and the review ground. Fructidor and Brumaire were as remote as
the Fronde.

V

It was natural that the Restoration should try to find in the Church a
popular support that it badly needed and feared, rightly, it could not
find elsewhere. From a Royalist point of view, the record of the

Church was not above criticism. It had, under papal leadership, accepted the Concordat with Bonaparte which meant abandoning the exiled King. A few devoted souls in the 'Petite Église' set up their schismatic tabernacle, but even the meagre patronage of the First Consul was better than persecution. It was worth paying a high price in servility, as the Imperial catechism, with its insistence on the duties of subjects, made plain. And if the Church turned against the Emperor, it was because of his treatment of the Pope, not because of his usurpation of the throne.

The Concordat had turned the once powerful Gallican Church into a branch of the government service. It had also, what was less noticed at the time, greatly increased the power of the Pope. For he alone had liquidated the old hierarchy, and if the new hierarchy was nominated by the Emperor, all bishops had to be instituted by the Pope. He could veto if he could not directly reward. What Bonaparte wished to restore was an auxiliary of his Government, bishops and priests preaching a morality useful to the Government. He could see the utility of nuns who worked as nurses and teachers, of missionary societies which spread French influence abroad, even of the famous seminary of Saint-Sulpice whose teachers, if not quite an order, were something more than a mere aggregate of secular priests. But the revival of real religious orders, not paid, not controlled by the State, was an intolerable abuse to him. And yet, the moment the tide of life stirred in the veins of what had seemed a moribund body, the desire for the religious life revived. The Jesuits reappeared, slightly disguised, and with the fall of the Empire, exiled regulars began to return to France.

From the beginning, the Restoration was faced with the problem of what to do about this revival. On the one hand, every sign of life in the Church was welcome. On the other, the revival of monasticism was abhorrent to the bourgeoisie whose Voltairian dislike of monasticism was made keener by the thought of how much monastic property had passed into lay hands. Yet the revival began. The Trappists, who had taken refuge with Mr. Weld in Dorset, returned to France. They were harmless enough, minding their own business with an extravagant determination. It was another matter when it was proposed to re-establish Benedictine houses on the lines of the old congregation of Saint-Maur, centres of learning and missionary activity. It was a secular priest who knew nothing of the religious life, the Abbé Guéranger, whom the dream of reviving the monastic life commanded most completely. He found the abandoned priory of Solesmes and he thought he had found a means of endowing it. For one of the monks of the great Abbey of Saint-Denis had received, as a trust, large sums from the last Prior. But Dom Groult, expressing a sentiment more worthy of Mahomet than of Suger, bluntly warned the young zealot against 'monkery'. The most famous secular priest, M. de Lamennais, pointed out to the Abbé Guéranger that monks had to sing the divine office in choir and was astonished to learn that it was exactly to do this that Guéranger wished to found his monastery. It was to be difficult to sing the Lord's song in this strange land. But it was done. Solesmes was founded, the seed of a great tree.

But if the revival of the religious life was a sign of health, monks were a luxury compared with parish priests. And they were few and growing fewer. After 1801, priests came back from exile in Germany and England, came out from the shadows in France; but there had been ten years' interruption of clerical recruitment and each year more priests died than were ordained. To fill the seminaries, so as to be able to fill the cures of souls, was the main aim of energetic prelates like Cardinal Cambacérès of Rouen. The exemption of clerical students from conscription forced on some vocations, but by 1814, there were fewer priests in France than in 1801 and, in many regions, traditional Christian habits had been permanently broken.

Since so much in the ecclesiastical policy of the Restoration failed, it is to be noticed that in one thing it succeeded: it turned the tide; the clergy of France grew steadily more numerous and younger. In such a situation it was impossible to insist on a high standard of clerical education. Lamennais, himself, received a very meagre intellectual preparation for the priesthood and most of the secular clergy, recruited from the peasantry, were barely competent to perform its sacred functions. And no doubt some of the recruits to the priesthood made the simple calculation of Julien Sorel: the way to power for a poor boy was now to bet on the black, not on the red. He could not become a marshal, he might become a bishop.

For the Government of the Restoration believed that its ally, the Church, could be useful only if it were powerful. It became known, or at any rate it came to be believed, that promotion, in Church and State, depended on the goodwill of 'the Congregation'. This mysterious body owed much of its prestige to the French talent for believing in conspiracies—of Jesuits and Jews, Masons and Republicans. There was never a 'Congregation' in the vulgar sense of the term. But the 'Chevaliers de la Foi', the monarchist parody of the Freemasons that had grown up under the Empire, had not been disbanded. Its support was worth having, or even the mere report of its support. Balzac's Abbé Troubert was able to triumph in Tours because he was thought to be the agent of 'the Congregation'.

The new priests, hastily turned out by the seminaries, were very different from the tolerant and 'enlightened' priests of the old regime. In the horrors that had befallen the Church of France, they saw the punishment of that tolerance. It was their duty to eradicate the tares sown by Voltaire and Rousseau, the bad habits bred by the interruption of Church authority. It was fully recognized that France was a mission field and the revived religious orders set out to reap in fields white for the harvest. The 'Missions', with their special sermons and ceremonies, conducted often enough by zealots hostile to all that had occurred since 1789, angered and frightened the bourgeoisie who, at best, regarded the whole business with the disgust that the Anglican clergy or the old school of dissenting ministers had, in eighteenth-century England, regarded the preaching of Wesley. That the Government supported the Missions was a black mark against both. It was religious persecution, it was held, to make all shopkeepers put out flags for the procession of the Fête-Dieu (Corpus Christi), for it imposed on Protestants and Jews a recognition of the Catholic doctrine of the Real Presence.

A less artificial grievance was the campaign of the clergy against Sunday work, for the closing of public houses during the hours of mass, against the nearly universal custom of public dancing. To that most representative member of the new clergy, Jean-Baptiste Vianney, curé of Ars, dancing was the most direct way to hell. Less saintly priests succeeded in putting down this diversion, with the aid of the secular arm. Paul-Louis Courier knew what he was doing when he contrasted the tolerant curé of the old school with the new curé of Azai, 'young, boiling-over with zeal, just out of the seminary, a conscript of the Church Militant, impatient to distinguish himself'. Paul-Louis Courier did not like any kind of priest, but he knew which kind was most disliked.

He would have disliked, even more, the priests of a more elevated social rank and more sophisticated intellectual approach such as were beginning to appear and to lead the assault on the still dominant Voltairianism, tempered by Gallicanism, of the bourgeoisie. The nobility, in its younger members at any rate, had learned the incompatibility of unbelief and high rank. The Comte d'Artois, after the death of his mistress, could risk being converted, and his friend Prince Jules de Polignac was equally changed from the frivolous and unbelieving young man so well known at Versailles. But in the next generation the conversions went deeper. The young Duc de Rohan, shattered by the death of his wife, took orders in a very different spirit from that which had moved the notorious Bishop of Strasbourg of the 'Diamond Necklace' scandal. As it was the policy of the Restoration 'to scrape the mud off the episcopate', he was rapidly promoted, becoming Archbishop of Besançon at thirty (where he over-ruled the boy's parish priest and admitted Gustave Courbet to his first communion). But Rohan was the friend of all that was living in the Church, especially of the young men won by the genius of Félicité de Lamennais. Lamennais, with his essay on indifference in religion, seemed, at first, just what the Restoration needed. Here was no deprecatory presentation of the minimum truths of Christianity in a form calculated not to shock the unbeliever. The most cherished Liberal doctrines were attacked at their very heart by the fiery Breton who claimed for the Church all that the Royalist doctrinaire, Bonald, claimed, and renounced the Revolution and all its works and pomps with as much conviction as, but far more literary charm than Comte Joseph de Maistre. Round Lamennais, the young men of zeal, priests and laymen, crowded. It was not yet clearly noted that it was really the Church, really God that he cared for, that the rights of the King were nearly a matter of indifference to him.

The Catholic revival faced very formidable obstacles. Women could be believers but, despite the official patronage given to the

Church by the State, it was almost outrageous for a schoolboy to keep the faith that he often brought from home to the royal colleges which had succeeded the imperial lycées. It took far more courage than was needed in Tom Brown's Rugby for a boy to practise faith or chastity in the state schools. Towards the end of the Restoration, there were chaplains in smart schools like Henri IV who had a genuine hold on some of the boys, but the names suggest that the zealous Catholics were for the most part young nobles.

It was no wonder, then, that pious Catholics, of whom there were still many, should prefer to send their sons, even if they had no intention of entering the priesthood, to the seminaries, since the fall of Napoleon, entirely under the control of the bishops or that the bishops, at their wit's end for teachers, should have turned many of their seminaries over to regular priests, above all to the Jesuits.

VI

It was a great personal triumph for Decazes that the King preferred him to Richelieu. But Dessolles was no shield as the great noble had been; the head of the Government was too visibly the King's favourite. Decazes knew how hated he was by the friends of the Comte d'Artois and he showed, by his use of the royal patronage, how resolute he was in combating them. The annual renewal of the Chamber swept away the candidates of the Pavillon de Marsan; a hostile House of Peers was swamped by lavish creations that brought back ornaments of the Empire to public life. An alliance of the King and the Liberal bourgeoisie was attempted. But the bourgeoisie refused to be won over; in 1819, the candidates of the Ministry were overwhelmed by the Liberals. And, sign of the times, one of the victorious Liberals was Grégoire, the most famous and distinguished of the bishops of the Constitutional Church. His very virtues made him the more odious to the Right. Although he had not voted the death of Louis XVI (if he had, he would have had to go into exile after Waterloo), he candidly admitted that he would have done so had he been present in the Convention. Such a defiance of the Royal cause was intolerable; and the fact that Grégoire was elected not solely by the Liberals of Dauphiné, but by the Ultras, pursuing that policy of extremes that was to become one of the bad habits of the Right, hurt the Ministry even more. In vain Decazes veered to the Right. He broke with his Doctrinaire friends; he proposed to alter the electoral law, to give a double vote to the biggest taxpayers, and to do away with the annual renewal of a fifth of the Chamber.

The Left was finally alienated, the Right not won over. And when a fanatic assassinated the Duc de Berry, the cup was full to overflowing. 'He has slipped in blood', wrote Chateaubriand. The King had to get rid of his beloved Élie; he made him a Duke, gave him the London Embassy, but Richelieu had to be recalled.

The assassination of the Duc de Berry threatened the now triumphant Ultras, for the heir presumptive was the Duc d'Orléans if the exclusion of the descendants of Philip V of Spain, provided for in the Treaty of Utrecht, was valid. The Comte d'Artois had already been alarmed at the possible succession of his kinsman; he had even hinted at his own second marriage as a solution, but destiny smiled, for the moment, on the elder line of the Bourbons. The Duchesse de Berry gave birth to a posthumous son, 'the child of the miracle'. He was given the title of Duc de Bordeaux in honour of the city that had first hoisted the white flag in 1814. But an ingenious courtier organized a public and formally voluntary subscription to buy for the infant prince the Château of Chambord, put on the market by the widow of Marshal Berthier. The subscription was, of course, a success (despite the most famous of the pamphlets of Paul-Louis Courier) and the baby prince acquired the title by which he was to be known to history.

If the birth of the Duc de Bordeaux heartened the partisans of the Bourbons, it was one of the straws driving the Liberals into the dangerous path of conspiracy. All Europe west of Russia was in movement. The Allied Monarchs were alarmed by the rumours of conspiracy in Germany, by the fact of revolt in Spain and Italy. They could not tolerate, in France, a Government that was not as hostile to liberty as they were. The new laws on the Press, the new laws on elections deprived the French Left of that inevitable parliamentary triumph that they had naïvely discounted. The news of the revival of the old cause in Europe bred new illusions. With a frivolity worthy of the Hundred Days, they planned a military rising in France that could at best have been a *pronunciamiento* on Spanish lines.

The birth of the Duc de Bordeaux, the double vote given the great taxpayers (most of them great landowners), the reduction of the taxes of nearly 15,000 voters (out of 110,000) gave the Ultras a new 'chambre introuvable'. The King, weary, tired, accepted the policy of the Comte d'Artois and the formidable leader of the Ultras in the Chamber, Villèle, entered the Ministry. In Europe, reaction triumphed. The Austrians easily disposed of the Neapolitan army; a military revolt, supported by the Prince of Carignano, was suppressed in Piedmont. The hopes roused in foolish breasts by the news of the 'Peterloo massacre' in England, which had led to cheers for 'our Manchester brethren', proved baseless; the dramatic news of the rising of the Greeks was followed by news of the defeat of the insurgent Hellenes. Only in Spain were the military leaders of revolt in uneasy power. The Spanish example went to weak heads, notably that of Lafayette. The death of Napoleon enabled Republicans and Bonapartists to co-operate. It was safe now to claim Napoleon's Glory; there was no danger that he might come back. The first conspiracy was discovered by the Government; the conspirators were more resolute and deliberately imitated the Italian conspiratorial society of the 'Carbonari' which recruited not only discontented ex-officers, but such rising intellectual lights as Victor Cousin, the philosopher. It was a condemnation of the policy of reaction that men as cautious as he were driven to nourish absurd conspiratorial hopes. Of the parliamentary leaders, only the egregious Lafayette believed in the possibility of overthrowing the regime by a military conspiracy. It failed; the Army remained loyal and the 'four sergeants of La Rochelle' paid with their heads for its failure. M. de Lafayette was not prosecuted.

It was time, thought the Ultras, in this in full accord with the Allied rulers, to end the centre of infection in Spain. Chateaubriand, now Minister of Foreign Affairs, was all for war. The King had let Richelieu go; the great noble was cheerfully betrayed by the Comte d'Artois; the real head of the Government was now Villèle.

The Minister shared his master's dislike of a gamble so great as

armed intervention in Spain. The thought of a new Spanish war was
as alarming as the thought of a new invasion of Russia. Villèle was
above all a financier, and war would risk weakening the laboriously
established public credit. Ferdinand was a poor prospect as a client
and—who knew?—the Liberals might be right, the Army might not
be reliable. But the Comte d'Artois and Chateaubriand had their
way.

The news of the war was bad for credit; the calling up of reservists,
still more the calling up of recruits who had been exempted on medical grounds, threatened to add the unpopularity of the Empire to
the unpopularity of the Royal Government.. The command of the
Army of Spain was given to the Duc d'Angoulême who was wisely
given Imperial officers to guide him. But it was Marshal Victor, the
Minister of War, who totally failed to provide for the supply of the
invading army. The Duc d'Angoulême was forced to deal with the
great speculator, Ouvrard, who drove a hard bargain. It was worth
it: like the Duke of Wellington, the Duc d'Angoulême paid his way,
so the Spanish peasants flocked to his camp. It was not the Emperor's
war. There were easy victories, more decisive than the Tudela or
Albufera. The only serious resistance was at Cadiz, but the strong-
point of the Trocadero was stormed (Charles Albert, Prince of
Carignano, expiated his Liberalism in the assault). Ferdinand VII
was restored to his full powers. He proceeded to behave according
to his character, despite the protests of his kinsman the Duc
d'Angoulême. He contracted to pay some of the costs of the deliver-
ing Army and of course did not. There was little to show for the
victorious campaign. There was the name of the Trocadero. There
was the more important fact that the new Royal Army had proved
its loyalty. At the Bidassoa a group of Frenchmen, among them
Armand Carrel, had waved the tricolour; the troops, without hesitation, had fired on it. The new Army, the Comte d'Artois and his son
thought, could be relied on (so James II had thought after the defeat
of Monmouth). But the whole policy of repressing revolt in Spain
had only one permanent result. The project frightened George
Canning, and from that fear came the Monroe Doctrine.

The royal power had now passed to the Comte d'Artois. The old
King was weary and defeatist. He had replaced his lost Decazes by

Madame du Cayla who was literally 'maîtresse en titre' and who insinuated Ultra doctrine into the mind of the dying King. The Ultras hoped, the Liberals feared. But when in 1824 the Comte d'Artois became Charles X, it seemed, for a moment, that his great office had sobered him. He set out to charm and he did. The Press censorship was abandoned and the King was popular.

VII

It seemed natural to give to the new reign a more splendid inaguration than had been possible for Louis XVIII in 1814. So Charles X, it was decided, would be crowned at Reims in a ceremony that would recall the splendours of the House of France and perhaps lead men to forget the coronation of the usurper in Notre-Dame de Paris. Traditionally, the most sacred rite was not the imposition of the crown but the anointing of the King. The Revolution had destroyed the sacred phial that held the sacred oil of St. Rémy but, miraculously, some had been preserved. All the ancient rites were to be carried out, but the great nobles of the Empire were to be associated with the great nobles of the old order. Thus, wrote the young poet, Victor Hugo (it was an age when all the young poets were Royalist, Catholic—and romantic) royalty would show that it,

> 'De la chaîne d'airain qui lie au ciel les trônes
> A retrouvé l'anneau perdu'.

But it was too late; the ecclesiastical atmosphere, for many, poisoned the ceremony. It was too late to secure that the people should not

> '. . . imprime en sa cervelle
> Le curieux discours d'une secte nouvelle'.

The French people, called on to burn what it had adored and to adore what it had burned, unlike Clovis, refused. The most popular poem was not Hugo's, but Béranger's 'Sacre de Charles le Simple'.

Behind all the reactionary measures of the Government, all the wild and whirling words of the Chamber, was the deep illusion that

the mass of the French people shared the nostalgia of the former
privileged classes for the old order or that, if they did not, the cause
was the poisoning of their minds by sophists and rhetoricians. If
the Government was only firm; if two-fisted Prefects, using all the
resources of Napoleonic centralization, acted with resolution, the
forces of disloyalty and irreligion would be crushed and the natural
devotion of the French people to the best of Kings and most loving
of Churches would find free expression. Royal theorists and practical politicians alike ignored the fact that, for the great mass of the
French people, of all classes but the nobility, the Revolution seemed,
in retrospect, a good thing. The vested interests of the bourgeoisie in
the Revolution settlement were guaranteed by the lesser interests
but very deep sentiments of the masses, that is, of the peasants. They
had not been transformed from serfs to proprietors; many of them
had been proprietors before the Revolution, and there had been no
true serfs. But they had escaped the grosser inequalities of taxation; they were not affronted by the more intolerable forms of
privilege. They cherished their new, legal equality, if they still
deferred to their betters. They rejoiced in the ending of the tithe,
even if they remained good Catholics (and millions had not remained
good Catholics). There were anomalies: the peasants of Venables
voluntarily paid tithe down to 1838. There were noble landlords
who were economically as powerful as, politically more powerful
than, they had been in 1789. But, as Napoleon insisted, the Revolution had *happened*. Only a small if fervent minority of Frenchmen
could tolerate its being undone.

Villèle has often been compared to Walpole. He had some of the
qualities of that statesman, but he was less attuned to the spirit of his
age than was Walpole. Even if he did not share, he accepted many
of the most dangerous prejudices of the zealous Ultras and his greatest
mistakes were to come from catering to them. He, like Walpole,
was jealous of power, and made enemies—for example, Chateaubriand whom he dismissed from the Foreign Office with calculated
brutality. And although an excellent financier of the old school,
with a notable regard for economy and solvency, he was totally out
of sympathy with the new world of business. He was a provincial
in Paris; his town house was in Toulouse and his heart on his

Languedocian estate. He knew little of the world of the Bourse and
the banks; he knew something of the old colonial commerce, but
nothing of the new industry. Above all, he was a man of the land.

The Revolution had changed the French landed organization in
many important ways. A great deal of land had changed hands; all
Church lands (in 1789 about a tenth of all lands) had passed into lay
possession and the whole complicated, degenerate feudal system had
been swept away. There was now only the naked title to land; the
old servitudes had been abolished; so had the medieval organization
of agricultural production. No longer was a villager bound to cultivate his land in the fashion of his neighbours; he could try new rotations, new crops. No longer had all villagers the right to general free
grazing after the crops were in. Of course, facts did not always accord
with the legal theory. There were survivals of the old order like
common lands and common forests; there were areas like the region
of Santerre in Picardy where a kind of 'tenant right' was enforced
against landlords by all the methods of Irish agrarian war, cattle
maiming, boycott, murder. But the absolute right of the owner of
land to do as he liked with his own was, in general, a social fact as
well as a legal concept.

In other ways the landed system had changed little. The begin-
nings of an enclosure movement, visible in the last years of the old
order, were stopped by the Convention. The community of the
open fields might have gone, but the strip system remained. A landed
proprietor often had his property in a score of strips which he let to
a score of tenants. Peasants coveted and often attained a strip of land,
a 'lopin', which they worked as well as the strips they rented from
bourgeois proprietors; even labourers sometimes had a 'lopin' of
land, although keeping themselves on the wages they earned from
richer peasants or from big proprietors. Other peasants were
'métayers', share-croppers, often victims of extremely hard bargains
driven by the owners of the land. Then there were farmers on long
or short leases, and there were some gentlemen farmers who lived
on their lands and, slowly assembling scattered strips, created
efficient units of production. But as a system of production the
French land system was less changed by the Revolution than the
English system was by the arrival of capitalist high farming and the

destruction of the smallholders. Rare in France was the landlord-farmer-labourer system that was normal in England, and which accounted for the wealth of the English countryside and the degradation of the rural population. For if the strip system left the utilization of the land of France to millions of petty proprietors, most of them illiterate, without either the capital or knowledge to apply new methods, the French peasant owner, ferociously industrious, avaricious, ambitious to add to his holding, was more of a man, less of a child, than the English labourer. So John Stuart Mill testified in one generation, Rowland Prothero in another.

There were, of course, improving landlords; there had been some before the Revolution; there were more now. English cattle, Spanish sheep were imported. Horse-breeding had suffered terribly during the Revolution and the Empire. The peasant foolish enough to have good horses saw them seized for the Army. Now good horses were an asset. But the general backwardness of French metallurgy prevented the general adoption of good tools—new ploughs, for example. Although the famines of the old regime were unknown, a bad harvest was a serious political risk, leading, as it usually did, to bread riots and disorder that were too much for the local police and could be suppressed only by the troops. The bad harvest of 1817 was an additional cause of anxiety for the Duc de Richelieu. Transport was bad, so there could be local shortages; and the landed interest usually, if not always, managed to keep out foreign, as a rule Russian, corn. Even good weather had its drawbacks, for windless weeks in the early summer, before the harvest was in, meant that the windmills could not grind and the 'soudure', the gap between harvests, became a time of crisis. But there were new substitutes for bread, above all the potato which began to spread under the Restoration; turnips had a harder fight against prejudice and routine. Slowly but regularly and generally, the food of the peasant became slightly more varied and everywhere more abundant. He seldom ate meat and wine was still a luxury, but he had memories of much harder times to console him and make him immune to lamentations for the good old days.

His housing was still atrocious. But peace allowed him to make improvements. The replacement of thatch by tiles and slates not only reduced the risk of fire, but improved the water supply; rain from the roofs was better than stagnant water from filthy pools that too often served as wells.

The amount of cultivated land steadily increased. Waste land was cultivated, primitive rotations of crops were changed for the better by the use of new grasses. The chronic weakness of French agriculture, the shortage of livestock, was slowly remedied. There were great schemes of improvement or, rather, schemes had a better chance of being brought to a fruitful conclusion. Thus in the seventeenth century, an English engineer with Dutch workmen had attempted to reclaim fertile land in Normandy by diking the Seine, but the Fronde interrupted the work and there was no great, prudent, far-seeing dynasty like the Russells to create something like the Bedford Level. All that the dike did was produce a new swamp; not until the nineteenth century was the work resumed and finished. All French agriculture was short of capital, for although the price of land rose, most buyers were mere moneylenders, not true investors. The old nobility were more likely to be improving landlords than were the new bourgeois proprietors, but both wanted favours from the Government and looked to it where their English counterparts often looked to themselves and to each other. The tariff policy of the Government was shortsighted, designed to protect all of the home market against any kind of competition. Even when it professed to protect industry, the motive was often the needs of the agricultural interests. The impossibly high duty on iron fostered hundreds of little open-cast iron mines, but, more politically important, provided a market for the timber of the gentry's woods which produced the charcoal for the primitive smelters.

The Government of Villèle was a government of landed proprietors. To the big landowners was given the control of local government under royal supervision. But they wanted the restoration of their old position. Even this Government could not dare openly to upset the landed settlement of the Revolution; it could only tamper with it. Villèle firmly believed that only by strengthening the position of the country gentry could France be given a stable policy. One way to do that was to provide that a father who had not specifically divided all his property among his heirs should be deemed to have left an extra portion to his eldest son. The Code Napoléon had allowed him to favour one child; the new bill would have forced him, unless he formally decided otherwise, to favour his eldest son. This project affected only the larger estates: 80,000 families out of 6,000,000 were involved. But a great conquest of the Revolution was threatened; the Chamber of Peers threw out the bill and there were significant cries of 'Down with the Jesuits' as Paris rejoiced.

More important was the proposal to indemnify the émigrés for their lost lands. Villèle had worked out an ingenious 'combination' whereby the bulk of the national debt, the *rentes*, would be converted from 5% to 3% (an operation justified by the rise in the stock market quotation of the *rentes*). Great bankers, not only Baring and Rothschild but that pillar of Liberalism, Lafitte, undertook to float the new issue. The alarm was given. Most of the *rentiers* lived in Paris. Their 'right' to 5% was threatened to recompense enemies of their country! The original project was defeated in floods of fallacious oratory. The Government had to pay the émigrés directly, in new stock, a sum calculated to recoup their losses. It was, roughly, a 'milliard' (£40,000,000). Since the émigrés were not paid at once in full, the actuarial cost was only 600,000,000 francs (£24,000,000). But there was a partial conversion; the *rentiers* were infuriated. And the émigrés were not grateful. Most of them had naturally and innocently an exaggerated sense of their losses; the compensation they got was often insultingly trifling. Nor were they pleased to notice that among the big gainers were Liberal noblemen like Lafayette and the rich and rapacious House of Orléans. The Government gained no strength from Villèle's boldest achievement.

France did. It was all very well for the Liberals in Parliament to declaim. In private, like Dupont de l'Eure, they had to take notice of the fact that 'family property fetched higher prices than national property'. The settlement of the émigré claims, if it bitterly disappointed the émigrés, at least secured the new wealth of the bourgeoisie who had done well out of the Revolution. The much decried policy of Villèle was a wise settlement of a burning question, a not so minor Edict of Nantes.

It was by its ecclesiastical policy that the Villèle ministry made most enemies for crown and the Church, stressed, in the most offensive form, the alliance of throne and altar. Thus sacrilege was to be punished with death and profanation of the consecrated host by the extra penalties laid down for parricide. To legislate like this was not only, as Royer-Collard said, to import into the civil law the doctrine of the Real Presence, but it was to awake all the fears and hates of the bourgeoisie, Voltairian by what was now a barely challenged tradition. The law of sacrilege recalled the execution of the Chevalier de la Barre, one of the two great crimes of the Church of the old order that had provoked Voltaire's famous war-cry, 'Écrasez l'infâme'. The law was never enforced but the damage was done.

The more intelligent members of the clergy recognized how limited were their successes in most parts of France. At Chartres during the great Mission of 1827 hardly any men, though many women of the bourgeoisie attended and as the sexes were rigorously segregated, the depressing fact was made more evident. True, poor men, porters, minor craftsmen, still, to some degree, observed the ordinances of the Church, but the bourgeoisie was busily converting them to its own infidelity; cheap editions of Voltaire were encouraged and so were very cheap editions of that anti-clerical masterpiece, *Tartuffe*. The virtues of the clergy were bogus, so it was insinuated, but, as Élie Halévy said of Molière, many of the sneers at clerical virtue came from men who would have disliked Tartuffe even more if he had been sincere.

There were material concessions that it was possible to make. Attempts to replace the Concordat of 1801 had broken down; there was no possible bargain that could both satisfy the Vatican and be accepted by any French Government. But the Royal Government could and did greatly increase the number of dioceses; thus Chartres again became an episcopal city and the present French ecclesiastical organization is much what the Restoration left it. The pious Government of Charles X gave complete control over elementary education to the Church. The schoolmaster was an employé of the parish priest; he was expected to be choirmaster as well as schoolmaster and, indeed, he usually needed the extra pittance to stay alive. But he was occasionally excessively versatile: one schoolmaster, near Illiers in the Beauce, was clerk of two communes, town-crier, choirmaster, bell-ringer, grave-digger. This was thought to be excessive.

The priests, even if they could command the schoolmaster to go to church and go to communion, could not so command the ordinary layman, and in many, many villages, hardly any men made their Easter duties and more and more celebrated Sunday in the village public-house rather than in the village church. But villages wanted to have a priest; it was undignified not to have one; it was also bad for business and a priest who took Talleyrand's advice and showed no excessive zeal might even be popular. But that significant sign of a decline in real religious fervour, the absence of vocations for the secular clergy, was as marked in the Beauce or Burgundy as in modern Rome. As Clausel de Montals, the pugnacious Bishop of Chartres, noted, the nobility, ready to send their sons into a rich Church, were not willing to send them into a poor one. So the clergy were recruited from the peasantry, often from the peasantry of remote, pious but backward districts, sent to try their zeal on the pagans of more favoured regions, where, the sword of the spirit producing no very impressive results, they relied on the secular arm. It was not refused them. All that mere power could do was done. The great mission crosses were often adorned with the fleur-de-lis. 'It is easy to see that the Son of God died 1,800 years ago to re-establish the Bourbons on the throne of France.'

This bitter and not unjust jibe came from no infidel wit, but from a scandalized priest, Abbé Gerbet, one of the new generation of Catholics whose leader was Lamennais. That fiery Royalist was now convinced that the alliance of 'Church and Throne' was disastrous for the Church, the living body of which must be cut free from the body of death of the Bourbon monarchy. What was living and awake to the problems of the age in French Catholicism was horrified by the political religion of the Government. And the Government was angered by the lack of dynastic loyalty of the young Catholic school. Yet if the Church suffered, so did the crown. The mourning colour of the House of France was violet, but when Charles X wore it he was suspected of being a 'secret bishop', and that intelligent and important people could be found to believe this fable showed how completely the links with the old order had been cut. Many Royalists knew that the King's public piety was a handicap; so was the charge that the Government patronized the Jesuits launched by an angry old

Gallican nobleman, the Comte de Montlosier, who became a hero of the Left. And despite lip-service to the principles of the Charter, the Royal Government was suspected, with some justice, of regretting the equality promised to the Protestants who had, on their side, the recent memories of the 'white terror of 1815' and (as Littré remembered) the not very remote family tradition of organized persecution. The Jews had even more reason to doubt the goodwill of the Government, but except in local colonies like that of Carpentras, they were not numerous anywhere outside Alsace, where Napoleon himself had had to recognize and allow for the anti-Semitism of the peasants.

The monarchy alienated most of the growing forces in France, alarmed the fearful vested interests of the beneficiaries of the Revolution, and, with all the levers of command more completely concentrated in the capital than ever before, it alienated also the only great body politic in France, Paris.

VIII

To Paris, the eyes of the ambitious young men of all schools turned as, in other days, they had turned to the Court. They came in their hundreds and thousands as students of medicine and law, as intending painters and poets. Their families invested in them, families of the *petite noblesse*, like the Rastignacs, giving up a third of their tiny income to launch their son with 1,200 francs a year instead of the 25,000 that, as Vautrin told him, he needed for his career as a dandy. Of course, there were medical students who worked as hard and ignored the pleasures of the town as completely as did, by his own report home from Paris, the young Oliver Wendell Holmes. But there were others, like Sainte-Beuve, for whom medical studies were a side-line. Paris, its men and women, its lectures and theatres, debates and literary *salons* like that of Charles Nodier at the Arsenal, were the main theme. The prizes were great. A successful play might make a man famous and rich overnight, as *Henri III et sa Cour* made the young Dumas; notoriety, power, money could be won by the successful journalists who undermined Royal authority despite the censor; the delights of discussions in famous cafés, of dinners with famous ladies of the town at 'Le Rocher de Cancale'—these were glittering prizes. The assault on Paris of the ambitious young man from the provinces became one of the great themes of nineteenth-century literature and life, in Balzac, Stendhal, Flaubert, Barrès, in Thiers, Gambetta, Zola.

It was the function of 'the Latin Quarter' to house, educate, entertain these young men, the Latin Quarter that was to get its new name from Henri Murger who christened that sea-coast (on which so many were to make shipwreck) Bohemia, with Mimi as the new Héloise. Of course, most of the temporary dwellers in 'the beautiful city of Prague' did not make shipwreck, returned to their provincial bases with memories no more disturbing than those of Justice Shallow. But while they were in Paris, they were a force, with at their head the élite of the French youth, the students of the École Polytechnique. They rioted in great rebellious manifestations. There were Royalist and Catholic students, but they were a minority.

Those of the students who were not mere playboys were open to many winds of doctrine. Even if they were not Catholics, Chateaubriand had marked them. They would not ask, as did Morellet, one of the last Encyclopedists, what *precisely* was meant by a famous passage of the master. The heart had its reasons they knew. And after Chateaubriand so many strange rivers flowed into the Seine, Rhine and Thames, Tweed and Danube. Old-fashioned and complacent Frenchmen like Napoleon's 'Grand Master of the University', Fontanes, might sneer in ignorant innocence at the pretensions of the Germans, but Charles de Villers and Madame de Staël had reported that strange things were stirring across the Rhine. The names of Kant, then of Hegel were heard.

It was less the ideas of Britain than its poets and artists that counted. Scott, then Byron, Bonington swept in on a flood-tide of Anglo-mania. Byron succeeded Napoleon as a symbol. (His dull translator, Amédée Pichot, made 40,000 francs, £1,600, more than many brilliant French men of letters did.) The first visit of a Shakespearian company, in 1821, was hooted off the stage by indignant patriots. It was very different in 1827. Already young Victor Hugo, at Reims for the coronation, had been converted. Shakespeare triumphed. Hector Berlioz fell in love with the poet and with Harriet Smithson. The rage for Shakespeare spread to other British authors. Tom Moore was seen as a great poet of the people, a more lyrical Béranger (which he was). Alfred de Vigny translated *Othello*, to the peevish surprise of M. Viennet, the well-known classical poet for whom all that could be made of that barbarous piece had been done by Voltaire who had turned it into *Zaïre*. Hamlet became a new symbol; so did Faust. Berlioz, Gérard de Nerval, Delacroix were only the leaders of the devotees of Goethe. And with Goethe came Beethoven. He was still hardly known; his name misspelled. Berlioz was taught counterpoint at the Conservatoire by a school-fellow of Beethoven's, but not until 1828 was Paris introduced to Beethoven's 'œuvres'.

At the most cosmopolitan times of the eighteenth century, Paris had never been so universally receptive as now. And this new spirit found its expression in *Le Globe* which deliberately, under Jouffroy and Dubois, set itself above the sterile battles of the Chamber and the polemical Press. More than religious dogmas die was the message and if the only newspaper read by the Duc d'Orléans was *The Times*, the only newspaper read by Goethe was *Le Globe*.

But this brave new world of new ideas had no links with the Royal Government. In the first amiable days of the new reign, it had seemed possible that the new reign and the new spirit were not quite irreconcilable. But the honeymoon had been brief. The Government was ineffectually hostile to 'the University', the Napoleonic creation that monopolized all forms of education from the 'great schools' of Paris to the secondary schools of small towns. It might be willing to leave the Church to educate the peasants, but it bitterly resented any attempt of the Church to educate the upper classes. Schemes of breaking 'the University' up into seventeen territorial universities were adumbrated. The Minister responsible for the University was usually a bishop. Its most celebrated teachers, like Guizot and Villemain, were silenced and the students were forced to formal observance of a religion in which few of them had faith. Engineers at the Polytechnique, like budding lawyers and doctors, were overwhelmingly Liberal. So were their teachers. A few savants like Ampère and Sylvestre de Sacy were Catholics; the great naturalist Cuvier was both a very orthodox Protestant and a bigoted Royalist; but what we now call the 'Intellectuals' were hostile and they helped to make the public opinion of Paris. All laughed at Sosthène de la Rochefoucauld (the first patron of Berlioz) for putting fig leaves on statues and lengthening the skirts of ballet dancers. The students, if not their teachers, were angered by the war against unlicensed brothels. Even the brief alliance between the poets and the crown was over. Hugo's play *Marion Delorme* was forbidden performance; it was irreverent to royalty. The poet was offered an increase in his pension as compensation. It was not enough. His revenge came when his new play *Hernani* was exploded under the old poetic order. The theatre was packed by the zealous young, marshalled by Théophile Gautier in a pink doublet. The new order won; the classical regime went down, for the moment, in defeat. In was 1830—and an omen.

There were other omens. The Government of Louis XVIII had undone part of the work of the Revolution by reorganizing the 'Institut de France', the federation of the Academies created by the Convention, and restoring the old pre-eminence of the Académie Française. But the Government of Charles X insisted on quarrelling with the Academy, which gained new prestige by its attitude of resistance. The attempt to impose the old Gallican doctrines of Louis XIV alienated many Catholics who were not blind devotees of papal supremacy, but knew the temper of the age. And, most serious of all, in a fit of pique, the National Guard of Paris was dissolved because, if it cried 'Vive le Roi' when the King reviewed it in 1827, it also shouted 'À bas les ministres'. It was a mistake to give the Guard the opportunity; it was a mistake (as Villèle realized) to react so foolishly. For the National Guard was a more representative body than the electorate. Its members, buying their own uniforms and equipment, solid citizens nearly all of them, were not a revolutionary force; they represented M. Joseph Prudhomme. His hostility to the Ministry might easily become hostility to the dynasty; at best he was now neutral.

The Army, if not neutral, was more obedient than loyal. Some of the promotions of émigré officers scandalized good Royalists like the Comte de Serre who noted their bad effect in a soldierly province like Alsace. A vacancy among the Marshals of France was filled, not by one of the leading Imperial generals, but by a Prince Hohenlohe whose military honours, such as they were, had been earned fighting in the armies opposed to France. The Austrian Embassy added oil to the smouldering fire by refusing to recognize Napoleonic titles taken from what was now Austrian territory: thus, Soult was not admitted to a ball as 'Duc de Dalmatie'. It was a loyal officer, member of a great family, General de Castellane, who noted, sourly, in his diary, 'This Austrian impudence is a little too much for those of us who served in the old Army, who have seen how humble these characters were under the Emperor.' The dilemma of the Restoration's attitude to the glories of the recent past was made most manifest at the funeral of Marshal Kellermann who had become a devoted Royalist (as his heir was after him). But his title was 'Duc de Valmy'. How could a servant of Charles X pronounce a funeral oration on a man whose title recalled the first battle in history in which a victorious French army had fought with the war-cry, not of 'Vive le Roi', but of 'Vive la Nation'? The Duc de Valmy was buried in silence.

IX

In the last years of his reign, Charles X moved with the confidence of a sleep-walker. The Ministry that replaced Villèle's had no formal head, but its spokesman was Martignac who hoped to reconcile the crown and the natural majority of any possible Chamber, that is the Deputies resolved not to permit the Revolution to be undone to the profit of the Court or the Church. He induced the King to accept the barring of the Jesuits from the seminaries into which some bishops had admitted them, a concession that Charles X regarded much as Louis XVI had regarded the Civil Constitution of the Clergy. He got rid of the most offensive officials of Villèle's administration. He proposed to make the Press laws more liberal and to introduce an element of election into local government. These measures, accompanied by soothing words, gained for the Ministry—and the King—a temporary popularity that Charles X noted and credited to his own private account. But the concessions infuriated the Right and did not satisfy the Left. The acceptance of Royer-Collard as President of the Chamber was humiliating for the Royalists; the refusal of the Ministry to submit all press cases to jury trial was made the excuse for violent polemics on the Left. For the Right to permit the election of local councillors was to weaken royal authority (the old belief that local electors would be easily manageable by the gentry had died); to retain the nomination of all mayors by the Government made the reform illusory for the Left. To retain such absurdly superfluous institutions as the arrondissements was simply a means of justifying the existence of those absurdly superfluous officials, the 'sous-préfets'. (This argument was to have a long life; so were the 'sous-préfets'.) The extreme Right refused to support Martignac and the Left, confident and aggressive, would not be content with half-measures. Neither would the King. He was pleased that his enemies had shown their hand. Martignac resigned and, although the politicians busied themselves with various combinations, even with a joint ministry of Villèle and Casimir Perier, Charles X brought back from his London Embassy Prince Jules de Polignac, an old friend even more religious and foolish than himself. Bourmont, the triple traitor, was made Minister of War; the two nominations were a declaration of war against the Charter. Or were they?

The opposition flattered the King and his Ministers in attributing to them a concrete plan of action. Polignac could not understand why his mere name alarmed the country. Had he not protested his loyalty to the Charter? Had he not great designs for the glory of France that would make the nation forget Waterloo? One of the few measures of the reign that were popular on all sides had been the intervention in favour of the Greeks. The three Allies, Britain, Russia, France, had destroyed the Turco-Egyptian fleet at Navarino, a triumph equally agreeable to the admirers of Byron and of Chateaubriand. A French corps had occupied the Peloponnese. But there had not been a joint Franco-Russian war on the infidel which would have enabled France to reopen the question of the Rhine frontier. England had opposed such a policy and the Government did not want a quarrel with England. Polignac, nevertheless, dreamed of preposterous diplomatic combinations such as one that involved sending the King of the Netherlands off to rule Constantinople so that France might recover Belgium! Nothing came, nothing could come of these preposterous schemes, save a general conviction in the cabinets of Europe that France, under the Bourbons, might be nearly as much an enemy of the *status quo* as under Napoleon.

Glory, however, was sought and found. A long squabble with the Dey of Algiers, culminating in that piratical monarch's slapping the French Consul with his fan, gave grounds for an expedition which would, the King thought, win him the needed popularity, or rather increase the popularity that, he was convinced, he already had. Only the journalists, the Doctrinaires, the permanent enemies of order were really discontented; the people was with its King and only the people was to be feared. The expedition sailed; the Algerines were defeated and on July 5 the French flag was hoisted on the Casbah of Algiers. Charles X had succeeded where Charles V had failed. But it was the white flag that had been hoisted and the victor was the most detested soldier in France, Marshal Bourmont.

Another war had broken out; 221 Deputies had voted an address to the King that he took to be a claim to dictate who should be his Ministers. (It was, in all but form.) The Chamber was dissolved and, for the first time since 1814, a Government failed to win the elections. In the restricted electoral body there was no support for the King. A young journalist turned historian, Adolphe Thiers, had laid down the policy of the opposition: 'Shut up the Bourbons in the Charter; they are sure to jump out of the window.' Others thought the same, although Royer-Collard, blinded by his Doctrinaire sagacity, believed that even Charles X could not be so foolish. Another young journalist, Armand Carrel, star of the most militant opposition journal, *Le National*, had already drawn the deadly parallel with England, with Charles X as James II. It was assumed that a *coup d'état* was in preparation. It was not. The Ministers prepared ordinances dissolving the new Chamber, again altering the electoral laws, imposing the most rigorous control of the Press; but no preparations were made to enforce them. The Ministers no more expected resistance than had M. de Dreux-Brézé on the day of the Oath of the Tennis Court. No fresh troops were brought into Paris. The Under-Secretary of War was not told and his chief was in Africa. The

command of the Paris garrison was earmarked for the second most
unpopular soldier in France, Marmont, but he was not told either.
The King went off to shoot at Rambouillet.

The news of the ordinances was like a thunderstorm on a sultry
day. The more ardent journalists decided to publish their papers as
usual; the Deputies of the opposition pondered legal methods of
expressing resentment and inducing the King to change course; no
one, not even Armand Carrel, thought of a revolution, of a change
of dynasty. The people of Paris took the matter into their own hands.
The ordinances threw printers into the streets (and printing was the
biggest single Paris industry). Other businesses shut up shop. The
unemployed began to pillage the gun shops; there was no National
Guard since its dissolution in 1827; the royal authority rested on a
small police force and a small and ill-prepared garrison. In the heat,
the troops tried to fight their way into the swarming, narrow streets
of the Faubourg Saint-Antoine; they failed; they wavered. The
King's complacency was unshaken, but the opposition Deputies
realized that it was not a revolt, but a revolution. The tricolour
floated on the towers of Notre-Dame; the King wavered and sent the
Duc de Mortemart to negotiate, but all the traditional intelligence
of his new Minister's family would have failed to save Charles X.
The question now lay between the Republic and the English
solution, the Duc d'Orléans. For the moment, the decision lay in
the hands of the great and empty symbolic figure of Lafayette.
He was won over to Orléans who was proclaimed Lieutenant-
General of the Kingdom by the Deputies and Peers, and then
nominated to that office by Charles X to save the throne of
'Henri V'. For even Charles X realized that Providence had turned
against him. He and the Dauphin, the Duc d'Angoulême, abdicated.
It was too late. A great mob poured out from Paris to drive the
King away from his capital. The household troops were as loyal
to Charles X as the Coldstream had been in 1688 to James II;
but all was over. The royal procession set out for Cherbourg. All
the pomp of the Court was preserved; the hated tricolour was kept
out of sight. At Laigle, there was only a round table in the château;
it had to be hewn square before the ex-King could sit at it. The last
King of France and Navarre reached Cherbourg, said farewell to

his guards (among them the father of Anatole France), and sailed to a new exile in Holyrood.

It is hard to be just to the Restoration. Its final follies were not less criminal for being childish. It wrecked whatever chances there were of uniting the two Frances. Yet its achievements were real. It 'liberated the territory'. It restored the public credit. It secured the position of France as an independent great power. It had such minor permanent achievements as the foundation of that glory of French scholarship, the École des Chartes, and the putting of the Army into red trousers. It did not, in fact, undo any of the achievements of the Revolution and the Empire; neither the monopolistic powers of the 'University of France' nor Imperial centralization suffered any real damage at its hands. The France that it left to its successors was solvent, stable, powerful. And, as was soon to be seen, the conviction of the rightness of the royal authority, an authority not based on popular will, still less on popular whim, was valuable. And it was 'digne', more than respectable, it was impressive. Not many of its successors could claim as much.

II

THE BOURGEOIS MONARCHY

I

LIKE Waterloo, the establishment of what was to be called 'the monarchy of July' was a 'damned, close-run thing'. The people of Paris, risen in arms, had had to be cajoled to lay them down. The great name of the Republic was again in the wind and many Frenchmen had begun to speculate on the future of the Duke of Reichstadt, once the King of Rome. It would take adroitness to keep Louis-Philippe on the throne on to which he had been pushed (as he hinted) or had deliberately climbed (as the partisans of the elder branch insisted). The new King thought that he had the necessary qualities. His education by Madame de Genlis had been more realistic than that of his cousins. He had fought in the armies of the Republic; he had lived in exile in a less restricted world than had Louis XVIII or Charles X. He was the first, though not the last, ruler of France to know the United States at first hand. He was a remarkable linguist. He was ready to say with Ulysses:

> 'Much have I seen and known; cities of men
> And manners, climates, councils, governments.'

He was very intelligent but, unfortunately, he knew it. He had no very high opinion of mankind and nothing that he was to see as King of the French was to raise it. For the alteration of the royal title was one of the concessions made to the heroes of July. Louis-Philippe was not the successor of Charles X. He had received a crown, not the crown, from Parliament; that was, formally, the base of his authority. It was a shaky base. It was hard to see why a Parliament elected on a very narrow franchise, and dissolved by the King who had called it into being, had constituent rights. But the bourgeoisie was frightened. All over France, it rallied to the new monarchy, less in love than in fear.

There was a wholesale replacement of 'Carlist' officials by old servants of Napoleon or old nominees of Decazes. From being rising young journalists or professors, men like Thiers and Guizot suddenly became powers in the State. For them, the Revolution of July had justified itself. But for the men who had raised the tricolour and the barricades, the solution of August 1830 was not a solution; it was a trick. Even if they, or their spokesmen, had accepted Louis-Philippe as being, in words put into the mouth of Lafayette, 'the best of Republics', they expected more than the meagre concessions grudgingly granted; the doubling of the number of voters (raised to a miserable 200,000 at the very moment when the First Reform Bill was transforming the oligarchic structure in England); the abolition of that preposterous institution, the hereditary peerage; the reduction of the salaries of bishops from 15,000 francs (£600) to 10,000 francs (£400). The blood of the Paris streets cried to heaven for vengeance, yet the heads of the Ministers of Charles X did not roll under the knife. The House of Peers (it survived though it was not hereditary) let them off with life imprisonment. An ostentatious celebration, at St. Germain-L'Auxerrois, of the anniversary of the death of the Duc de Berry led to riots in which the palace of the extravagantly Royalist Archbishop. Monseigneur de Quélen, was pillaged. The new King took the hint and removed the fleur-de-lis from his arms. But the spectacle of licensed disorder, not repressed by the Prefect of Police or the Minister of the Interior, frightened the real victors of July, the upper middle classes. They found their man in Casimir Perier and, with him, the policy of 'resistance' was begun. For the lesson, the apparent lesson of July, was being learned by the discontented in Paris and in other cities. Barricades could be erected against more powerful tyrants than Charles X; the workers of the great cities were beginning to ask for more than 'freedom', to protest against more wounding privileges than those of the old nobility. Such a representative of the new ruling class as Casimir Perier had no use for the sentimental temporizing of Odilon Barrot or Jacques Lafitte. The first battle of the social war was won.

Another war was avoided. The fall of Charles X had been the signal for revolutionary effervescence everywhere. In Italy, in Poland, the settlement of Vienna was challenged in arms. It was challenged in a more dangerous form when the southern Netherlands rose against the rule of the House of Orange. To some of the victors of 1815, the revolt of Belgium, the threat of its annexation to France, was the omen of a reopening of the great war. So it was to many hopeful Frenchmen. But Louis-Philippe was not among them; neither were his Ministers. The rickety Government of July could not stand a war. Belgium was made independent; a French army besieged the Dutch garrison in Antwerp; the throne, offered to a son of Louis-Philippe, was refused; Belgium accepted Prince Leopold of Saxe-Coburg who married a daughter of Louis-Philippe (he had earlier married the daughter of George IV). No other settlement would have been accepted by England and only the alliance with England could prevent the revival of the alliance of the Four Great Powers that had dethroned Napoleon. It was a settlement worthy of the diplomatic talents and sense of reality both of Palmerston and of Talleyrand who had been sent as Ambassador to England. But it was not a settlement to appeal to the hearts of the young men who were beginning to see the wars of the Empire through a haze of rhetoric. A chance to avenge Waterloo had been lost. Nor was it the only opportunity lost. For the Poles were crushed and in a disastrously unfortunate phrase the Minister of War, Marshal Sébastiani, announced that 'order reigns in Warsaw'. The revolted Italians of the Papal States were left to their fate. That revolt was unimportant in itself, but it had long-term consequences for France. The 'King of Rome' had died in 1831. His death removed the most formidable candidate for the throne of Louis-Philippe. But the heir of the Bonapartes was a handsome, energetic prince, the eldest and only undoubted son of Louis Bonaparte. He died in the Italian revolt and the next heir was his younger brother, silent, secretive, conspicuously unlike any other member of the Imperial family. He, it was universally thought by the prudent, could be disregarded. The prudent were wrong.

They were more afraid, for the moment, of the dangers of a Royalist restoration. There were plenty of partisans of the Bourbons everywhere. Were there not organizations of armed Royalists in such unlikely places as La Ferté-Vidame where, in 1793, the local Jacobins had thrown the coffins of the great Duc de Saint-Simon and of his wife into the ditch? There were Royalist zealots among the non-commissioned officers as there had been Republican zealots under Louis XVIII. But the danger was not real. Briefly brought back into the national life, the old nobility was now self-exiled. The 'émigré of the interior' became a familiar figure, sulky, hostile, living in a world of dreams and resentments. He was idle unless he had enough land to occupy him, and enough industry and intelligence to farm it. Few were as lucky as an officer of the Guards who married a woman of the Macintosh family and founded, in Clermont-Ferrand, a little rubber business that became, in due course, the great firm of Michelin.

The catastrophe of 1830 demoralized the Royalists. The Restoration of 1814, even the Restoration of 1815, had had a miraculous character. Fifteen years of royal favour, only briefly interrupted, had bred or revived habits of golden expectation. These were abruptly broken. In every part of France, the bitter enemies of the recent past triumphed. The Royalist monopoly of office, the Royalist control of local government, ended. Even had the gentry been willing to accept the new King, they would have had to share his bounty with men and groups they detested. But they were not willing. Only in the Army did Royalist officers (often after deep heart-searchings like those of young Patrice de MacMahon) consent to serve France even if it meant serving the usurper, and many refused to do even this. Alfred de Vigny went out; Colonel Bugeaud came in. The Royalist officer, unemployed, increasingly embittered, became a figure in the Legitimist society of most local capitals. We can see him, the equivalent of the Bonapartist half-pay officer, through the eyes of young Lucien Leuwen in Nancy. But he was to be found in the Saint-Pierre quarter in Nantes, in the upper town of Angoulême, sulking like the Jacobites of Fielding or Scott. Of course, the new monarchy could not last; it would be overthrown by the Republicans and then the King would come into his own again. It would die of its own unworthiness. For the Legitimists firmly believed that their social disapproval was a political force. Ridicule kills in France, and what could be more ridiculous than the usurping monarch with his bourgeois Court? But it was the Legitimists who were becoming figures of fun.

They were worse than that. They were 'Carlists'. For the old King seemed to have forgotten that he had abdicated. He was again Charles X, King of France and Navarre; all rightful authority was in his hands in Prague. It was the enemies of the old monarchy who insisted that the Legitimists were 'Carlists'; the very name was like a knell. It recalled to all the inexcusable follies of the last King. By a miracle, the sacred phial had been put in his hands. With a pathological clumsiness, he had insisted on dropping it. Yet, by their own creed, the 'Carlists' could not blame King Charles. He had not only been King; he had been *their* King. He had avoided all the faults of Louis XVI, so his fall could be explained only in terms of conspiracy and treason, above all by the treason of the Duc d'Orléans, a treason hereditary in that rotten branch of the royal house. To the Carlists, the fury of the mob at St. Germain-L'Auxerrois was more encouraging than frightening; there was no choice between the rightful King and the rule of the mob. The French people would come to see that. In 1832 this theory was put to the test by the Duchesse de Berry who attempted to raise La Vendée in rebellion. But even less than in 1815 were the devout peasants of La Vendée ready to fight for the King. The scuffle (it hardly deserved a more dignified name) ended with the flight of the Duchess, her discovery and her imprisonment at Blaye under the guardianship of General Bugeaud. The temperament of the Spanish Bourbon women did the rest; the Duchess was soon pregnant, was released, married an obscure Italian nobleman, and remained an even greater nuisance to the supporters of her son than Marie Louise had been to the partisans of the King of Rome.

II

The Church had now to pay for its exorbitant claims under the Restoration. There was more visible, popular rejoicing over the downfall of the clergy than over the fall of the elder line of the Bourbons. The King was in exile; the bishops were at hand. The fiery Bishop of Chartres, Clausel de Montals, tried to remove a parish priest popular with his flock, if only because he was unpopular with the Legitimist and authoritarian bishop. The new parish priest was chased out of his presbytery and the mob marched on Chartres and pillaged the episcopal palace under the complacent eyes of the revived National Guard. In Paris, Monseigneur de Quélen consecrated the new Bishop of Le Mans at midnight, in real or simulated fear. Priests dared not wear clerical dress in the streets; the crucifix was removed from the court rooms; churches were closed on week-days. The Trappists at La Meilleraye were dispersed by armed force, most of them taking refuge in Ireland where they founded the Abbey of Mount Melleray, destined to render, in that country, services the very opposite of those rendered by the monks of La Grande Chartreuse in France.

But the new order soon found it had more formidable enemies than the Church. The crucifixes came back to the court rooms; the churches were reopened. The new Government began to take the nomination of bishops seriously and the noble prelates of the Restoration were slowly replaced by a new middle-class type, by former professors in the big seminaries, by court preachers. The new bishops were not well received by the old nobility and they began to take into their hands the administration of Church charities, to impose their authority against both the gentry and the clergy. For the priests had, except for a small minority, 3,000 out of 60,000, no fixity of tenure. A famous pamphlet asserted that they were worse off than the village schoolmasters. A zealous reforming bishop, like Olivier at Evreux, might be thwarted by his chapter, but the parish clergy were at his mercy. A generation later, it was the same story. Cardinal de Bonnechose of Rouen was not exaggerating when he said that each bishop commanded a regiment and when he gave the order, it marched. These ecclesiastical centurions had much to do and they did it well. But they were almost as much cut off from their rural subordinates as the noble prelates had been. The parish priest saw in his bishop possibly his father in God, but seldom a spokesman of his needs and passions.

The Church was finding new and irregular spokesmen. Félicité de Lamennais had foreseen the downfall of the crown and the danger to the Church. He drove home the lesson in his newspaper, *L'Avenir*. The future of the Church was with the people. And round Lamennais rallied the most energetic of the young clergy and laity; priests like Lacordaire, laymen like Montalembert. The Breton country house of La Chesnaie was all—and more than all—that Newman's Littlemore was to be. Lamennais was not a thinker of Newman's rank nor of the rank of Maine de Biran (although, as Renouvier was to say, he would have been taken more seriously as a philosopher if he had written in German). But he was an incomparable influence. Both the Legitimist bishops like Monseigneur de Quélen and the new Government feared him. He appealed to Rome, made his pilgrimage, and saw his paper and his doctrine condemned. He submitted, formally, but his heart overflowed and in the *Paroles d'un Croyant*, the new Pascal turned from the official Church. But his disciples did not. Lacordaire was called on to preach the Lenten sermons at Notre-Dame, and, for the first time in a century, sermons were news and a force. This was not the tepid official eloquence of Maury or Frayssinous. Lacordaire could touch the hearts of a generation formed by the romantics. He did more. He defied the eighteenth century by setting out to restore, in France, the Order of Preachers, the order of the Inquisition as it was pointed out. He explained away the responsibility of the Dominicans for the Inquisition ('A gentleman does not deny his escutcheon,' said Dom Guéranger); but the appearance of a friar in his robes in Notre-Dame was followed by the appearance of a Jesuit, the Père de Ravignan. Was the work of the National Assembly to be undone?

The mere name of the Jesuits rallied the enemies of the Church. Few remained genuine Catholics like Montlosier, seeing in the Society the bane of religion. They had no use for religion or at any rate for the old religion. They were content with the naïve deism of Voltaire or were hankering after the reconstruction of French society on a new religious, but not necessarily theistic, basis. Meantime, the adroit defenders of the old religion must be discredited. For the mass of the bourgeoisie and for the more literate workers, Eugène Sue in *Le Juif Errant* had, in his portrait of the monster of intrigue, the Jesuit Rodin, shown up the Society for what it was. At the Collège de France, the two young professors, Edgar Quinet and Jules Michelet, in more and more impassioned and uncritical lectures, undertook to cure France of Catholicism. The Government, now conservative and reconciled with a Church less and less devoted to the cause of the old dynasty, silenced the two orators. It also secured the public dispersal of the Jesuits by a deal with the Pope. But neither Louis-Philippe nor Guizot could still the battle, even if they could disarm, for the moment, some of the combatants.

III

The parliamentary life of the July monarchy was brilliant but sterile and, in the long run, demoralizing. The debates of the Restoration had been often pedantic, excessively solemn, more a series of set speeches than of real debates. But they had been impressive; Bonald, Royer-Collard, General Foy had raised great questions. They ceased to be raised under Louis-Philippe. Even the great 'Carlist' spokesman, Berryer, was more a lawyer pleading a difficult case than an apostle preaching a militant creed. The 'legal country' was so small —and so fearful! The debates were sometimes on great issues of peace and war, but it was difficult to believe that that really meant peace and war. The clash of personalities and ambitions was dramatic, but it had many of the faults of the romantic theatre. All finished, if not in songs, in new combinations of ambitious orators. Thiers, Guizot, Molé, then the poet Lamartine were what the French were to call 'tenors'. There was no 'moment of truth'; no real *corrida*. There was at most a 'course royale', with a portfolio as prize. 'La portefeuille' became a stock epithet of the French comic stage. The artificiality of the political system was made manifest by the role allotted to Marshal Soult. He was now old, respectable if not venerable. He had been too many things to too many men to inspire reverence. His very ostentatious conversion to Catholicism under Charles X had caused a sensation, as had the conversion of Turenne under Louis XIV. (The Duc de Dalmatie, like the Vicomte de Turenne, belonged to a Protestant family.) But he was not taken so seriously as a convert as was Turenne, any more than he was taken as seriously as Marshal-General, an office held by Turenne and revived for the soldier called by the politicians 'the illustrious sword' and by an irreverent public 'the illustrious scabbard'. But sword or scabbard, the Marshal was a tool in a more adroit hand, that of the King.

Louis-Philippe might pay lip-service to the doctrine of the July monarchy, 'the King reigns but does not govern'. But he had no more intention than Charles X had had of being a 'roi fainéant'. He had some excuse for refusing to remain above the battle, for the parliamentary battle was a scuffle like the last scene of *Hamlet*: though the combatants did not exchange anything so dangerous as swords; they exchanged places. In this mêlée, it was difficult to find or keep an effective Government. The King thought it his business to see that the national business did not suffer, and the safest way to make sure of that was to do it himself. As long as the parliamentary forms were observed, as long as a figurehead like Soult, and an effective Minister to work through him, could be found and supported, the King, who could nominate a Minister and put the royal patronage at his disposal, had the last word.

The drawback was that this comedy wore thin, the pretence of a merely constitutional monarch became less and less plausible. The French people, inside the small body of electors and outside it, were forced to contemplate their chosen monarch. What they saw pleased them less and less. Louis-Philippe was intelligent but he was not wise. He was greedy but not thrifty. He had great confidence in his own political skill but appeared to have little in the stability of his regime. No sooner did he become King than he defied the laws of the House of France by transferring his immense private fortune to his family, instead of letting it fall into the royal domain. It was reasonable to argue that things had changed since 1789. But to do so was also to imply that Louis-Philippe was not the embodiment of the French State. It was tempting to accept the legacy of the last of the Condés, Chantilly and its dependencies, but that involved apparent collusion between a Prince of the Blood and an English harlot, Sophie Dawes. And the French saying that 'a good family man is ready for anything' was exemplified in the candid greed of this model husband and father. Again and again, his Ministers had to haggle with Parliament over endowments for his numerous and attractive children; and, equally revealing, an important scheme for the improvement of the French canal system was held to ransom by the King who, as Duc d'Orléans, was owner of an indispensable link in the system. Only too completely did the King personify the spirit of his supporters, the rising bourgeoisie. He not only dressed like them, in trousers, top hat, umbrella; he thought like them and lived like them. True, the ostentatious egalitarianism of the first years of the reign diminished as the King felt more secure. The Tuileries became more like Buckingham Palace and less like the Mansion House—or the White House.

The young princes, intelligent, handsome, brave, contrasted with their parent, 'the Father' as they called him in their candid private correspondence. The Prince de Joinville served with success in the Navy; the others, the Duc d'Orléans, the Duc de Nemours, the Duc de Montpensier, served in and successfully cultivated the Army. And the youngest, the Duc d'Aumale, by his talents, his courage and his success in love and war, almost justified the inheritance of Chantilly.

It was necessary to secure the succession and it was difficult, if not impossible, to marry the heir into any of the great Catholic houses that had provided brides for the Bourbons. So the intelligent if not beautiful Princess Helen of Mecklenburg-Schwerin was chosen. She was a Protestant, but for many of the supporters of the monarchy that was an advantage. She produced an heir who was given the original title of the House of France: he was 'Comte de Paris'. Then fate struck. In 1842, the Duc d'Orléans was killed in a driving accident. In his will, the Prince Royal (he had not claimed to be the Dauphin) dedicated his child to the Revolution. But it was far more important that the heir was a child, even younger than the Comte de Chambord had been in 1830. Good Orléanists might have murmured (some did), *Absit omen*.

If there was danger, it would not come from the Comte de Chambord. His father, his uncle were dead, at last. He was 'Henri V'. But the education he had been given made him no fitter to be a successful Pretender than had been his cousin, the King of Rome, educated by Metternich. He was not allowed to speculate on the reasons for the fall of his grandfather (other than the treason of the Duc d'Orléans). He toured Europe and, in Belgrave Square, received delegations of loyalists, now 'Legitimists' not Carlists any longer; but to all except the faithful, his was a lost cause.

To the shortsighted, another Pretender's cause was even more lost. For Prince Louis-Napoleon Bonaparte, formally heir to the Emperor (despite doubts about his paternity) had twice tried to imitate the tactics of the Hundred Days. At Strasbourg in 1837, he had tried in vain to win over the garrison: after a brief hesitation, the new discipline of the Army told; the Pretender was arrested and exiled. Louis-Napoleon's next attempt was at Boulogne in 1840; it was more elaborately planned (there was a tame eagle). Again it failed: discipline was too strong. This time the Prince was tried before the Chamber of Peers; and he was defended by the great Legitimist barrister, Berryer. Berryer found it easy to impale the time-servers of the regime on the dilemma. Would they have served the Empire if the plot had succeeded? Everyone knew that most of them would. Perhaps only Berryer could have dared to put the question. The Pretender was condemned to perpetual imprisonment. 'There is nothing perpetual in France', said the condemned man. He was imprisoned in the fortress of Ham, carefully guarded but not rigorously treated. He was allowed to read, to contribute to the Press, to correspond; he was not even denied the pleasures of love or, at any rate, of sex. He thought, he wrote, he dreamed. And history worked for him.

Or historians worked for him. The more remote the Empire became in time, the easier it was to forgive the Emperor. His great effort of propaganda from St. Helena was more successful after his death than in his life. The willow under which he was buried provided more and more relics. Béranger was only one of the balladmakers who exalted the man of the 'grey riding coat'. Cheap prints, 'Les images d'Épinal', kept his glory fresh. Fresher, perhaps, than it had been when the narrator of La Vie d'un Simple reported the ironic retort of the peasant of the Bourbonnais at the prospect of the return of the King of Rome to 'kill lots of people and lay countries waste like his father'. The Arc de Triomphe was a gigantic evocation of the epic story. And Thiers, in his overwhelmingly successful Histoire du Consulat et de l'Empire, retold the story in a style that was brilliant, clear and dazzlingly uncandid. In a moment of folly, the Government and the Chamber, despite the warnings of Lamartine, decided to appeal to Britain and to bring the Emperor back to Paris among 'that people' which, so he had mendaciously asserted in his will, he 'had so much loved'. The Prince de Joinville was sent to bring back the body. It was received in Paris with all possible parade. Victor Hugo noted, angrily, that 'there were three different welcomes given the Emperor. He was received by the people . . . piously, by the bourgeois . . . coldly, by the deputies . . . insolently.' But only the welcome of the people counted. And Victor Hugo went on to wonder whether 'among the veterans who guarded the catafalque there was not one of those grenadiers who had seen the deputies of the Council of Five Hundred (they were insolvent too) jump out of the windows of the Orangerie' (at the *coup d'état* of the 18th Brumaire which had made General Bonaparte First Consul, then Emperor). It was not quite true to say 'The Empire is made', but it was in the making.

IV

It is not very profitable to speculate on what would have been the evolution of French industry had there not been the great solution of continuity caused by war. Thanks to the war, to the constant distortion of economic life that it caused, France, in 1814, was industrially little changed while England had been revolutionized. James Watt (very sympathetic to the Jacobins) was a greater revolutionary than Robespierre.

In 1814, Britain had made the fundamental changes that we call 'the industrial revolution'. Mechanical power was the secret of the new society, mechanical power generated by the new steam engine designed in the University of Glasgow and made available for general use by the skilled workers of Birmingham. Steam power and iron were the heavenly or diabolic twins that had transformed Britain. They had not yet transformed France. And the France of the Restoration took over an economy where steam engines, power looms, the use of iron instead of wood were only in their first infancy. The first signs of the new age can be seen at Mulhouse in 1812. But it was only with the coming of peace that the new machines began to replace the old. And the names of the makers of the machines show how foreign was the new technique: Manby, Wilson, Waddington, Collier, Dyer, Dixon. By the end of the Restoration the main task was accomplished: the old looms of oak were a thing of the past; so, though less completely, was the old cottage industry, replaced by 'the dark, satanic mills' of the new order.

The change was effected slowly and expensively, for the rigorous protectionist system made iron two or three times dearer in France than in England, a basic cost from which the whole French economy suffered. The iron industry suffered too, from the fact that its ores were scattered in hundreds of small deposits, that its fuel for smelting was usually wood, since French coal suitable for coking was scarce and bad and the importation of foreign coal was highly penalized. Moreover, the best French coalfield, a part of the Belgian field, was not yet developed, and only in a few regions round St. Étienne and Le Creusot was there a happy conjunction of raw materials. Despite protection, infant industry involved many risks; some of the English pioneers paid for their boldness by bankruptcy, and even at Le Creusot it was not until the Schneider family took it over that the integrated industry there began to pay. And Decazes, exiled from politics, was not only a rare pioneer in investing his own and his friends' money in the new iron 'company town' of Decazeville in the Aveyron; his investment for a long time gave meagre results. All the profits were ploughed in, and the example was not very encouraging to other members of the ruling classes.

The dispersion of French industry made transport of the first importance and, in 1814, French transport was in a bad way. The Imperial road system, planned and maintained chiefly for war purposes, was in a poor state and the thrifty Government of the Restoration only very slowly repaired and extended the main roads; local roads remained few and bad. The transport of raw cotton by road from the French ports to Mulhouse added greatly to the manufacturing costs, and the monopolistic system of commerce kept Mulhouse from importing its cotton by the Rhine from Rotterdam.

It was natural, then, to look for a substitute for the roads, and the first charge on such funds as could be spared for improvement was the utilization of the rivers and the building of canals. On the map, the river system of France was admirably designed to link all regions together. But the map was deceptive. All the great river systems had their own drawbacks. The Seine was too winding, the Rhône and the Garonne too rapid, the Loire too sandy. Moreover, the availability of the rivers varied from week to week and from year to year. There was a great and disastrous difference between the maximum and minimum movement of freight that the shipper could calculate on, and this was reflected in delay and high freight costs. Barges could seldom be safely fully loaded and sometimes could use only a fifth of their capacity.

Canals were not, in theory, open to such objections. But not only were most canals designed to supplement river traffic, there were among them great differences in depth, width, in the size of locks, in the length of journey possible without breaking bulk. The State, nevertheless, spent a great deal of money, by the standards of those economical days, on canals. Mulhouse was connected with the Marne and so with the Seine and the sea. It was in financing such enterprises that bankers like Greffulhe rendered their greatest services and secured satisfactory profits.

But the application of steam to water transport changed the whole scene. Many of the existing canals could not be adapted to the use of steam power and there were many obstacles, even on great rivers like the Seine, that were now intolerable nuisances. Bridges had to be rebuilt, weirs and other obstacles removed, the rights of fishermen disregarded or bought out. The work was done though slowly (the improvement of the Seine navigation was not completed till 1888). But tugs pulling barges made of Paris a great river port; with the clearing and straightening of the channels of the Seine and the Loire, new life came to Rouen and Nantes, and by the time the monarchy of July was firmly established passengers used the rivers more than the roads. So it was by steamer that on September 15, 1840, Frédéric Moreau returned from Paris to Nogent-sur-Seine.

By 1840, the short reign of the river steamer was threatened by the new invention of the railway. But the threat or promise was slow in affecting French life. Viennet rejoiced, ironically, that Spain existed so that it could not be said that France was the most backward country in western Europe in the use of railways. She was decidedly backward. There were several causes. The protectionist system made the price of iron and so of iron rails prohibitive without exciting such an expansion of the iron industry as to lower prices or, indeed, provide the rails. The competition of railways was bitterly opposed by all vested interests; coach owners, inn-keepers, above all everyone interested in river and canal transport. The admirable but excessively cautious service of the Ponts et Chaussées had not only (like the

Army Corps of Engineers in the United States) a vested interest in
river and canal improvement, it imposed very rigorous standards on
the projectors of railways that they found it difficult and expensive to
meet. The first railways were, as in England, designed solely for
goods traffic in local industrial centres like Roanne and St. Étienne.
Not until 1837, when railways were normal in England, the United
States, and Belgium, did Paris have its first line, to St. Germain (more
exactly to Le Pecq; it did not climb the hill). Some of the most eminent figures in French life still refused to see, in the railway, anything
but an expensive and probably ruinous luxury. It was also dangerous
and unjust to existing methods of transport. There was a competition
in silliness; the winner was probably that eminent scientist in politics,
François Arago. The first serious railways out of Paris were to Versailles; there was one on each bank of the river so neither paid. But
scepticism had to give way in face of the rash of lines spreading all
over western Europe and the United States.

There were bitter debates in the Chamber on the legal foundations
of the new railway systems; there were able arguments for ownership
and operation by the State. The final decision was for a system in
which the State provided the permanent way and the main fixed
equipment; the companies, to which concessions were given, provided rolling stock and rails; and the State had the right to purchase
after a relatively short period of time. By 1844, France was beginning
to pursue if not catch up with her neighbours. She had escaped the
waste of competitive lines, of mere speculation; her new system of
main lines, radiating out from Paris, was symmetrical and rational.
All that had been lost was time—which has a price.

One cause of the slowness of the growth of the French railway
system was the difficulty of raising capital, itself a product of the
slow development of the French money market. The railways were
the first great capital consuming enterprises of the nineteenth century, the first enterprises that could not be financed by private bargains. They called on not only the national but the international
money market; it was as railway financiers that the Rothschilds first
made a deep mark on French economic life, and one ostensible reason
for caution in dealing with the projected railways was the danger of
the swamping of the nascent French industry by English capital. The

railways brought the average Frenchman face to face with big business for the first time.

'For the immense majority of Frenchmen', so Balzac asserted in *Les Illusions Perdues*, 'the working of one of the bits of banking machinery, if well described, will be as interesting as a chapter of a travel book about a foreign country.' There were several reasons for this, but two were of primary importance. Banking, as a system, was new and it was foreign. The very word was taboo under the old regime, ever since the calamitous collapse of the 'Royal Bank' of John Law of Lauriston. The Revolution was even more hostile to banks and bankers than the Monarchy, and although the necessities —and the desires—of the Directory brought about the creation of private banking houses, the beginning of the modern banking system, as of so much else, goes back to the Consulate. In 1800, the First Consul became one of the first and most important shareholders in the new Bank of France. Inevitably, the new bank had to face competition. It triumphed over its rivals, thanks to the support of the Government, but, in turn, it had to give up its cherished aim of being a totally independent bank; it had to accept a Governor from the Government and, soon, its chief customer became the State—sometimes master, more often client. Apart from the general control by the State, the Bank was ruled by its two hundred biggest shareholders, and these 'two hundred families' became, in myth and in reality, what was to be called 'the high bank'. A large proportion of those families were Protestants (often of recent Swiss or Dutch origin) and became the hard core of the 'H.S.P.', the 'haute société protestante'. To this nucleus were added the great Jewish bankers, of whom the Rothschilds were the most eminent and symbolic, and, although there were 'Catholic' members of this oligarchy like Stendhal's schoolfellows, the Periers from Grenoble, the banking system was distrusted by Catholics and Jacobins alike.

Banking grew slowly outside Paris and so did the national money market. There were local banks, some flourishing, like those of Bordeaux and Lyons, but in most French towns, the supply of credit was in the hands of local usurers, even if, at Saumur, M. Grandet had a banker, M. des Grassins, for his cover. There was no equivalent of the Quaker brewers and millers who created the English local banking system. Naturally enough, after the Revolutionary experience, the Frenchman was chary of bank-notes. The local banks of issue confined their activities to their own departments, and not until 1845, and after the Bank of France had begun a successful war against the local banks, was the whole note issue of the Bank taken up all over France. One cause of the slow industrialization of France was the slow development of her banking system.

There were some inadequate substitutes. The notaries, in return for the payment of high caution money, secured from the Government of the Restoration the right to sell or bequeath their 'études', and with this continuity assured they could undertake to run the investments of their clients, often, as Balzac insisted, to their clients' ruin. Another group of even more privileged agents of the State, the 'Receivers-General', who collected and remitted local taxes, acted as a loose national banking system. If not as important as the Farmers-General of the old regime, they were more useful. They, too, had to give very serious guarantees of respectability and solvency. So Armand Duval's father, who was a Receiver-General, could afford, even less than an ordinary bourgeois father, to have his son entangled with 'the lady of the camelias'.

The Receivers-General were not the only important and privileged body. There were the 'agents de change' whom it would be wrong to call mere stockbrokers. They were a small and limited corporation dealing, at first, in French Government securities. At the beginning of the July monarchy, less than fifty stocks were dealt in on the Paris Bourse, ranging in importance from the French *rentes* to the less stable public debt of Spain and Haiti. Ten years later, the range had been greatly extended: American securities were quoted, so were 'industrials'; and by 1847 there were nearly two hundred stocks on the market. And an 'agent de change' was now a person of great respectability, high in the bourgeois hierarchy. The fact that the father of Charles Swann had been an 'agent de change' placed his son, in Combray, more definitely than it would do in modern Surrey or Fairfield County.

Although Paris was on the way to becoming a great international money market, the main business of the Bourse was still the handling of the national debt and the health, prospects and stability of governments were tested by this simple barometer. It had been noted as a sign of the realities of French life that the *rentes* rose at the news of Waterloo and, despite all the signs of a gathering storm and the visible beginning of a great economic crisis, the *rentes* in the last year of Charles X's reign were at a premium of nearly 10% —and less than a year later, under Louis-Philippe, under par. It was, in fact, a very unreliable barometer, for if nearly all the *rentiers* were Parisians, the Parisians whom governments had to fear were not *rentiers*. They were the 'people'—those who were to be called the workers and, later, the proletariat.

v

The word was new; so was the thing. As the industrial revolution took hold in France, the social problem of the town workers began to perplex and distress the humane and the critical. If the new factory workers represented progress, was progress worth the price? They were often unemployed, not merely idle; their old craft status was destroyed by the new machines; real wages steadily fell; the habits of rural life were deadly in the towns. The cellar slums of Lille became an exhibit of the horrors of the new society. Hard times, too, became a feature of the new society, as ominous as famine had been in the old days. Hard times was one of the immeasurable forces making easier the revolution of July. That revolution, by drying up the market for luxury goods and causing a further restriction of credit, made the position of the workers worse than it had been before the successful defence of liberty by those same workers. So they rose in their own defence, not only in Paris but in Lyons. They were not very clear what they were fighting for, but they knew what they were fighting against. They fought desperately, round the Cloître Saint-Merri and in the Rue Transnonain where the infuriated troops slaughtered men, women, children, and gave Daumier the chance, in his most famous picture, to rival Goya.

There were lights as well as shadows in the picture. Not all textile towns were as deplorable as Lille. There were few examples of the totally new industrial town—perhaps only Roubaix and Mulhouse qualified; and, in Mulhouse, poor German and Swiss immigrants created some of the problems created by poor Irish immigrants in Liverpool and Glasgow. Nor did the new machines necessarily lead to a concentration of industry in the towns. Much of the weaving in Lyons was now sent out to the neighbouring villages. There was no hard and fast division between the town and the rural worker. He moved from the land to the factory and back again. What became the typical garment of the town worker, the blouse, was simply the peasant smock. Even less than the English factory worker was the French worker reconciled to urban life and factory discipline. He remembered, or thought he remembered, a happier day. The State did little to mitigate the horrors of the new order. The first primitive factory act was enforced by inspectors paid by the employers; so it was ignored. Even so upright a man as Waddington, the cotton spinner (he sent his son, the future Prime Minister, to Rugby), confessed, candidly, that he did not observe the acts because no one else did. Napoleon had marked the special and inferior status of the factory worker by making it compulsory for him to have a workbook, the much hated 'livret' which listed all his previous employers. The law of the 'livret' was not rigorously enforced, but its existence was bitterly resented.

Trade unions and strikes were illegal, as they had been in England until 1825, and, as in England and America, the law of master and servant discriminated against the worker. In certain skilled trades like building, the old 'compagnonnages' served as trade unions as well as insurance and self-improvement societies. But they were divided among themselves by meaningless, traditional quarrels. They represented the old pre-Revolutionary order (some were zealous observers of the religious traditions of the old guilds). In vain Agricol Perdiguier, 'Avignonnais-la-Vertu', tried to make peace between the trades and make of the 'compagnonnage' a school of virtue and professional competence. At best, they were a kind of poor man's freemasonry; at worst, mere excuses for drinking and brawling.

It was not proletarian leaders who made the most effective criticism of the new economic order. The most influential, Comte Henri de Saint-Simon, believed that Charlemagne was his ancestor. Saint-

Simon, soldier, speculator, prophet, saw in the anarchy of the industrial process its greatest weakness and sin. He was a prophet of the managerial revolution. Science had put the possibility of wealth into men's hands; the only obstacles were an obsolete and irrelevant political and social system. The French Revolution had brought the opportunity to deliver men from the curse of poverty. But Saint-Simon, if a believer in the control of competition, in the abolition of industrial anarchy, was no believer in equality. Talent (and capital) deserved a higher share of the greatly increased product. It was not surprising that the disciples of Saint-Simon were to include some of the boldest businessmen of the next generation. Nor was equality, or political freedom, the main preoccupation of Auguste Comte, Saint-Simon's most original and rebellious disciple, whose 'positive philosophy' was to provide a doctrine, if not a practice, for the bourgeoisie of Latin America, and whose invention, the word 'sociology', was to cover a multitude of systems. The self-taught Fourier found in the principle of sympathetic harmony the clue to wealth, for men and women doing the work for which God had designed them would be, as producers, vastly superior to the slaves of the ungrateful taskmasters of the old order. Compared to these visions of easily attained wealth, the drab egalitarianism of Cabet attracted few but fanatics.

Yet it was not the disciples of Saint-Simon, founding a new religion in Montmartre, or the disciples of Fourier dreaming of the wonders of his Utopian societies, the 'phalansteries', who best expressed the spirit of the rebellious French workers, but the printer, Proudhon, who opened his most famous tract by declaring that 'property is theft'.

That too famous sentence as much misled the public as did the first sentence of *Du Contrat Social*. But although Proudhon spent most of his life explaining the philosophical sense in which he meant his famous dictum to be taken, the French workers took it literally. Their employers were robbing them of their natural rights. Their resentment was not tempered by a common religious faith, such as bound Methodist employer and worker in England. There was no effective propaganda for the services of the entrepreneur. Economists might demonstrate the necessity of inequality, but they could not win for the businessman moral acceptance. For one thing, the representative success story in the France of Louis-Philippe was not that of a French James Watt watching a kettle and inventing the steam engine or even of Jacquard inventing his loom; it was of Jacques Lafitte picking up a pin and being launched on his brilliant career as a Liberal millionaire banker. There was no French Samuel Smiles or Horatio Alger to write the new hagiography. The businessman was often a foreigner and seldom fully received by French Society. There were towns like Le Creusot dominated by the Schneider, or St. Quentin dominated by the Seydoux family where business ruled. To have inherited a share in the great eighteenth-century iron and coal company of Anzin, a 'denier d'Anzin', like Victor de Pressensé of the famous Protestant dynasty, or the Catholic Grégoire family in Zola's *Germinal*, was to have inherited worth as well as wealth. It was even a great asset to marry into Anzin, as the poor journalist-politician, Adolphe Thiers, proved. But in regarding the French businessman with suspicion, the old aristocratic and the new revolutionary traditions were at one.

The misery of the workers was explained, for many of their betters, by their bad habits, drinking, gambling, sexual looseness. The upper classes tended to idealize the simple rural life that Zola was later to describe in *La Terre*. It was in the new factory quarters, in the new railway settlements, that bad politics and bad morals went hand in hand. It was assumed, rather than proved, that the town workers drank more than the peasants, that the public-houses, the 'cabarets', were centres of immorality as well as of sedition. But most of the licensed premises were in villages and hamlets; in some regions most houses in villages sold wine and spirits, even if only on fair days. Otherwise it would have been hard to account for the half-million of licensed dealers. There was no necessary connection between drunkenness and the number of licences to sell wine or spirits. There were great regional differences; the South where wine was not a luxury was more sober than the North. Then, as now, Normandy was a land of heavy drinkers.

There were well-meaning attempts to limit the evil. Protestants tried in vain to introduce total abstinence societies on the English odel. Seeing in the 'cabaret' the main source of evil, some philanthropists tried to make it easier for the worker to buy wine in small barrels to drink with his family, instead of letting him tipple with his comrades in the cabaret. This kindly thought was not notably well received. There was a steady rise in the amount of wine consumed if not in the amount of drunkenness.

Catholics concentrated more on the widespread sin of concubinage. A married man gave hostages to fortune that many workers had no intention of giving. He preferred to 'marry at the *mairie* of the XIIIth arrondissement' (a joke that lost its point when, in 1860, eight new arrondissements were added to the original Parisian twelve). The Society of Saint-François Régis tried to induce couples to regularize their situation in the sight of God and the law. It had some success; but many men, from prudence and principle, preferred to ignore both.

The factories introduced a new moral danger, for the sexes worked together in most industries and foremen often exercised a 'droit de seigneur' over the female workers. Reformers sometimes got the sexes separated and in some factories workers were supervised by nuns; but such paternalism was not universally popular. It smacked too much of patronage.

So, indeed, did most charitable effort. Under Louis-Philippe, some zealous Catholics began to realize that the urban workers were outside the Church which must go and seek them out as, in the time of Theodosius, it had sought out and converted the barbarians. The most striking example of this new concern for the unchurched poor was the Society of Saint-Vincent de Paul founded in 1833 by one of the most intelligent of the 'romantic' Catholics, Frédéric Ozanam. The object of the society was the sanctification of its members; charity was the means, not the end; but the young men who made up the 'conferences' learned, in visiting the poor, a great deal of the miseries of the new industrial world and very slowly began to perceive the existence of problems that charity, however holy, could not solve. That this was so was not appreciated by all. In that once famous monument of upper-class piety, *Le Récit d'une Sœur*, Mrs. Craven (*née* La Ferronays) could talk complacently of 'a power of charity which no need, no poverty have escaped'. Those who knew Paris better than she were not so optimistic. Nor did the work of bodies like the Society of Saint-Vincent de Paul necessarily do much to bring Christian life to the poor. As the President of the Chartres conference reported to headquarters, 'In general, our poor give us little consolation from the essential point of view', the work of faith.

One cause was the failure to involve the workers in their own salvation. The best 'conference' of Saint-Vincent de Paul was very inferior, as a means of Christianization and as a social bond, to a Methodist class. The French workers, less than most, wanted good done to them. Yet the Catholics, clergy and laity alike, refused to see this. They knew that, in Germany, very successful associations of Catholic workers had been set up. Their founder, the Abbé Kolping, was brought to Paris to explain his success. He insisted that one basis of it was the rigorous exclusion of the employers from the associations. 'The worker does not like having the employer's eye on him, outside his work' and 'in these intimate meetings, the inequality of status, being certainly too much felt, would drive out the workers'. What was true of German workers was truer still of French workers. But the Catholic leaders, the Catholic employers, would not learn. They had tens of thousands of young men in their 'patronages', but among them no leaders of the workers. Indeed, it was generally thought that Catholicism and such leadership were incompatible. Buchez, the Saint-Simonian and historian of the Revolution, was converted to Catholicism but refused to 'practise' since that would destroy his influence. Some of the priests most deeply convinced of the urgency of the task found themselves drifting away from the Church and it was necessary to reassure priests who found themselves denounced by the rich as 'communists'. But all efforts failed, and in 1856 a report made to Archbishop Sibour estimated at a million the number of Parisians totally outside the influence of the Church.

There were areas where the complete paganism of the Paris suburbs was not the rule. In places like Nîmes, dislike of Protestant employers kept the faith alive; there were areas in which the peasants brought to the growing towns a faith that they found it hard to keep. There were employers who, from genuine conviction, made the factory a centre of more or less voluntary adhesion to the traditional faith. A saintly employer who was also wise and magnanimous, like Léon Harmel, could be a kind of Catholic Robert Owen. The lady who then thought that she was Mrs. John Ruskin noted the different degrees of religious fervour in various regions, the church filled with men at Mortain in contrast with the absence of men at Abbeville. Formal respect for the Church was now the mark of good society. In the last years of the monarchy of July, it would not have been necessary for the Duchesse de Langeais to snub Eugène de Rastignac for his irreverent conversation. It became a mark of good tone in certain circles not to eat meat on Friday. But the men of the ruling class were still Voltairian, still cut off from the Catholic tradition. At the funeral service of that representative figure of the July monarchy, M. Dambreuse, most of the mourners had to be told when to stand and when to kneel.

VI

Of very great importance for the intellectual and political future of France was the revival, as part of the educational programme of the monarchy of July, of the École Normale Supérieure. This institution was designed to provide teachers for the lycées and for the university faculties. It was entered by competition, and all through their lives at the school the 'Normaliens' were in constant, feverish competition. 'Normale' provided admirable teachers (as Matthew Arnold testified), but it did more than that. It offered to poor and ambitious boys of the bourgeoisie, and even of the tradesman class, something of the opportunity the Church had offered before the Revolution. A Normalien had to undertake to teach, as a seminarist had to take orders; but for many of the ablest this meant no more of a vocation for teaching than entering the Church had meant a vocation for the priesthood for young men like Sieyès or Raynal. Of the group of six Normalien contemporaries with whom his biographer associates Taine, only one remained connected with teaching; four became men of letters or journalists; one became a cardinal.

But it was rare for a Normalien to be a practising Catholic, much more to become a priest. Prévost-Paradol was both shocked and astonished, when he entered the school, to discover that there were practising Catholics among the students. Formal respect for the established religions was insisted on, but that, in itself, made the position of the believing student more difficult. It was not until the school was freed from the weight of official religion that the 'talas', the practising Catholics, could expect to be respected by their comrades. Most of the Normaliens, if superior to vulgar Voltairianism, despised all forms of orthodox religion; those of them who had a sense of mission saw, as part of it, the liberation of France from dogma. The highly competitive atmosphere of the school produced brilliant polemical writers rather than scholars. Taine, as self-confident as Macaulay, if with far less knowledge of the world and a much wider and more superficial range of omniscience, was the representative Normalien at his best. Edmond About, clever, cynical, unscrupulous, was a not totally unrepresentative Normalien. For all but a few had to make their way in the world. Taine was exceptional in having private means; Prévost-Paradol in having important family connections (he was a bastard Halévy). But the poor, kinless, ambitious boy, with no vocation for teaching, learned at Normale that the race was to the clever, especially to the clever manipulator of words. There can have been few of the brilliant young men of the school in the mid-nineteenth century who suspected that the Normalien teacher whom the world would best remember was that pious and reactionary Catholic, Louis Pasteur.

The École Polytechnique, despite the rise of the École Normale, preserved its old prestige. To its professors like Carnot came brilliant young foreigners like William Thomson of Glasgow and Peterhouse, later to be Lord Kelvin. It was the temple of the religion of 'scientism'; the fact that its pupils were destined for the Army, or the State service as engineers, attracted boys who would not have wished to enter Normale. From it came some of the most original minds of the age; it was the spiritual home of the Saint-Simonians. And that the 'X' wore a brilliant military uniform added to his prestige in society and in love. The militant youth of the 'schools of Paris' saw in the Polytechniciens their natural leaders.

Not as much could be said for the university, in the ordinary sense of the term. 'The Sorbonne', the faculty of letters of Paris, provided a platform for brilliant lecturers. But it was not a university in the

German or even the English sense. The standards for the degrees, the 'licence', the equivalent of the bachelor's degree in England, were not high, and those for the doctorate were not rigorous. (Michelet was received as a doctor at twenty for a thesis of twenty pages on Machiavelli.) At the Collège de France, brilliant orators could entrance non-specialist audiences. But there was little advanced teaching and less research.

The provincial faculties were worse. There were respectable law schools. Montpellier had preserved its fame as a medical school; Strasbourg still kept in touch with German scholarship. But the faculties of letters provided sinecures for young men making their way, or for older men resigned to mediocrity, giving elegant courses of lectures before a mainly female audience. Cournot at Lyons, Walras at the lycée of Évreux, were men of talent out of place. A young literary man like Sainte-Beuve might aim at a chair at Besançon to tide him over a gap or as a springboard, as with Prévost-Paradol at Aix; but often the ambitious young teacher preferred a post in one of the great Paris lycées, at the heart of things, to the exile of a more dignified professorial chair in the provinces.

The intellectual standards of the State secondary schools rose steadily as the École Normale did its work, and the best of the Paris lycées, and of the lycées of the greater provincial cities, gave an admirable if too purely literary education. But they had serious defects. The 'professors', often brilliant, rising men of letters, were not merely too often lacking in a vocation for teaching; if they had a vocation, it was solely for teaching. The other parts of education, discipline, the organization of the scanty leisure of the pupils, were left to ushers, often of a much less impressive intellectual and not always of a very creditable moral standard. In some of the most famous schools, a boy was as neglected, as open to vice or bullying, as if he had been at Thackeray's Charterhouse. The existence of 'pensions' where boys were fed, supervised, housed better than they were in the lycées (which did the mere teaching) mitigated these drawbacks and seriously augmented the incomes of the lycée teachers who ran them. But for a zealous Catholic, these were poor substitutes for Christian training.

The State schools had chaplains; there were formal religious obser-
vances; but education, apart from much Latin, some Greek and
mathematics, and the teaching of French composition, culminated in
the class of 'philosophy'. Here it was impossible to avoid taking sides,
but the official doctrine, the 'eclecticism' of Victor Cousin, got as
near to that ideal state of neutrality as possible. Common sense plus
a dash of Kant and an insistence on the truth and relevance of a
vague theism, made up this course in the French schoolboy's diet. It
was not offensive; it was null. For that reason it was suited to the
monarchy of July of which its author was so representative a figure.
Cousin had had his moments of passion. He had been a *carbonaro* and
his mistress, Louise Colet, was a formidable woman of letters who
later took over Flaubert. Only people with strong beliefs could object
to M. Cousin's doctrine. There were now people with strong beliefs
to do so.

The Catholics wanted a specifically Christian doctrine (it would
be too much to say philosophy) taught and Catholic practices made
part of the very life of the school, not an extra like English. They
could not get such education from the State system, so they demanded
liberty to found their own schools. Liberty of teaching was one of
the rights guaranteed by the new Charter, but the jealous defenders
of the University did not expect it to be taken seriously. The State
might not strive to suppress independent schools but it would and
should do nothing to make life easy for them. Nevertheless, the independent schools grew. The most famous of them was officially only
the junior seminary of the archdiocese of Paris, Saint-Nicolas-du-
Chardonnet. But its director, the Abbé Dupanloup, had wide ideas.
'The young people destined for the ecclesiastical estate and young
people destined for the first rank in society ought to be educated
together', so Dupanloup's most famous pupil described his ideal. The
fees paid for the education of rich boys, destined for the world,
helped to pay for brilliant poor boys destined for the Church. The
young gentlemen would be the better Christians, the young Levites
the more effective preachers of the word, for this early association.
So the boy Ernest Renan was brought from his remote Breton
seminary to Paris. So the great noble families sent their sons to be
educated, not merely taught, by Dupanloup who was after all,

it was believed, a Rohan 'of the left hand' and had succeeded in the diplomatic masterpiece of making a treaty between the Church and the dying Talleyrand. Saint-Nicolas-du-Chardonnet flourished, as was natural in a snobbish world. It was also a climbing world and Voltairian fathers succumbed to the pressures of believing wives. It was deplorable from the point of view of the old, dogmatic apostles of the Enlightenment or of the new 'scientism'. But the Catholic schools flourished, even when they had no Dupanloup to run them or social promotion to offer. For they could and often did give an education, not merely lessons. The State system could give a chance to great teachers, but it could not give a chance to a great head-master like Dupanloup or, later, Lacordaire at Sorèze. There could be no Rugby, no Dr. Arnold in the lycée system.

Of course, all the fears and hopes that the growth of the Catholic schools provoked were not well founded. Many a boy of a good Catholic family lost his faith at the school he was hopefully sent to, his religion there being hardly a more serious thing than it would have been at a lycée. The same sad truth was learned by the parents who sent their boys to the famous Protestant school of Sainte-Foy; zeal and faith could not be commanded. But it was by the schools that Christian faith began to creep back into the ranks of the male members of the bourgeoisie. It was recognized as a necessity for women by nearly all of their fathers and future husbands. For them the convent was sufficient. There were old convents like the famous school of the Dames Anglaises where the future George Sand learned the importance of tea, but there were a score of new orders, and by the end of the reign of Louis-Philippe there were more nuns than under the old regime and the children of the bourgeoisie usually received not only different but opposed educations, according to sex.

VII

The attractions of Paris for the outside world grew daily. German princes and English nobles settled there. Russian grand dukes began to visit the seductive city; so did Russian enemies of grand dukes.

'In Paris', wrote Alexander Herzen, 'the word meant scarcely less to me than the word "Moscow". Of that minute I had been dreaming from childhood. If I might only see the Hôtel de Ville, the Café Foy in the Palais Royal, where Camille Desmoulins picked a green leaf and, fixing it on his hat for a cockade, shouted "À la Bastille".' In Paris, Heine found that liberated city he had glimpsed when he saw the Emperor ride across the princely turf in Düsseldorf. There were other lovers of Paris drawn there by less noble motives. There was Lord Henry Seymour, brutal, eccentric, fabulously rich, to whom the Parisians gave the title 'My lord l'Arsouille', coveted and usurped by others. But Seymour was the son of either General Junot or of Talleyrand's friend, Montrond. The devotion of his English half-brother, Lord Hertford, son of Thackeray's Lord Steyne, was more of a tribute. So was the permanent affection of Thackeray. It was not only because you could live there for 'a whole month upon five pounds' and buy 'a waistcoat out of it'. What he appreciated even more was that being an artist was a serious matter, not something to be ashamed of if you were determined to be a gentleman as well as an artist. By his time, it was unthinkable that a serious art student from England or America should any longer go to Düsseldorf or Munich; even Rome was dead.

The Paris noblemen and artists inhabited was a first, rough sketch of the Paris we know. The Emperor had had grandiose plans for his capital; an immense palace for the King of Rome on the hill of Chaillot, a great monument to his triumphant armies on the hill of the Étoile. But he was busy and he had adorned Paris, cheaply, with his trophies. The famous bronze horses of Venice and the Lion of St. Mark were only the most famous. A Temple of Glory was designed on a site that Napoleon had, for a moment, intended for a temple of money, for it was to have housed the Bourse and the Bank of France. The temple became the Madeleine and was finished in 1842. The only completed monuments of Napoleon's reign were the overbearing Column in the Place Vendôme, to be more famous in political poetry than in art, and the elegant 'Arch of Triumph of the Carrousel' whose superb narrative text departs less from the truth than is customary in lapidary inscription. But the greater Arch of Triumph was left unfinished and there was a comic decision that, in

1823, it should be dedicated to the triumphant arms of the Duc d'Angoulême. Not until 1836 was it completed. And, in the same year, the obelisk of Luxor was erected in the Place de la Concorde, on the site of the statue of Louis XV and of the guillotine. Round it were the statues of the great cities of France. One of them, that of Strasbourg, was to know a double celebrity; it was to be a centre of patriotic mourning and its model was Juliette Drouet, the 'maîtresse en titre' of Victor Hugo for the greater part of his long, glorious and amorous life.

But statues and monuments were not all. The Emperor at least gave Paris the rudiments of a good water system; gas began to light the streets and, in 1828, the Duchesse de Berry, greatly daring, took the newfangled omnibus from the Madeleine to the Bastille. The great problem of Balzac's poor young men paying court to great ladies on rainy days was how to keep their shoes clean; it was made easier. And the life on the cleaner, better-lit streets was one of the great Paris sights. The boulevards had come into their own. So had the cafés like the Café de Paris or the Café de la Renaissance. The Palais Royal still had its restaurants and its gambling hells where Rastignac staked, successfully, the money of Madame de Nucingen. But the empire of fashion and vice took its westward course. Even the shops like the pioneer department store, 'Les Trois Quartiers', went west. The Boulevard des Italiens and the Rue Napoléon that had become the Rue de la Paix were now, for many women of all nations, the centre of the world.

But the old Paris remained; much had been destroyed in the Revolution, much to make room for streets like the Rue de Rivoli and the Rue de Castiglione. But most of Paris was narrow, dirty, as labyrinthine as Lyons. There had been no clean sweep like the Great Fire of London. It was still a largely Gothic city.

The word Gothic was no longer a term of abuse. If the grandparents of the French Gothic revival were Scott and Chateaubriand, the father of the Gothic revival in France was Baron Taylor whose *Voyage romantique et pittoresque* reminded the more opulent French of the treasures and last enchantments of the Middle Ages. It was time, for the Revolution and its profiteers had made a clean sweep of so much. Where was Cluny, 'mater et caput' of so many great religious houses? It had disappeared and so, reflected M. Prosper Mérimée, picnicking under the crumbling walls of Vézelay, would other great medieval buildings do, too. The work of saving was begun by the Service of Antiquities and by private owners. Indeed, preservation hardly does justice to what Viollet-le-Duc did at Carcassonne and Pierrefonds; even in Paris, if he saved the Sainte-Chapelle, he did more than that for Notre-Dame, where the ravages of enlightened eighteenth-century canons and of Revolutionary iconoclasts were repaired with a boldness that few would emulate today. But gas, buses, the free use of cast iron in building were not the most important changes in Paris; for the first time since the Fronde, it became a fortified city. Tenaciously, Louis-Philippe fought for his project; Soult and Thiers got it through a hostile Chamber. The new girdle of walls, unlike the customs 'barrier of the Farmers-General' was a real military obstacle; outside 'les fortifs' lay the new suburbs, the villages that were yearly being swallowed up. And also outside the wall were the forts, one of which, Mont-Valérien, was to become almost as much a symbol as the Bastille. Not until after the first world war did Paris break through the confining strait-jacket given to her by the timid bourgeois King.

VIII

The news of the fall of Charles X came to Algiers where the victorious Marshal Bourmont gave up his command and where the Restoration left to the new regime a problem to which no thought had been given. Was Algiers to be treated as a conquest or was it sufficient that the peccant Dey should be deposed? Should a few coastal towns be held like the old Spanish *presidios* (the precedent was not encouraging), or should some native authority be found to accept French tutelage? There was, in France, a party in favour of simple abandonment of the conquest; its power grew as the difficulties of any solution became more apparent. There was no Algerian state; there were a number of independent principalities round citadels like Tlemcen and Constantine. There were tribes, nomadic and sedentary;

there were religious fraternities. For years, the French sought to find native rulers with whom to deal. Finally, they invented one, Abd-el-Kader. He had many claims on their support; he was intelligent, capable, pious; he was a member of a family of hereditary saints, a member of an important fraternity. Some Frenchmen saw in him a new Mehemet Ali who would do for Algeria (under French tutelage) what Mehemet Ali was thought to have done for Egypt. Abd-el-Kader thought this too, but he wanted no tutelage. He dealt with General Bugeaud; he extended his authority over western Algeria; and, strengthened by French recognition and gifts, he launched war on the infidel.

Year after year, the war continued. At the beginning, the French were pinned into Algiers and ports like Bône. The first attack on the rock fortress of Constantine failed. The war seemed endless and expensive. The troops, cooped up in the forts, were demoralized by idleness, drink, disease.

But a new school of soldiers replaced the old Imperial generals like Clauzel. They were 'the Africans'; there were Bugeaud and Changarnier, and the boldest of them all, Lamoricière; there were the Princes of the Blood, Orléans, Nemours, Montpensier, and Aumale. The war of strong-points was replaced by a war of the type waged by Abd-el-Kader. He ravaged the lands of the allies of France; the French, in a series of 'razzias' (the word and the thing were new), swept in the cattle and the crops of the 'rebels'. The war became harder and harder to sustain. The Emir was driven west into Morocco whose Sultan could not or did not prevent the use of his territories as a base. The Prince de Joinville seized Mogador with his naval squadron; Marshal Bugeaud, at Isly, routed the Moroccan horsemen as completely as Wellesley had routed the Mahrattas at Assaye. The Duc d'Aumale, in a bold charge, seized the Emir's camp, the 'Smala', his wives, his treasure. The victor was a year younger than Condé had been at Rocroi. He had earned Chantilly.

The Emir was still at large; but Algeria, by 1845, was conquered. In 1844 England sulkily admitted this at last by accrediting consuls, and the preachers of a policy of abandonment were resigned to the conquest if not to its cost. But what was to be done with the conquest? Marshal Bugeaud, now Duc d'Isly, wished to treat it in the high

Roman fashion and to establish colonies of veterans in the manner of
Caesar (or of Alexander I of Russia). The military colonies failed.
But colonization set in; with the soldiers came the sutlers, the women,
the land speculators. Most of them settled round camps, in the new
French quarters of the towns, and by 1840 there were a hundred
thousand settlers, barely half of them French, the rest Italians,
Spaniards, Maltese, Germans. Some began to settle on the land, to
live on a frontier more dangerous than Kentucky's 'dark and bloody
ground' had ever been, one that recalled, indeed, the frontier of New
France in the great days of the Iroquois. Slowly, the colony struck
root and dreams of settlement in Algeria as a solution of French
social problems began to cloud the public mind.

There were other clouds coming up from Africa. Marshal Bugeaud
could boast that 'it is quite certain that no army in Europe has at this
moment as many experienced officers as we have'. But the experience gained in the Algerian campaigns was very different from the
'grand tactics' of Napoleon. Again and again, General de Castellane
noted the demoralizing effects of African experience on the training
and ideas of the French officer. It was a school of war, but was it a
good school for European war?

Others wondered at the political effects on 'the Africans' of the
endless, ruthless campaigns. Marshal Bugeaud, though he did not
defend all that was done by rough-and-ready campaigners like
Pelissier, deplored the debates they caused in the Chamber of Deputies. These produced 'a very painful impression on the Army',
which found in Africa reasons for despising the 'pékins', the civilian
population in France as well as in Algeria—as their fathers had done
in Germany and Spain. But for one minor problem Algeria had provided a solution. In the collapse of the revolts of 1830 and 1831, Poles,
Italians, Spaniards had drifted or fled into France; the soldiers among
them were embodied in a new formation carrying on the old traditions of the foreign regiments of France and, at Sidi-Brahim, the
Foreign Legion gained its first battle honours in a forlorn hope.

Slowly, the colony took root. Romantic dreams of its future became common. Disciples of Saint-Simon and of Fourier, encouraged
by officers like Lamoricière and Walsin-Esterhazy, saw in it a field for
experiment. There were pockets of resistance in the mountains but,

by 1848, it did not seem absurd to think of France as restoring the Roman peace to Roman Africa. Abd-el-Kader finally surrendered to the young Governor-General, the Duc d'Aumale. The proud had been conquered; it was time to spare the weak and impose the habit of peace.

IX

Nostalgia for the glories of the Empire grew. The failure to over-throw the 'treaties of 1815' was one of the crimes of the regime in the eyes of the reviving Jacobins and sentimental Bonapartists. There was talk of making a customs union with Belgium. But not only would England have objected to a move that threatened the independence of the new kingdom, Belgium was by far the most advanced industrial power on the Continent. Louviers had unpatriotically rejoiced at the exclusion of Belgian competition in 1814 and had no desire to see it renewed in any form. And there were scores of towns like Louviers.

It was simpler to dream of extending French power in the East. French sympathies went out to the ambitious Pasha of Egypt, Mehemet Ali, in his war against his suzerain, the Sultan. But both Russia and Britain acted to preserve the Ottoman Empire (though from different motives). France was faced again with the union of the four victorious powers of 1815. It was war or surrender. Louis-Philippe surrendered. It was prudent, but it was not glorious. There were other causes of friction with England. It was necessary to compensate an English missionary, Pritchard, for wrongs he was alleged to have suffered in the French annexation of Tahiti. This alienated the bellicose, but it also alienated the Catholics for whom Tahiti was a prize and for whom the name of Chanel, the proto-martyr of Oceania, was sacred. England was again the hereditary enemy, and too few Frenchmen noted, in the Egyptian crisis of 1840, how the threat of a general war had provoked a violent explosion of German patriotism. The Rhineland no longer regarded reunion with France as promotion.

The drabness of the decaying regime was made the more manifest by the contrast not only with Imperial, but with Revolutionary glories. For the great and unending inquest on the Revolution was in full swing. It was no longer a matter of seeing the necessary liberties of 1789 preserved in the institutions of July. The cold and lucid treatment of Mignet was replaced by passionate vindication of the Revolution. The means for the study of the great convulsion were provided by the Catholic Socialist, Buchez; the flood of more or less authentic memoirs never ceased. But it was three men of genius who provided the tinder and the flame. Louis Blanc, the most critical of the three, rehabilitated the once odious memory of Robespierre. Robespierre had had his defenders, the pupils of Buonarotti and the other heirs of the Jacobins. But it was Louis Blanc who made Robespierre the hero, Thermidor not a happy deliverance, but the betrayal of the great hope of the people, the prelude to the deceptions of the rule of the bourgeois. It was Michelet who, without defending Robespierre, launched the great myth of the Revolution as a new Incarnation, with the people hypostatized, their work of redemption for France and the human race still going on, thwarted by the English and the Jesuits. It was Lamartine, with his lachrymose prose, who made not only the Girondins but the whole *dramatis personae* interesting, *sympathique*. He has 'gilded the guillotine', said Chateaubriand. It was Lamartine who had the most immediate effect (he got £40,000 for his pains). *The* Revolution was a great and moving event; *a* revolution, what might it not be?

What could the drab system of Louis-Philippe offer? It was more and more conservative in its foreign policy. Here was no memory of '92, not to speak of '93. The old King had long forgotten he had been a soldier of the Republic. He and his Minister were now the closest and most trusted allies of Metternich, joint guardians of the established order. The tacit alliance with the English was over, the 'entente cordiale' dissolved in acrimonious disputes over a scabrous diplomatic combination. The throne of Spain was occupied by Isabella II, joint protégée of France and England. She had to be found a husband and, in his old age, Louis-Philippe was more and more a Bourbon. But the English would not permit an open renewal of the Family Compact. The matrimonial future of the young Queen was the subject of a transaction. She would be married off to a prince not closely connected with the King of the French; her sister could later, when the succession was assured, marry the Duc de Montpensier, the son of Louis-Philippe. But the prince chosen as consort was the Duke of Cadiz, believed by many to be impotent. Not only was this doubtful but it was irrelevant, for Isabella had all the temperament of the ladies of the Spanish Bourbons. Alarmed, or professing to be alarmed at the suggestion of a Coburg candidate, the French Government rushed the marriages. The English Government was furious—not only Palmerston, but the Queen who thought she had been tricked. She had come to Eu as the old King's guest. She had been duped. She did not forgive. The whole history was ludicrous. Isabella II provided several heirs quickly and it is possible that at least one of her children was her husband's. The Duc de Montpensier was not destined to be a new Duc d'Anjou. The Pyrenees were as high as ever. All that had been attained was isolation of the July monarchy from its natural ally.

The speedy crushing of the Catholic cantons of Switzerland in the brief civil war of the *Sonderbund* prevented Guizot from appearing openly as the ally of Metternich and the Jesuits. And, last stroke of unpredictable ill fortune, the new Pope, Pius IX, was a liberal! He talked of reforms, of constitutions; he did not discourage the hopes of the Italian 'New Guelphs'; he was feared and deplored in Vienna, popular in Milan and Venice; was seen as useful by the *carbonari* and their heirs. The European order in which Louis-Philippe had invested so much was collapsing around him. Catholics and Republicans, Legitimists and Bonapartists alike rejoiced in his discomfiture. The Bonapartist pretender, Louis-Napoleon, had escaped from Ham. More serious for the moment, the National Guard was now all for Reform, for 'votes according to qualifications', for votes for people with university diplomas, with certain responsible jobs, for officers, for members of the National Guard. The old King was as firm or obstinate as Charles X. There would be no reform. The Chamber was dissolved and the usual method of running elections paid—as it had not done in 1830. The Government got an increased majority; Soult ceased to be the formal Prime Minister. Guizot took the rank as well as the power. The 'legal country' had spoken; the King had won the trick according to the rules. He was safe, if the opposition played the game according to those rules, and he was right in thinking that the orators of the Chamber were not revolutionaries. But they were not the whole country. When the Legitimist hero of *Les Rois en Exil* saw the old King drive out from the Tuileries amid the sullen silence of his subjects, he could not refrain from crying 'Vive le roi'. But he had few imitators.

Bad times added to the stresses that were shaking the jerry-built political structure. In France as in England, 'the hungry forties' were harsh on the poor. The full effects of the international trade cycle were beginning to be noted. A slump in New York or London was felt, deeply, in Paris or Lyons. To the misery of the poor, the rich had only conventional answers. The necessity of economic inequality and so of political inequality to protect the economic disparities was preached with all the confidence of the old political economy. But it was not preached quite confidently. The English manufacturers who talked of the iron law of wages and of the beauties of competition were willing to practise what they preached. They welcomed free trade, for which they felt fit. The repeal of the corn laws removed the most obvious use of English State power to benefit a class. The spectacle of the only great famine in western Europe taking place under British rule in Ireland was offset by the great reforms of the Peel administration, income tax and free trade. There was no such consistency in France. It was only to the workers that the natural law applied in its fullness. French business, French landowners shuddered at the thought of competition. All the follies of protectionism that attracted the sprightly wit of Bastiat could be illustrated from his own country. This insistence on law was ironically received by the dispossessed. For them, as Victor Hugo was to put it, the bourgeoisie, once arrived in power, had pulled up the ladder to prevent the people's following them.

The ruling class was not even notably moral itself. One of the highest judges was convicted of gross corruption (the briber was a general); there was a series of scandals in high places; a banal murder case convinced many that Marie Lafarge was not a poisoner but the victim of aristocratic venom; and, on August 18, 1847, in the heart of the Faubourg Saint-Honoré, the Duc de Praslin (he was a Choiseul) murdered his Duchess (she was the daughter of Marshal Sébastiani). The murderer poisoned himself. Who gave him the poison to escape trial? Or did he poison himself? Had he not been smuggled out to London where he was living in opulent sin with the governess for whom he had killed his wife? People were willing to believe everything and anything. There was even farce to discredit the regime. The Vicomte Hugo had been made a peer; it was an honour for the drab upper house and it opened to the poet (he believed) a political career equal to, greater than Chateaubriand's. But a suddenly jealous husband surprised the poet in his love nest in the Rue Saint-Roch. French law and public opinion then took proved adultery seriously; the erring wife was imprisoned; the poet was cut by his peers, and Chancellor Pasquier had a comic scandal to lament with all the others. What Lamartine had called 'a revolution of contempt' seemed to be on the way.

x

The monarchy of July in its old age was stricken with a disease that Proudhon called 'immobilisme', and that at a time when all but the political system was in movement. French Protestantism was as much affected as French Catholicism by the spirit of the age. The great movement of 'the awakening' spread all over Protestant Europe and entered France from Switzerland. The British and Foreign Bible Society sent hundreds of colporteurs selling the Bible into every region of France. What the French intellectuals loosely called 'Methodism' revived evangelical faith and even made some Catholic converts, although the Plymouth Brethren (founded by John Nelson Darby in Dublin and known in France as 'Darbistes') were far more numerous than the Methodists. Even Catholicism produced its unorthodox prophets and seers, of whom Vintras was the most influential.

The invention of photography by Daguerre and Niepce hastened the great revolution in art that was to make of Paris the new Florence. If such dregs of the romantic wine as Hugo's *Les Burgraves*

deservedly soured the public, the classical repertoire received a new
lease of life when a young Jewish actress made Racine modern. After
all, it was so representative a romantic poet as Alfred de Musset who
fainted when he heard Rachel begin:

> 'Ariane ma sœur par quel malheur blessée.'

But if the romantic drama had lost its first fresh appeal, romanticism
was not dead. For at the beginning of 1844 the *Siècle* began publish-
ing a serial by the flashy dramatist Alexandre Dumas, for which the
editor, Desnoyers, had found the innocuous title, *Les Trois Mous-
quetaires*. The world received and adopted overnight one of the great
symbols of France. As Hugo was to write:

> 'Tu rentras dans ton œuvre éclatante, innombrable,
> Multiple, éblouissante, heureuse, où le jour luit.'

At best, Louis-Philippe recalled the old age of Aramis.

The cry, the pressure for 'reform' grew in vehemence. Reform
meant many things. It meant a 'moralization' of the system, and that
involved the barring of placemen from the Chamber. Nearly a third
of the Deputies were officials and often important officials, like
prefects and even judges. They often secured election not only by
official pressure, but by corruption of individual electors and of com-
munities. The prudent voters of Arcis naturally hesitated to oppose
the candidate supported by the administration when that might cost
the town a new bridge. But reform meant mainly an extension of
the right to vote, to officers of the National Guard, to all the National
Guard, to people with certain educational qualifications, to taxpayers
who were worthy citizens, even if they could not meet the very high
qualification of 200 francs of direct taxation. But the King and his
Minister were adamant. 'Get rich', said Guizot in an unfortunate
phrase which made the right to vote a reward for pecuniary success.

More and more elements in French society joined in the reform
movement. Even the Legitimists took up this stick with which to
beat the usurper, and at the banquets which became the chief means
of propaganda care was often taken to see that no toasts or songs that
might offend Legitimist feelings were proposed or sung. Gérard de
Nerval, in prison for disorderly conduct, had noticed, long before,

that the Legitimists could sing 'Vive Henri IV' and the Republicans 'La Marseillaise', but the monarchy of July had no songs. Its head did not think he needed them. He admired himself even more than did M. Lieuvain who, at the agricultural show at Yonville, had celebrated the ruler who 'directs at one and the same time with a hand so wise, so sure, the car of State among the perils of a stormy sea'.

The sea was getting stormier. The bad harvests of 1845 and 1846 had been followed by the collapse of the railway boom. The workers discharged from the railway camps were a social danger; so were the craftsmen and shopkeepers affected by hard times and a freezing of credit. Faced with one of the great crises that seemed inseparable from the new industrial 'progress', the more literate victims listened with faith to such preachers of a new order as Louis Blanc whose 'organization of work' called for positive action by the State quite outside the wildest dreams of Louis-Philippe—and of his political critics who had become his enemies. For the King was too obviously the obstacle to change. At banquets, more and more reformers refused to drink his health. What would happen at the great banquet arranged for Paris in February? The King was not alarmed and few in either House shared the dark apprehensions of Alexis de Tocqueville. The banquet was banned.

The bourgeois reformers had no intention of challenging authority, but the Paris 'people'—or mob—began, on a small scale, one of the Paris 'days' that had punctuated the reign. Had the Government stuck to its guns and used the Paris garrison, it might have won; it was far better prepared than Charles X had been to deal with what, at the beginning, were merely rioters. But the King relied on the National Guard, and the citizen soldiers, except in the very rich quarters, were at best sulky and neutral. In some districts they were mutinous. The defection of the National Guard broke the old King's nerve. He dismissed Guizot, calling first on Molé, then on Thiers. The rioting died down; the rioters might have done no more than impose a change of ministry (the National Guard was far more representative of solid middle-class opinion than the Chamber). But troops outside the Ministry of Foreign Affairs (then in the Boulevard des Capucines) fired on the crowd. The blood of the people had been spilled; all Paris rose. The King abdicated; the Duchesse d'Orléans took the little Comte de Paris to the Chamber which was ready to accept him, but authority had passed to the people of Paris, to the Hôtel-de-Ville where, in 1830, the monarchy of July had been founded. The Republic was proclaimed. Charles X had departed surrounded by his guards; the bourgeois monarchy ended fittingly with the flight of the King in a cab.

III

THE INTERIM REPUBLIC

I

THE fall of Charles X had been foreseen, provided for. The Chamber remained in existence and the Duc d'Orléans was slipped on to his cousin's throne. But no such transaction was possible in 1848. Parliament went the way of the King; the parliamentary leaders were as much taken by surprise as the King and his Minister. There had been no life in the system that collapsed in February 1848; Louis-Philippe excited no loyalty and little pity. The monarchy of July that began as a device ended as a dodge. The Republic was proclaimed and rapturously received, at any rate in Paris and the big towns, but what was the Republic—a new system of government or a new system of society? Almost at once, the poet made Foreign Minister in the Provisional Government had to make his most famous speech to prevent the tricolour being replaced by the red flag; but Lamartine's eloquence could not bridge the gap between those who welcomed or accepted 'the Republic' and those who clamoured for the 'social Republic'. Few had given much thought to what this meant, but it meant, at the least, a State that assumed more positive duties than had any government since the fall of the old regime. The workers of Paris were ready, so it was said, to give 'three months of hardship' to the Republic; at the end of that time it must deliver the goods, end poverty, 'organize labour'.

How was this to be done? By the flowering of the spirit of fraternity. For the first result of the ending of the drab, unenterprising, materialistic rule of Louis-Philippe was a restoration of faith. 1789 was come again; again 'bliss was it in that dawn to be alive'. The memories of the Revolution clouded the minds of the workers and of their leaders. Would the bourgeoisie be ready to imitate the abnegation of the nobility of 1789 who (according to a highly misleading legend) had voluntarily given up their feudal privileges on the 4th of August? The answer was most decidedly no! The bourgeoisie

93

was frightened but it was not in retreat; its conscience was good. To welcome the Republic, attend the planting of trees of liberty, applaud the highly republican sentiments of so many of the clergy, that was one thing. To give away economic power and wealth, richly deserved as the classical economists pointed out, was something very different.

If the possessing classes did not give way, was the State to make them? Only if it were coerced by the armed workers. For it soon became evident that the revolutionary passions of the cities were but sparsely represented in the countryside. Elections to an Assembly to give France a new constitution were soon seen, rightly, as a threat to the 'social Republic'. In vain the new Minister of the Interior, Ledru-Rollin, sent out Commissioners, equivalents of the 'Representatives on mission', to encourage Republican zeal and establish Republican authority; these emissaries were often ill received; they were often unknown; sometimes too well known; often young talkers like Émile Ollivier who was made Commissioner for two departments (including Marseilles) when not yet twenty-three. In vain Carnot, the new Minister of Public Instruction, encouraged the village school teachers to preach the new gospel. France was not yet republican in spirit. Paris was. It was full of clubs of all kinds: imitations of the Jacobins, religious clubs, socialist clubs. Every panacea found its believers. The wave of sentimental socialism that had mounted high in the last years of Louis-Philippe approached its crest. There had been Flora Tristan (the grandmother of Paul Gauguin) who had known the Chartist leaders; there had been George Sand who had patronized Agricol Perdiguier, the reformer of the 'compagnonnages'; there had been Eugène Sue as well as those more reflective students of the social problem, the disciples of Saint-Simon, of Fourier, of Proudhon. Engels, coming to Paris on the eve of the revolution, had been impressed by the energy of the Paris working population but struck by the fact that few or none of its spokesmen could read English or knew anything of the society where these problems had been more profoundly studied and existed in a more advanced form than in France. Paris was exciting but, compared with Manchester, it was backward.

Concessions were made to the workers. Hours of work in Paris were reduced to ten, to eleven in the provinces; a commission to study the labour question was set up in the Luxembourg under Louis Blanc. The unemployed were set to work in 'National Workshops', which were not in the least like Louis Blanc's design for government-supported rivals to the new capitalist factories, but simply gangs, for the most part of skilled workers, employed in futile tasks like levelling the Champ-de-Mars. (In Marseilles, where most of the unemployed were navvies from the unfinished railways, Ollivier was able to find more useful things for them to do.) But when the elections came, only 100 out of 876 'Representatives of the People' had any sympathy with the hopes and necessities of the townsfolk. Overwhelmingly rural, at least one-third illiterate, the French adult males, given the vote in a fit of mystical faith in 'universal suffrage', had repudiated the fond hopes of February. It was a new conservative 'windfall chamber' like that of 1815, chosen by millions of frightened and docile electors. The new 'Representatives of the People' were very like the Deputies of the condemned order of Louis-Philippe. The chief difference was that there were many more open Legitimists, hoping that the chance for the restoration of 'Henri V' had come. But the conservative majority had something more important to conserve than the rights of princes. It had property to save; property new and old. Property-owners, heirs of the Crusaders, heirs of the Jacobins, were frightened; they had reason to be.

1848 was not only a year of revolution in France, it was *the* year of revolutions. Beginning in Palermo, spreading to Paris, revolt broke out in places as far apart as Venice and Ireland. The news of the fall of Louis-Philippe was the signal for an explosion. Metternich, Guizot and Prince Wilhelm of Prussia were all exiles in London at the same time. Austrian power was reduced for the moment to Radetzky's camp, as Grillparzer put it. The 'Tedeschi' were driven out of Milan and Venice; King Charles Albert of Piedmont, the *carbonaro* prince, took up arms; the Pope refused to imitate him and was soon an exile. All things seemed possible. All the old Jacobin fervour and illusions revived. Everywhere, 'le peuple souverain s'avance', or so it seemed. There was a foolish movement to 'liberate' Belgium in which that typical Jacobin fanatic, Delescluze, was involved; it failed ludicrously; there was a movement to aid Italy, although Carlo Alberto was to announce that 'Italia farà da se'. There were the old dreams of the restoration of the Rhine frontier, although the German radicals of Berlin, or even of Vienna, were aggressive German nationalists as well. There was above all Poland. Russian rule in Poland, like Austrian rule in Italy and English rule in Ireland, was one of the great, admitted European scandals. The suppression by the Austrians of the free city of Cracow in 1846 had scandalized even Guizot. It was necessary to 'do something for Poland'. But nothing could be done for Poland without a general, revolutionary war that the timid majority of the new Assembly had not the slightest intention of launching, in this being faithfully representative of their voters.

They were representative in another way. France was still overwhelmingly a peasant country with little knowledge of and little sympathy with the problems of the city workers, above all the formidable workers of Paris. The illusions of February had gone, especially when the Provisional Government, at its fiscal wits' end, raised the tax rate by the famous and disastrous 'forty-five centimes'. This was collected, more or less successfully, in the wealthier departments, but in the remote and poor regions, the local Mayors refused to co-operate and the tax collectors were mobbed. In non-co-operation with the tax gatherers, the Lot led, but was widely followed.

Rumours of war, constant 'days' in Paris, invasions of the Assembly by the bands of Barbès and Blanqui, frightened all property owners, and there were millions of them. It also intensified the economic crisis and made the solution of the problem of Parisian unemployment more difficult. The conservative leaders saw their duty—and their opportunity. It was falsely reported that the mob that had invaded the Assembly on May 15 was mainly recruited from the National Workshops, and the Assembly, led by the Comte de Falloux, decided to take the chance to end this dangerous experiment. Falloux was a grandson, 'on the left hand', of Charles X; but he had far more brains than his ancestor. Intolerable terms were offered to the workers—service in the Army for the bachelors; dismissal, or exile to the provinces, for the married men. Workers' Paris rose in what, up to that date, was the most desperate and bloody of Paris insurrections. General Cavaignac was given dictatorial power. Troops were brought in, the 'mobile' National Guard, paid servants of the Assembly, was called out.

The fighting was savage, far more bitter and bloody than in July 1830. The workers had something more dear to defend than the Charter; the attackers had more to fight for than a mere matter of military discipline. The Army had to avenge the humiliations of February; the bourgeois National Guard had fear as well as hate to spur it to action. The XII arrondissement saw the worst fighting. But it was at the Hôtel-de-Ville that a captain of the National Guard replied to Armand Marrast who saw the bodies piled up, 'Never fret, not more than a quarter were innocent.' And Meissonier in *La Barricade* drew civil war more candidly and brutally than he was to draw foreign war in the nice tidy battle pictures that made his fame. Victor Hugo could see the brighter side of things. 'To save civiliza- tion, as Paris did in June, one might almost say is to save the human race.' Flaubert was to put it another way. 'It was an outburst of fear. They took vengeance on newspapers, clubs, meetings, doctrines, on all that had exasperated them in the past three months. . . . The public mind was upset as after great natural disturbances. Intelligent men were made idiotic by it for the rest of their lives.' Michelet noted simply in his diary, 'Excidat illa dies.' And the beaten workers of Paris submitted and remembered.

II

The real beneficiary of the June Days was not 'the Republic' or the Republican general, Cavaignac, who had crushed the workers. Still less was it Lamartine or the original leaders of the Provisional Government. It was not even the Royalist majority of the National Assembly. It was Prince Louis-Napoleon Bonaparte. He had escaped from his captivity at Ham in 1846 and had returned to France after the fall of his gaoler, Louis-Philippe. But the time was not then ripe. It now was. The great mass of the peasant electors knew only one name to set against the name of the Republic: Napoleon. For mil- lions, his name was a programme. Louis-Napoleon began to culti- vate the legend and shrewd men began to take him seriously. He was helped by the folly of the Assembly. It drafted an absurd constitution providing for the direct election of the President of the Republic by the millions of newly enfranchised voters. A drab lawyer, Jules Grévy, saw the danger, but the rights of 'the people' were saved by Lamartine, who still had delusions of popularity. There were other credulous believers in the infallibility of universal suffrage; there were other credulous believers in their own popularity. Opposed to the popularly elected President there was to be a single Assembly, inevitably jealous of the rival power. As the more objective spectators had foreseen, Louis-Napoleon Bonaparte won easily; he got over 5,000,000 votes, easily out-distancing Cavaignac and Ledru-Rollin, the candidate of the 'Mountain', the extreme Left. Lamartine got a handful of votes.

It was not only the illiterate peasants or disgruntled workers who voted for Louis-Napoleon. There were plenty of conservatives, even Legitimists, who thought him the best bet, for the moment. Cavaignac was too firmly Republican and he was too capable. The new President would be unimportant. 'Stat magni nominis umbra.' He had no force or strength of his own. He could and would be taken over by the 'Burgraves', the great parliamentary leaders; they would use him and, when the time came, discard him. It was easy to underestimate the President. He was small, unimpressive (except on horseback; unlike his uncle, he was an excellent horseman). He spoke all languages, it was unkindly said, with a German accent, except German which he spoke with a Swiss accent. He reminded Prince Albert's brother of a cultivated prince from a minor German court. In a talkative city, he was silent; he doodled while others talked. So he was written down or off.

The new President moved into the Elysée with his handful of faithful adherents. He had to create a party, to gain support for himself, not merely for his name, and he had to give the Burgraves time enough to discredit themselves. Slowly, the President asserted his right to know what the Ministers whom the Assembly foisted on him were doing; more slowly, he acquired the right to interfere with them; more slowly still, he acquired the right to choose his own Ministers. Whether the President formed the design of overthrowing the Republic as soon as he entered the Elysée, no one knew then and no one knows now. He had sentimental, 'socialist', even 'republican' ideas. He genuinely wanted to do *something* for the workers. He knew that their wrongs were real, not the invention of wicked men. He even dallied, to his Ministers' horror, with the infamous income tax which he had seen at work in England. He had seen a great deal of the world; he knew that a great many things were done better elsewhere than in France. Indeed, compared even with Thiers, not to speak of mere windbags like Odilon Barrot, the new President was an intelligent citizen of the world, free from the Chinese complacency of so many Parisians. He needed time and he needed more intelligent and well-connected partisans than the devoted but inadequate Fialin, called Persigny. He also needed money. He had drawn on the generosity of his cousin, Princess Mathilde, daughter of King Jerome of Westphalia and Catherine of Württemberg. But he needed still more. He was deeply in debt to others, notably to his English mistress, Miss Howard, whom he flaunted in the face of French bourgeois prudery with the insouciance of Charles II. He had to subsidize newspapers, Bonapartist leagues, organizations of Imperial veterans. So he was forced to live beyond the handsome means the Assembly provided for him—and to ask its suspicious politicians for more.

For a time, collaboration between the President and the Assembly was necessary. For one thing, there was 'the Roman Question', an insoluble problem that was to bedevil French politics and foreign policy for a generation.

Pius IX had been, for a brief period, a hero to the 'Liberals' of Europe and Italy. He was no longer a hero to the Italian nationalists. He refused to join in a holy, patriotic war against Austria. He was driven out of Rome and a Roman republic was set up whose prophet was Mazzini and whose sword-arm was Garibaldi. A Roman republic, by its origin anti-Austrian, was a political windfall for France as a secular power. But a Roman republic that expelled the Pope from his lawful territories in the name of Jacobinical doctrines of popular rights and new doctrines of the rights of nationalities was detestable to French Catholics—and to French conservatives like Thiers who hated Mazzini, the friend of French 'reds' like Ledru-Rollin. The recovery of Austria made it certain that Rome, like Vienna and Budapest, Prague and Milan, would be brought to heel—and a Pope restored by Austrian arms was, by the rules of the traditional foreign policy, a danger to rightful French influence. The exclusion of France from any part in Italian politics, enforced by the settlement of Vienna, was one of the intolerable servitudes of 1815. There was thus a secular as well as a religious case for restoring the Pope by French arms. The 'eldest daughter of the Church' could both rescue the Sovereign Pontiff and undo the work of Metternich. But a war to destroy a republic, especially this republic, was deeply criminal in the eyes of the Left, a crime against the Constitution of 1848 as well as against the Spirit of 1793. The Constituent Assembly had been succeeded by a new Assembly even more to the Right—but, and this was noted, there was far less discrepancy between the popular vote than there was between the number of seats won. The 'reds' had shown alarming strength, not only in the great cities, but in the countryside—and in the Army.

Despite their defeat, the 'reds' were full of hope; the old Assembly lingered on and its elected successor was condemned by monumental asses like Félix Pyat to being the 'Legislative' Assembly that had been swept away in 1792 to give way to the heroic Convention. Less foolish men than Félix Pyat (there were none more foolish) shared his illusions. Even Engels thought seriously of a junction of the French Army, carrying on a new revolutionary war, and the armies of the rebel Magyars. But the tide was running the other way. Sardinia had re-entered the war, to be crushed at Novara; Russian power was gathering like an avalanche to crush Hungary; and the Roman republic, after a heroic defence, was conquered by a French army. The Pope was brought back, cheerfully resisting all good advice from the President who yet got some credit for offering it. The Papal States again became a disgrace, reminding some visitors of the desperate poverty of Ireland. Pius IX had made his last concessions to the Spirit of the Age. And France had now to underwrite his follies.

All folly was not on the side of the Pope. Ledru-Rollin allowed himself to be bullied into a foolish demonstration that was represented as being an attempt at revolution. 'I am their leader, I must follow them' were the words put into his mouth. He fled; the Assembly acted. By a new and rigorous election law, 3,000,000 voters were cut away, like cankered timber, from the voting lists. There were numerous Press persecutions and a war against the colporteurs who sold books, pictures, tracts, Bibles. The Assembly was against all stirring up of the countryside, even by the sale of Bibles. The Republic was dying; the only question was who would give it the *coup de grâce*.

It is possible that the monarchists might have brought about a restoration if they had not been disunited and unduly contemptuous of the President. Louis-Philippe had died, but the royal house was still divided. The Duchesse d'Orléans was not ready for the unconditional submission of her son, the Comte de Paris, and the Comte de Chambord was not a convert to a parliamentary monarchy. The Assembly, if it had been united, might have put off the decision until the President's term had come to an end, or it might have bought him off by amending the Constitution and allowing him to succeed himself. But the Republicans were more afraid of the Royalists than of the President, and the Royalists were more afraid of the general elections of 1852 than of the President. Men talked, it is true, of a *coup d'état*, but as months went by and there was no open move, they began to laugh at their fears. As the Duc de Guise had said when told of the threats of Henri III, 'He would not dare.' So men talked of Louis-Napoleon. They had, they thought, more serious things to be afraid of.

How frightened the bourgeoisie had become was made manifest by the abandonment of the monopoly of teaching claimed, and to some extent exercised, by the University. It was no longer enough to see that children of the poor received a Christian education which would make them resigned to their lot in life. Socialism had made its ravages in all classes. So M. Thiers and the Abbé Dupanloup, soon to be Bishop of Orléans, combined with the adroit Comte de Falloux to destroy the monopoly of the University, one of the few achievements of the Second Republic which have never been undone. 'Free schools' were given a legal status, and bishops and other Church dignitaries were brought into the governing body of the University. There was no Church monopoly such as the Restoration had aimed at, and the failure of the Assembly to create such a monopoly angered zealots like Louis Veuillot. The 'Loi Falloux' was to be and is a stumbling-block to the disciples of Voltaire. But he would have fully understood the motives which induced Thiers to combine with the more enlightened clergy against an enemy more formidable than the Jesuits—'Socialism'.

The successive triumphs of the Right inside the Assembly, the collapse of such scarecrows as Ledru-Rollin, did not reassure the timid majority. What Romieu was to call 'the red spectre of 1852' frightened them. What would the voters do in that fateful year when France would have to elect a new President and a new Assembly? There was little hope that she would prove as wise and scared as she had shown herself to be in 1849. The republican idea was making progress even in the countryside. The socialistic sensational novelist, Eugène Sue, was triumphantly elected in Paris. There were some conservatives of sufficiently strong nerves to dismiss the danger. Dom Guéranger appealed to the example of his favourite saint: 'Cecilia will teach us how to get rid of the feeling of fear.' But others, perhaps remembering that the saint had not managed to save her own Trastevere from the revolutionary tide, were less easily reassured.

The fears on the Right were equalled by confidence on the Left. The exiles in London and Brussels looked forward to a speedy reversal of fortune. The secret societies were busy with planning for the day, and the new Jacobins, 'the Mountain', recalled the good old days. A political publican in St. Étienne kept a model guillotine in his back shop which he demonstrated to the faithful. The fearful were ready to believe any stories. Thus, it was well known that the 'reds' had wormed their way into the fire brigade, and when the signal was given and Paris set on fire, they would play oil, not water, on the flames! Victor Hugo's mistress told him that she had dreamed that she saw a 'great omnibus in flames that galloped at full speed. The horses had taken the bit between their teeth.' It was 1852, said her lover; memories of 1793 no longer frightened him. In a phrase worthy of Hégesippe Simon, he noted that 'when day comes, the ghosts vanish'. For others they walked.

III

The President kept his counsel. He proposed that the excluded millions should be restored to the voting lists; the Assembly refused. The President was now the friend, or at any rate a friend, of 'universal suffrage'. As the Assembly wavered and havered, more and more sagacious men began to dally with the idea of a *coup d'état* legalized by an alliance with the conservative majority of the Assembly, an alliance that would put off the evil day of the elections of 1852. But Louis-Napoleon would not play the game of M. de Montalembert. He had studied the *coup d'état* of Brumaire which had almost failed because General Bonaparte had allied himself with too many politicians. The idea of seizing supreme power during the parliamentary holidays was discussed and rejected. The dispersed Representatives would be so many centres of resistance. The higher administration was in safe hands; the Army had at its head a new War Minister, General de Saint-Arnaud, a bold adventurer who had been given a chance to earn some cheap glory in Algeria. Other reliable generals were put in the great commands. A vigorous though, as the event proved, easily panicked Prefect of Police, Maupas, was found. Above all, M. de Morny was available.

Morny was the son of Hortense, Queen of Holland and mother of Louis-Napoleon. His father, the Comte de Flahaut, was a bastard of Talleyrand's. The doubly illegitimate if illustrious ancestry did not impede Morny's rise. He had a brilliant military career in Africa where he became a friend and protégé of the Orléans Princes. He entered the Chamber of Deputies where he was soon known as the lobbyist for the nascent beet-sugar industry. He was equally at home on the battlefield, on the Bourse, and in the boudoir. He had some of his paternal grandfather's preternatural calm and worldly wisdom, but he recalled in his courage, egoism and ruthlessness his Spanish contemporary, Narvaez. What Morny planned was the perfect *pronunciamiento*. He needed secrecy, speed and competent agents. He had, above all, to overcome the scruples of his half-brother who was so unlike him and whose romantic and vacillating temper endangered the great enterprise on which Morny was staking his life. There were to be no mistakes; there were very few. On the night of December 1, the President held one of his usual receptions at the Elysée. He was as calm, silent, inscrutable as ever. Guests who had been sounded out were taken into a private room. There was the plan of the *coup d'état* in an envelope marked *Rubicon*. Morny was the life and soul of a party at the Opera. In the darkness of the morning of December 2, the conspirators moved. It was the anniversary of the coronation of Napoleon I and of Austerlitz.

The early risers in Paris went about their business and found the walls placarded. The Assembly was dissolved; universal suffrage was restored; and the French people were summoned to approve or reject the dictatorship of the President.

There was to be no chance of organized resistance. Troops poured into Paris, troops well fed and soon to be well provided with drink. The drums of the National Guard were found to have been burst in; there would be no 'rappel' calling the citizen soldiers to defend the Republic, or rather the Assembly. The Palais Bourbon, where the Assembly sat, was seized; it had been carefully reconnoitred; a list of leading Representatives had been drawn up; they were quickly and effectively arrested in their own or other people's beds. All printing plants were in the hands of the troops.

The Paris workers were not indignant; they were even amused by the adroitness of the seizure of the pompous legislators. The execution of the *coup d'état* was not quite perfect. The Palais Bourbon was not secured; Representatives drifted into it and talked of organizing resistance, of calling on the High Court to depose the President. Representatives of 'the Mountain' tried to organize resistance in the eastern arrondissements. Centre and Right-wing Deputies met and chattered in the Town Hall of the Xth arrondissement. There were a few barricades; in a skirmish, an obscure Representative, Baudin, was obscurely killed. He was to be remembered. The Right and Centre did nothing. Some 'Representatives of the People', on their way to Vincennes, vehemently refused to be rescued by 'the People'. And the Republican Representatives not only deposed the President but dissolved the Assembly. It was one revolution against another. There was no doubt which would win. But the troops, trigger-happy or merely drunk, fired on the highly respectable bourgeois crowds on the boulevards; there were many deaths and a cry of genuine indignation. The victims were not workers; they were respectable spectators. There was horror; but Paris was cowed. Louis-Napoleon was not Louis-Philippe. He meant business.

It was not in Paris, indeed, that the *coup d'état* was most effectively resisted. It was not in the great Republican cities like Lyons and Marseilles. It was in the countryside. There were sporadic peasant revolts all over the centre and the south. The Republic, a mere name perhaps, had yet been a name full of hope for poor sharecroppers, tenants, labourers, the 'reds', the 'Jacobins', the enemies of the Church and the gentry, the forces that had rallied to Napoleon I during the Hundred Days. The revolts were futile. Courts martial were set up and many village hotheads who saw themselves as village Hampdens were imprisoned, sent into exile in Algeria. Lambessa became a name of dread, the number of colonists increased, and the new colony, a kind of French Siberia, was made highly Republican in sentiment. Many of the victims of the military courts were the men who had been boasting of their bloody triumph in 1852. Many were illiterate, simple-minded victims of local jealousies, of the determination of squire, priest or notary to teach the 'socialists' a lesson. In departments like the Allier, where the land war was endemic, the victims were numbered in thousands. General Canrobert was especially noted for his rigour and vigour. The new order started, like so many other French new orders, with a proscription. Exiles, hopeful and credulous, filled Brussels, London, Geneva. Since Balzac had died on August 18, 1850, Victor Hugo was the undoubted head of French literature. He was exiled, leaving an immense vacuum which was soon filled with the great polemical collection, *Les Châtiments*. The new regime had its ambiguous heroes but the Republic had the *vates sacer*.

Morny and the President had made one odd mistake. The plebiscite which was to ratify the *coup d'état* was to be held on a system of open voting. This was to make the restoration of 'universal suffrage' a mockery indeed. It was an unnecessary error and the plebiscite was held under secret ballot rules. There was, of course, vigorous official pressure, but there is no reason to doubt that the overwhelming majority of 'yes' votes represented the sentiments of the vast majority of the French people. Monarchists and Republicans alike had bored and frightened them. Outside France, there were many moral protests, but the *coup d'état* was approved of by the Tsar, by Lord Palmerston and by Walter Bagehot.

The dictatorship of the Prince-President was obviously only a halting-place on the way to the Empire. The dictator had to be seen by the country. Even before the *coup d'état* he had presented himself on semi-royal tours (embarrassing prudish officials by taking Miss Howard around with him). Mrs. Browning had seen him 'in cocked hat and with a train of cavalry, passing like a rocket along the boulevards'. His courage, as well as his horsemanship, was impressive, and if he was no parliamentary orator, he could be an effective public speaker. 'The Empire is peace', he promised at Bordeaux and he may have meant it.

Meantime, the new political organization was completed. The model was the Consulate. All executive power was in the hands of the President, aided by Ministers and by the Council of State. There was a Senate of notables, appointed for life, to guard and amend the Constitution. There was a 'Corps Législatif', only a third of the Assembly in size, with no power of initiating laws; with its presiding officer appointed by the President; with the public informed of the activities of its legislators only by the report of the presiding officer. It was, apparently, as futile a body as the Corps Législatif of the First Empire. But the deputies, docile, hand-picked, indifferent to great issues, represented, all the same, the tenacious, thrifty, frightened bourgeoisie and the Catholic, conservative, formally Royalist gentry. Both sections had one thing in common: a firm determination not to abandon the control of the purse to Louis-Napoleon and, still less, to countenance his dangerous ideas like income tax and free trade. One liberty won by the Revolution was jealously guarded by this counter-revolutionary body. The French were no longer to be 'corvéable et taillable' at the whim of the ruler. It was about the only liberty that survived.

There was no Press censorship, but a system of warnings worked as well. A paper that was warned was in danger of suppression. A journalist who was warned was in danger of prison. The prison might be very mild, more of an advertisement than a punishment if the offender was someone like the smart Orléanist journalist, Prévost-Paradol. But really determined enemies of the regime, like Delescluze, found that it had teeth and claws and was ready to use them savagely and unscrupulously. So Proudhon found, even though he had at least tolerated the *coup d'état*. Leading articles had now to be signed, a custom that survived. The University was tamed. Philosophy classes were suppressed and teachers were forbidden to wear the dangerously suggestive beards. The Institute of France sulked, so did good society. For the President had signalized his new powers by confiscating the property of the Orléans Princes that, he argued, should have fallen into the royal domain in 1830. Good society was deeply shocked. Morny resigned. He had been a friend of the Princes; he was a gentleman—and the Orléans Princes had many friends in big business which Morny wanted to cultivate and to win for himself, if not necessarily for the regime. The workers, the peasants, some of the Legitimists were not shocked, and after a decent interval Morny returned to power. The Empire needed him, for on December 2, 1852, Louis-Napoleon took the title of Napoleon III, affirming thus the legitimacy of the nominal reign of the King of Rome. All the powers acknowledged the 'new-born majesty'—the Tsar Nicholas, slowly and sulkily: it was one thing to applaud the dictator, another to welcome the sovereign.

IV

THE SECOND EMPIRE

I

IT was desirable that the new Emperor should have an Empress and an heir. For the moment, the heir presumptive had to be Prince Napoleon who had one asset (he looked very like Napoleon I) but several liabilities: he was a Republican, an atheist, quarrelsome, changeable. It was not easy to find a suitable bride for the new Emperor, even more difficult than it had been to find one for the Duc d'Orléans. Through Stéphanie de Beauharnais, Grand-Duchess of Baden, the family of the Emperor's mother was kin to several royal and princely lines in Europe, but none of them seemed anxious to share the fortunes of their kinsman. While negotiations were going on and speculation was rife, the new Emperor settled the matter by falling in love with and proposing marriage to Eugenia de Montijo, Condesa de Teba. The object of Imperial favour came of a great Spanish and a good Scots family; but the blue blood of the Guzmans had been some-what diluted. Her mother was a well-known figure on the edge of Paris society; her sister had married the Duke of Alba; and Eugenia, if poor and not accepted everywhere in the very best society, was astonishingly beautiful. On the Emperor's side it was a love-match (gossips suggested that marriage was an after-thought). On the side of the future Empress it was doubted if she could sincerely have said that

> 'Moi qui, loin des grandeurs dont il est revêtu,
> Aurais choisi son cœur, et cherché sa vertu.'

The marriage was unpopular with the people and with the new Imperial ruling class. It was romantic; but a King Cophetua who had himself, not so long before, been a beggar man, was ill-advised to choose a beggar maid. Eugénie had, indeed, reached the then advanced age for a spinster of twenty-seven without any serious scandal; but Eugénie's mother was believed by many to have been the mistress of Prosper Mérimée—and others—and her son-in-law was to prefer to keep her out of France.

But, and it was an important but, the new Empress was very
beautiful indeed and she gave to the Second Empire a note that it
never lost in the popular imagination. Thanks to Eugénie, the new
Court was splendid. True, there was something factitious about the
splendour. The royal gold and silver plate had disappeared in 1848
and the new Emperor, when he found what it would cost to replace
it, settled for the new and ingenious system of electro-plating for all
but the most splendid of occasions and guests. Little that glistered at
the Tuileries was gold. But the glitter was dazzling enough. As
Bagehot pointed out, the Imperial Court had to be splendid. It could
not afford to erect dowdiness into a system of government, as Victoria did. Money was spent lavishly, and as much as in the seventeenth and eighteenth centuries the French Court set the tone. It had
its elaborate ritual: the season in Paris; the season at the remote seaside
village of Biarritz (the French Balmoral); the great hunting season at
Compiègne. The Court was not exclusive; it could not be. It called
on the Imperial nobility to provide it with its ceremonial figures,
although it had in M. de Cossé-Brissac an hereditary courtier of the
most relevant lineage. It welcomed foreigners like the beautiful Miss
Moulton of Cambridge, Massachusetts. It delighted many princes,
above all the young Prince of Wales. And the great court dress-
maker, Charles Worth, born in Lincolnshire and trained by Swan
and Edgar in London, quite eclipsed such predecessors as Rose Bertin
who had served Marie Antoinette, and founded the great dynasty of
Paris men-milliners who served and serve 'the happiness of women',
as Zola was to put it. The Second Empire was, in a way, a paradise
of women, of women of all kinds; great ladies like the wife of the
Austrian Ambassador, Pauline de Metternich; great if shady ladies
like that Contessa di Castiglione who was the not very secret weapon
of the Conte di Cavour; the famous and amiable light actress, Hortense Schneider; the great English courtesan, Cora Pearl. That world
had its not quite respectable artist, Constantin Guys, and its official
painter, Winterhalter. But the real charm of the Imperial Court—and
of its fashion, the crinoline—is best conveyed by the little Boudin that
shows Eugénie and her ladies at Trouville, moving against the breeze,

'Sails filled and streamers waving,
Courted by all the winds that hold them play,'

II

As characteristic of the new Empire as its flashy and brilliant Court was the new Paris made by the Emperor and his Prefect, Baron Haussmann. In the remaking of Paris, the Emperor had an idea to which he clung with his usual tenacity and he had an executant whom he trusted and supported with more than usual constancy. Haussmann was a brilliant administrator and he had more ideas than most brilliant administrators. (As a boy, he had been thought to show more poetic talent than his schoolfellow, Alfred de Musset.) A decidedly orthodox Protestant, he was not an orthodox financier. He had grasped the truth that great speed and great scale are often true economy. He would transform Paris, quickly; the profits of one great development paying for the next. The city (which had no elected council) could borrow on its expectations, and Haussmann discounted the future of Paris with American boldness. The rebuilding of Paris was pushed on, despite the opposition of lovers of the old, of vested interests of all kinds, of rival speculators, of prudent financiers. The old project of joining the Louvre to the Tuileries was taken up again, and the Rue de Rivoli was made. The great new Boulevard de Sébastopol was driven through the old, revolutionary areas and continued, in nearly a straight line, across the river in the Boulevard Saint-Michel. The improvements were justified from a political point of view: they provided work, increased real wealth, and made the repression of revolt easier.

They had other less desirable consequences. They made the class divisions in Paris more visible. The rich left the Marais. It took one Paris family 'three hundred years to get from Notre-Dame to the Porte Dauphine', but the big jump was made under Napoleon III. Whole new quarters were developed, round the Boulevard Malesherbes and on the Plaine Monceau. Madame Victor Hugo, in exile in Guernsey, found the news that her kinsfolk had left the Faubourg Saint-Germain for some remote spot beyond 'les Ternes' so astonishing that she had to come to Paris to see for herself. The Boulevard de Sébastopol was more than an artery; it was a frontier. To the west lay the 'smart districts', to the east, the workers' districts, visibly cut

off from the new, brilliant, lavish life of the west. As that barrier
went up, an old one went down; the Emperor pushed through the
annexation of the villages and towns and the great river port of La
Villette that lay between the old barrier of the city and the new fortifications. It was a most necessary step, bitterly opposed by the Liberal
and Republican opposition. They saw in Haussmann a vandal, des-
troying old Paris (and he *was* too fond of symmetry; he made too
many hills into plains). They saw, in Napoleon III, an extravagant
Anglomaniac and the Emperor *did* want Paris to have a west-end like
London and, in the Bois de Boulogne, something like Hyde Park.
But if the new buildings were more impressive than beautiful, the
new streets were soon full of the fast-growing chestnut trees and
catalpas that gave Paris its air of being more than mere miles of stone.
It was this brilliant new Paris to which all the world turned and which
all the world, and especially the wives and daughters of the world,
wanted to visit. And it was given its accolade by the wittiest of Bos-
tonians. 'Good Americans, when they die, go to Paris', said Tom
Appleton.

When they got to Paris, they found a new city. The new railway
stations, the new hotels, the new theatres made Paris the model for
cities of Europe as Versailles had been for Courts. The Government
itself was part of the show. The 'Cent Gardes', immobile giants at
the doors of the Tuileries, suggested the pomp of the lavish Court
receptions to which entry was not difficult. The annual art shows
impressed the orthodox. The opera was splendid, if musically behind
the times. And the 'can-can' was one of the great Parisian sights.
The young men of *Trilby* saw in the heroine dancing the can-can 'et
vera incessu patuit dea'. It was a different goddess who was worshipped at the Bal Mabille in the Chaillot quarter or, in a slightly
more respectable fashion, in the Rue de Vaugirard. The great
'cocottes' driving in the Bois de Boulogne or the Avenue de
l'Impératrice were almost as much a part of the show as the Empress
with her outriders. And in 1869 was founded what was to be a great
Parisian institution, Les Folies Bergère, destined to so great and
democratic a fame.

The Paris of Napoleon III had a good deal of the Venice of *Candide*.
It had its constant procession of Kings and Princes in masks and of

Kings and Queens in exile. There was the immensely wealthy Duke of Brunswick and at 19 Avenue Kléber, in the new fasionable district of the Étoile, Isabella II of Spain. But it was also the age of Thomas Cook. There was the conducted tour as well as what was to be called the 'tournée des grands ducs'. Bismarck and Mark Twain were both visitors to the Great Exhibition of 1867 and, for tens of thousands, the great new railway stations, the Gare du Nord and the Gare Saint-Lazare, were the gates of a dangerous paradise.

The Paris of the Second Empire had its bard. A German Jew, Offenbach, in *La Vie Parisienne, La Belle Hélène, Orphée aux Enfers* expressed the spirit of the city in music, as did Constantin Guys in his drawings. The team of Meilhac and Halévy represented the spirit of Paris in a purer, more French form. The great achievement of Berlioz was better appreciated in Germany than in Paris, but the dying master lived long enough to secure for the young Saint-Saëns a prize at the exhibition of 1867.

The Paris stage delighted the world. The younger Dumas turned current problems into current problem plays. M. Scribe, despite the jibes of the adoptive Parisian, Heine, was admired and imitated. Nowhere in the western world was the theatre, at that time, a serious art form. At Paris it was at least a successfully frivolous art form, fascinating so serious a soul as Matthew Arnold and soon to be given the necessary stimulus of a great personality by Rachel's successor, Sarah Bernhardt. Meantime there was Hortense Schneider at the Variétés.

Social life was more organized than it had been. The great clubs were a rival to the Imperial Court. The Travellers, the Union, the 'Cercle de la Rue Royale' that admitted the cultivated Jew, Charles Haas (whom the world was to know as Charles Swann), were fruits of the Anglomania of the upper classes. So was the Jockey Club that regulated the increasingly important sport of horse racing. That was no longer confined to the cramped Champ de Mars where Frédéric Moreau had his misadventure. Longchamps and Chantilly began to rival Ascot and Newmarket and, in 1865, 'Gladiateur', a French bred and trained horse, won the Derby and went on to win the St. Leger, the first swallow of a long summer. But the Jockey Club did more than try to 'improve the breed of horses'. It became a social arbiter, *the* social arbiter. (It was taken as a proof of the depth of humiliation caused by the disasters of 1870 that the son of the Duc de Gramont was blackballed by the Jockey Club simply as the son of his father.) If the Imperial Court was often snubbed by the members of the great clubs, it was to Napoleon and Eugénie that Vichy owed its new and greater fame, and the remote Basque village of Biarritz its notoriety. And with the annexation of Nice and Mentone in 1860, the Riviera, the 'côte d'Azur', was prepared for its great destiny. Paris and its pleasure satellites were Corinth as well as Athens.

It was under the Second Empire that the new glory of French painting appeared above the horizon. But it was also under the Second Empire that the cleavage between the taste of the man in the street (of all classes) and the taste of the pioneering artists and of their partisans became more and more evident. It was a cleavage that affected all the arts, but was most visible in the visual arts. It was not a mere matter of a change in styles, of a progression from David to Ingres to Delacroix. That progression still went on. But the recognized artist of eminence ceased to be the artist whom the next generation would honour. The old certitudes were gone. When the Duc de Morny called on Meissonier at 15 Quai de Bourbon, he was calling, he knew, on a great artist, perhaps *the* great French artist. When his half-brother, the Emperor, visiting the Salon in 1863 before its official opening, demanded to be shown the pictures that had been refused and ordered the opening of the 'Salon des Réfusés', he was, as he so often did, showing an independence of judgement rare in rulers. And by being shocked by Manet's 'Déjeuner sur l'Herbe' he was also in character; the picture was morally dangerous and the Emperor (as a ruler) was a moralist. The clash of 1863 was to be repeated again and again. The official Salon refused, monotonously, the offerings of the painters whom posterity was to cherish. Yet the official painters were famous, and not only in France. Meissonier and Millet, the later Corot, at a lower but equally popular level Rosa Bonheur, were world artists. A little later, with rather less universal applause, Carolus Duran and Bouguereau were world artists. To their Paris to be applauded and received came Sargent to paint Madame Gauthereau. To Paris came emissaries from Boston to secure the services of Puvis de Chavannes to rival Sargent in decorating the

Public Library. To Paris came pupils from France, from America, from all parts of Europe, even from Japan.

But artistic life had turned into another channel. It was with the painters that were to be called, ironically, 'the Impressionists'. New names that evoked ridicule were talked of. Manet and Monet, Sisley and Seurat, even names whose persistence defied all the principles of the official schools, Cézanne and the Douanier Rousseau: the rich man who could not be taught; the ex-Customs House official who had not been taught. These rebels had many bitter moments, but some, like Degas and Cézanne, were rich; some had been, for a time at any rate, well off. Others found patrons like the publisher Charpentier, and so Renoir's 'Madame Charpentier' entered into rivalry with Sargent's 'Madame Gauthereau'. And as they fought for recognition, the new, heretical painters made the Île-de-France, with its lofty sky and noble clouds, its woods and smooth-sliding rivers, Yonne and Oise, Loing and Marne, all converging on Paris, 'subterlabentia muros', as much the representative landscape of European painting as Tuscany and Umbria had been in the fifteenth century. But their achievement added nothing to popular culture. The French workers had admired in Delacroix his evocation of the Revolution of July. They admired, on trust, the painting of Courbet; it was at the service of the people, it was anti-clerical. They would have admired Meissonier and Detaille if they had commemorated a revolt or a great strike. But what to them was Moret or La Grande Jatte or La Montagne Sainte-Victoire? The taste of the bourgeoisie was no better; the prestige of the official schools, of the Academy was great; the bad judgement in choosing the annual Prix de Rome almost infallible. The artists were alienated from the State and from the people. The story of the Impressionists and the Post-Impressionists, of the sterility of the Salon and the Académie was to be used as a further illustration of the alienation of true culture from its official patrons. The State was *bound* to be philistine; its mistakes were indefensible, as bad as the mistakes of the Académie Française. So the official artists were forgotten, like Henner (whom Henry James admired and who, in turn, saw merit in Renoir), and few remember that Matisse came to Paris to study under Bouguereau, and Dufy to study under Bonnat.

III

'The Empire is peace', Louis-Napoleon had promised. Within two years of the promise, France was at war, a war scarcely intelligible in 1854 and almost totally unintelligible now. The Crimean War had more than one cause. Some were frivolous or seemed so in an agnostic age, like the French and Russian claims to protect the Holy Places. Some were based on sentiments very natural at the time but forgotten now. The Russia of Nicholas I was detested by the Left as the embodiment of tyranny, the crusher of the Revolution of 1848, the great slave state. It was detested by many on the Right as the oppressor of Catholic Poland. It was detested by Bonapartists as one of the two powers that had brought down Napoleon I—but not, as a rule, as much detested as was the other, England. But Napoleon III had determined not to quarrel with England, and he entered into war with Russia to protect what was more a British than a French interest, the integrity of the Ottoman Empire.

The war was in many ways preposterous. By the time the Anglo-French armies got to Turkey, the Russian invasion had been repulsed. It was necessary to call off the war or find a battlefield. So the armies sailed off to the Crimea to capture the great Russian naval base of Sebastopol. At the Battle of the Alma, the Allied armies were victorious, but it was not even a victory like Borodino; Sebastopol, unlike Moscow, did not fall.

Perhaps it would have done so if the victory had been exploited, but Lord Raglan, though a veteran of Waterloo, had never commanded troops and Saint-Arnaud had only the glory and experience of an artificial victory in Algeria. The two armies settled down for a siege, the British, with bad luck and bad judgement, choosing the harbour of Balaklava as their base. Sebastopol was besieged but not invested. Russian armies marched across the steppe, suffering great losses, to attempt to drive off the besiegers. They failed, defeated by the military virtues of the Allied rank-and-file rather than by any skill of the commanders. Saint-Arnaud died and was succeeded by Canrobert; Raglan died and was succeeded by General Simpson. But only the great Russian engineer, General Todleben knew his business. The war was costly, in money and men, and more and more unpopular in France. The Allied navies made empty demonstrations in the Baltic; the Turks held their own in Asia Minor; the astute Count Cavour sent a Sardinian contingent to fight in the Crimea. Diplomats negotiated at Vienna; and Napoleon III, with his new and lovely Empress, visited London, the Queen and the Prince Consort visited Paris. Victoria was charmed by Napoleon III (in many ways he was so like Albert), but Albert was not charmed by the new Emperor or dazzled by the new Empress. A new French commander-in-chief, Pelissier, was horrified at the threat of the Emperor to take command in person. So were the Emperor's Ministers and Allies.

The army of the chief Ally had been destroyed; its empty ranks filled with raw recruits, poor substitutes for the men of 'the thin red line' killed by the War Office. A last Russian attempt to drive off the besiegers was brilliantly defeated by the French (with some over-advertised Sardinian aid) at the Tchernaya. The Tsar was dead. The war must be ended. The first assaults on the fortress failed, but Pelissier did not lose heart. The next attack succeeded, that is, the French part did. General MacMahon, on the mined tower of the Malakoff, said or was said to have said: 'Here I am and here I stay' ('J'y suis, j'y reste'). The British attack on the Redan not only failed, but failed disgracefully. Lord Palmerston, who had forced his way into office to win the war, wanted to win it in a fashion that would redound to the credit of Britain. Napoleon III had all the glory he needed. Peace was made. The showdown between Russia and Turkey was postponed for twenty years. Limitations on Russian armaments were imposed; they lasted fifteen years. The real victor, if there was one, was Sardinia which had got useful publicity and a claim on the gratitude of Napoleon III. But the Peace Congress was brilliant. Paris, in 1856, filled the more simple-minded with dreams of restored glory. There was now an heir to the throne, after several miscarriages. The young Prince Imperial was baptized in Notre-Dame and, like the Comte de Chambord and the Comte de Paris, was promised a brilliant future.

The alliance with England was immediately tested. The new Tsar courted the parvenu his father had snubbed. Morny was all for a reversal of policy, for an alliance with Russia. A devoted Italian conspirator, Orsini, organized the assassination of the Emperor. The attempt failed, costing many innocent lives; Napoleon III showed his usual phlegmatic courage and, far from bearing Orsini a grudge, remembered that he, too, had been a *carbonaro* and had fought for Italy. He was ripe for Cavour's plucking.

As a by-product of the Orsini attempt came a quarrel with England. The murder plot had been planned in England; the explosives manufactured there. The Empire reacted vigorously. For a moment it seemed that 1851 had come again. There were mass arrests, mass deportations. New wounds were inflicted; old wounds re-opened. Yet there was no revolutionary danger. It was not only that the Imperial police were vigilant, easily catching incompetent conspirators like Delescluze; there was no revolutionary temper. The indefatigable Blanqui dreamed, still, of his small, dedicated party, seizing power in one blow; but it was a dream, a dream to know its realization in 1917 in Petrograd.

Lord Palmerston introduced legislation to make conspiracies like that of Orsini more difficult, but the British public would have none of it. More people than Meredith's Nevil Beauchamp were angered by the tone of the French official Press and of the officers of the Imperial Guard. Palmerston was overthrown and the Derby-Disraeli Government had no sympathy with Italian aspirations. But Napoleon III was firmer on the subject of Italy than on other projects. The difficulty was to find a reason for war. Austria obliged by sending an ultimatum to Sardinia, and France, that is, Napoleon III, came to the aid of his Ally.

The war was detested by many of the elements of French society that had strongly supported the Empire, but it was welcomed by many enemies of the Empire. Napoleon III landed at Genoa; it was 'roses, roses all the way'. At Magenta the firmness of MacMahon saved the day, endangered by rashness and stupidity. Milan was entered and victory shone on the plains of Lombardy where, in 1796, the star of the House of Bonaparte had first soared into the empyrean. But 1859 was not 1796; Napoleon III was no 'lord of the ascendant'. His staff noted with horror that he could not read a map. (Neither could some of his generals.) The Austrian Army, muscle-bound and defeatist as it was, was better commanded. But the *furia francese* (and the superiority of the new French rifled cannon that the Emperor had provided) prevailed. At Solferino the Austrians were again defeated. Then the world learned with astonishment that the two Emperors had made an armistice at Villafranca. Italy was not to be liberated 'from sea to sea'. Venetia was to remain Austrian; the princes driven out by their subjects were to be restored; all that Sardinia got was Lombardy (minus the great fortresses). Italy was to become a confederation under the Pope. Many explanations were found for the Emperor's decision. He was said to have been horrified by the slaughter of Solferino (Henri Dunant, a young Swiss who saw the battle, was also horrified, and from his horror came the Red Cross). There were other reasons. The great fortresses of the Quadrilateral were still in Austrian hands. They had not fallen after Lodi, and Solferino was Lodi, not Rivoli. Prussia was threatening. France had no allies. Honour had been won; something had been done for Italy. The future was unknown, but no question was settled by the settlement. It might not last; it did not. Meantime, there was glory. Another of the victors of 1814 and 1815 had been defeated.

On August 14, the Army of Italy marched into Paris. Its reception was overwhelming. For the moment, the Emperor was almost accepted in the Faubourg Saint-Antoine. He could now wear laurel wreaths on his coins and, in celebration, a general amnesty was proclaimed. On August 18, the most illustrious of exiles replied. Victor Hugo would only 'return with Liberty'.

The Emperor had more to trouble him than the rebuke from Guernsey. Italy had not been freed from sea to sea. The Pope was totally cured of his old weakness for Italian patriotism. The Emperor dreamed of an Italian confederation of which the Pope was to be the head; but Pius IX could not see himself as the partner of Victor Emmanuel II. He clung, with desperate energy, to the whole papal territory, in which the liberation of Lombardy had naturally bred hope of liberation from the incompetent and unpatriotic papal government. All over Italy the nationalists were on the move. The princes of Tuscany and Modena, the weak young King of the Two Sicilies, were all threatened. The final push that brought down the rickety structure was given by Garibaldi. He landed in Sicily with 'the Thousand', conquered the island and invaded the mainland.

There was no doubt that the settlement of Villafranca would be overthrown. All that was in doubt was by whom. Nor could the Emperor of the French really resent the continuation of the work to which he had put his hand in 1859, or consent to let Austria put an end to it. Cavour knew how essential was this French veto on Austrian intervention; he was willing to pay a high price for it and he shuddered at the thought of Garibaldi's resuming the disastrous policy of 1848. Italy, he knew, could not 'farà da se'. As Garibaldi moved north, it was essential for Cavour to move south. Between the two lay the Pope. He still lived in a world of illusion. He formed his own army of Catholic volunteers and the command was given to the most brilliant of the 'Africans', Lamoricière. Catholic volunteers came in from Ireland, Belgium, France. It was to be a new crusade. But for all the drum beating, the response was not impressive. Only five hundred French 'papal zouaves' were at hand when Cialdini swept away the papal army at Castelfidardo. As a crusading leader, Pius IX recalled Pius II more than Urban II. It was only too clear that if the Pope was to stay in Rome, it would be by the good offices of Cavour and Napoleon III, and Cavour would hold his hand only to please the Emperor.

Pius IX was not grateful, for Cavour had annexed to Sardinia the greater part of the Papal States. And he had proclaimed the 'Kingdom of Italy': 'the great name was out and its enemies had heard it'. The Pope, if he had been a wise man, might have said 'Addio grassa Bologna', but he was not a wise man. His political rule was reduced to Rome and the 'patrimony of St. Peter', and he did not forgive any of the men who had humiliated him. The Catholics of the entire world were asked to regard the Pope as the victim of a great crime; the defence of what was left, if not the restoration of what was lost, was now the chief aim of papal policy to which many more important things were sacrificed.

One of these was good relations not only with the French Government but with the French people. They were asked to disregard the Imperial triumph of securing Savoy and Nice as the price of non-intervention, the first breach made in the system of the treaties of 1815 to the direct advantage of France. All French foreign policy was to be judged by zealous Catholics in terms of papal needs. The fact

that it was French pressure that made the successors of Cavour keep
Garibaldi from Rome, that it was a French garrison that did what
the Pope's own army would most certainly have been unable to do
—keep Rome free from Italian rule—was not accounted to the Emperor for righteousness either by the saintly Pope or by his very
unsaintly (and lay) Secretary of State, Cardinal Antonelli. By moving
the Italian capital from Turin to Florence, the new kingdom at any
rate postponed the solution of the Roman question, although no
Italian government dared finally renounce the hope of Rome as the
capital of Italy. The Pope had been deceived.

    He had other troubles in France. As long as the Imperial Govern-
ment had been worthy of the traditions (as seen from Rome) of 'the
eldest daughter of the Church', the steady increase of papal power
in France had gone on unchecked, except by a few old-fashioned
bishops. But papal imperialism had been resisted, and now the
Government was ready to favour the resisters. Pius IX was as much a
centralizer as Napoleon I, and he had often the same good reasons for
the extension of his authority. He wished to impose the Roman
breviary on France. It was perhaps time. There were twenty-six different usages in the French Church; one diocese had five. If there was
to be uniformity in worship, the uniformity must be that of the
Roman rite. So Dom Guéranger argued with much vehemence and
some lack of scruple. Thus he denounced the breviary of Chartres as
the work of Sieyès. He was shown to be wrong, but did not withdraw this charge with any grace. It was one thing to replace the
eighteenth-century coat and breeches with the cassock, to deprive
the canons of Notre-Dame of their traditional pointed bonnets; it
was possibly magnanimous not to make the wearing of the 'Roman
collar' compulsory. The local rites had deep roots. To replace them
by the Roman rite was to evoke all that dislike and contempt of the
papal court that was traditional in the Gallican Church.

    The old Gallicanism was dead. How dead was seen by the univer-
sal acceptance of the proclamation in 1854, by the sole authority of
the Pope, of the long-contested doctrine of the Immaculate Conception. Henceforward December 8 was a great and popular feast. The
new dogma had been ratified, so many of the pious thought, by the
appearance of the Blessed Virgin to a peasant girl, Bernadette

Soubirous, at Lourdes in the Pyrenees. The heavenly visitant had
announced, in the local *patois*, 'I am the Immaculate Conception.'
This was not the only reported apparition. But the scepticism of the
most famous of French priests, the curé of Ars, had kept La Salette
from anticipating and rivalling Lourdes. Miracles, in the mid-
nineteenth century, were not only 'to the Greeks foolishness', they
presented serious administrative problems. Nothing could have been
less in the spirit of the Concordat. And the Imperial officials were
tempted to imitate the royal officials of the eighteenth century, to
announce their own version of:

> 'De par le Roy, défense à Dieu
> De faire miracle dans ce lieu.'

But the popularity of the new shrine was too much for them. The
spirit of the age was defied successfully. It was also defied less successfully by the Pope. The heirs of Lamennais had not given up hope of
reconciling the Church with the age. They hoped that the Pope had
learned from his experience of Napoleon III not to put his trust in
princes, but rather to throw himself into the arms of 'liberty'. This
was the politics preached by Montalembert among the laity and by
Bishop Dupanloup among the clergy. They pointed to the example
of England, Ireland, Belgium. They pointed in vain. The Pope denounced their project and in the most rigorous terms, listed and condemned in the 'Syllabus' of 1864 the most cherished beliefs of the
times. It was war on the spirit of the age, a war deplored in bitter
silence by the discomfited Catholic liberals, welcomed by militant
Catholic propagandists like Veuillot and by the numerous Frenchmen who delighted to see the Church, as they thought, digging its
own grave.

The betrayal of the Pope by the Emperor had put an end to the
love match between the imperial regime and the Church. Pius IX
told the French Ambassador that the Emperor was a crook, and that
was the view of Catholic zealots. The Legitimists noticed, with sar-
donic pleasure, the distress of the clergy. The militant Veuillot prepared for battle and, as he expected, *L'Univers* was suppressed. So
was the Society of Saint-Vincent de Paul, which not only was
suspected of serving as an instrument of Legitimist propaganda, but

which had refused to accept a chief nominated by the Emperor. The Freemasons had done so, why not the allegedly purely charitable body? So asked Persigny who was not totally displeased to see the Empire turn away from the clerical embrace. The imperial administration now began to indulge in a policy of pin pricks, of disciplining turbulent priests. The anti-clerical comedy, *Le Fils de Giboyer*, was cried to the heavens as a new *Tartuffe*, Augier as a new Molière. The radical Bonapartists, like the circle round the Prince Napoleon, rejoiced. Sainte-Beuve at last was made a Senator. And it was discovered that in regions where there was strong, popular Bonapartism, like the Charentes, the Empire gained in popularity. Even soldiers were not averse from noisy demonstrations of anti-clerical feeling. The breach was not all loss for the Empire, and it revealed how artificial was the prosperity and power of the Church.

The coldness between the Empire and the Church made it possible for the Emperor to give to his Minister of Education, Victor Duruy, more support than he would otherwise have been tempted to give, despite his agreement with Duruy's aims and their common interest in ancient history and archaeology. Like the Emperor, Duruy was impressed by the superiority of the German university system and, unable to make a frontal assault on the existing order, he added to the array of 'great schools' the new research institute, the École des Hautes Études. If this foundation implied criticism of the existing university institutions, that interested few outside academic circles.

It was very different when Duruy encouraged communes to make their elementary schools free, when he abolished the limit on the number of free places, when he restored the classes of philosophy and modern history in the lycées. The State was now competing with the Church, and competing effectually. But in one field, Duruy and the Emperor both failed; they could not shake the monopolistic hold of the Church on the education of young ladies. There was plenty of grumbling about it. Taine, writing in *La Vie Parisienne* as 'Frédéric-Thomas Graindorge', complained that there was 'an enormous disproportion between the education of men and women. As a result, there's a lack of subjects of conversation; women can no longer talk of religion as in the seventeenth century, nor of philosophy as in the eighteenth.' But it was not only Bishop Dupanloup who did not want young ladies to be taught subjects of conversation by young men. The average bourgeois father, if he still thought religious faith rather shameful in his sons, was alarmed by the lack of it in his daughters. The Empress sent her nieces to attend courses in the Sorbonne, but Duruy's university teachers, in Paris and the provinces, were kept by a strike of parents from educating or corrupting the future wives and mothers of the bourgeoisie.

The apologetic position of the Church had altered for the worse. The old-fashioned anti-clericalism of M. Homais was bad form. Voltaire now seemed superficial and naïve. (So also did Monseigneur Dupanloup.) Eloquence in the manner of Chateaubriand or Lacordaire was no reply to the German historical school whose influence was just beginning to be felt. The Faculty of Protestant Theology of the University of Strasbourg kept in touch with the movement of ideas across the Rhine, and the theories debated in the *Revue Germanique* made that a more important and exciting periodical than the old *Revue Britannique* had ever been. It was, of course, a time of intellectual ferment and revolution everywhere; the age of *The Origin of Species* and *Das Kapital*. Prehistory with Boucher de Perthes, comparative religion with Burnouf, turned the flank of some old arguments. Bishop Dupanloup was as much lost in this world as was Bishop Wilberforce.

The French Church was, in its intellectual equipment, out of date. Various Church leaders had attempted to give it an intellectual high command. But the École des Carmes, founded by Archbishop Affre, had not lived up to its promise; neither had the revived Oratory; neither had Solesmes. The Theology Faculty of the Sorbonne was highly suspect at Rome. It was believed to be Gallican; it was certainly not Ultramontane and its Dean, Monseigneur Maret, shared the views if not quite the learning of Bishop Hefele and Professor Döllinger. Napoleon III had wanted to create in France something like the great Catholic faculties of Germany or like Louvain. It was not a project that interested Pius IX. Of course, there were hopeful signs. The massed volumes of Migne's *Patrologia Latina* and *Patrologia Graeca*, if not monuments of modern scholarship, showed that the old appetite for learning that had been one of the glories of the Gallican Church was not dead.

But much of that learning was irrelevant. How irrelevant was made evident by the storm that burst when, in 1863, Ernest Renan, recently appointed to the chair of Semitic Languages at the Collège de France by the favour of the Emperor, published his *Vie de Jésus*. What he had to say was not new; Strauss's life had been translated by Comte's disciple, Littré, in 1835, before Marian Evans had translated it into English. But it was Renan who suddenly brought the mass of the cultivated French public face to face with an attack on the basic doctrine of Christianity far more fundamental than Voltaire's and written with an elegance that, in its own way, was as masterly as Voltaire's prose. That Renan had the greatest respect for the Church, for the teachers he had known at Saint-Sulpice, altered nothing in the fact that, as he was to say, 'Monsieur Homais was right'.

The doctrine of the divinity of Christ was defended by vehement orators. The irreverent were amused, the wiser among the orthodox alarmed by the spectacle of that great dogma defended in the Senate by Marshal Canrobert. The few Catholics who were abreast of the controversy, like the Abbé Meignan, lamented. 'In Germany they laugh at Renan but they also laugh at us.' But most Frenchmen of the educated classes agreed with Renan; they saw the sea of faith ebbing, heard only

'Its melancholy, long withdrawing roar'.

The Imperial Government suppressed Renan's chair but that was mere politics. Humanity was left to

'the vast edges drear
And naked shingles of the world'.

IV

One of the causes of the depression of the winter of 1847–48 had been the ending of the railway boom; renewed railway construction would have been the most effective 'national workshop'. But political disturbance froze up the stream of credit and bitter discussions of the ways and means of giving France that railway system already possessed by Britain, Belgium, Prussia delayed action. Railway directors were excluded from the Legislative Assembly as corrupting influences; so they resigned, formally, from the boards. Attempts to make the Government builder and owner of the railways were defeated. (In this cause, Lamartine achieved his last great oratorical triumph.) But there was still no system. Naturally, the new dictatorial Government, banking on public confidence, conscious of the need for creating employment and more alive than any of its predecessors to the technical needs of society, at once put in hand the completion of the schemes projected and begun under Louis-Philippe. For the plans were there; there were fragments of the great design in existence; it remained to unite the fragments.

This was the theme preached by the speculative brothers Péreire in the *Journal des Chemins de Fer*, of which the proprietor was another speculator, Mirès. The brothers Péreire were Jews and Saint-Simonians. They believed that if France were rapidly given the necessary capital equipment, the increase in wealth that would follow would make the boldest policy of borrowing prove the wisest. It was not only a matter of railways, but of ports, of steamship lines, of warehouses, of reconstructed cities. The instrument of finance was to be the 'Crédit Mobilier'. It was a holding company which would invest freely in every promising enterprise, its shares would represent the whole range of the new capital development; this stock would be the 'omnium', the representative claim on the new wealth. There was one flaw in this system, as more conservative financiers like James de Rothschild pointed out. The Crédit Mobilier would tend to have some of the weakest and most speculative issues in its portfolio, since the absolutely sound enterprises could be financed without calling on its services. But, for the moment, the wind was from the south.

The saving of society on December 2 had reassured the timid; money was plentiful and cheap. In the next five years the great schemes of the railway planners of the July monarchy were carried out. It was necessary, at times, to buy out the owners of strategically placed links in the incompleted chain, but that was a necessary cost. The State guaranteed a minimum rate of interest; if more was earned, the profits were to be divided. The Government was a sleeping partner in the future profits and as the system grew, the profits began to come in. This was especially true of the region served by the Nord where the new Pas-de-Calais coal-field was being exploited and where a real industrial revolution was in progress. The line from Paris to Lyons and the Mediterranean, the P.-L.-M. as it was to be known, came next in present yields and future expectations. The other lines were less impressive investments and the State guarantee, though not called on, was necessary to their financing. But the old doubts about the utility of railways were dead; so were the hopes placed in canals and river improvements. Each year saw more and more steamers give way to railways, barges to trucks. The Bank of France was forced to deal in railway paper; stock was very widely distributed (selling it was one of the duties of a stationmaster on the P.-L.-M.). Railway securities were second only to *rentes* in respectability, and on the boards of directors could be found the names of great nobles: Noailles, Lorges, Cars, Ségur. Their ancestors had had the right to ride in the King's carriages; directorships of the railways were the current equivalent.

Mirès, the Péreires had a wider view than that bounded by the French frontiers. One of the great handicaps of French commerce was the absence of good natural ports; the coming of the steamer made the lack more serious. Bordeaux might rely complacently, and foolishly, on its river, but Marseilles and Le Havre could not grow if pinned into their old areas. The citadel of Le Havre had to be razed to make room for docks; the old Phocian port of Marseilles was eclipsed by the warehouses on the made land, sheltered by the great new sea-walls that sheltered the new docks. Marseilles not only began to exploit the existing trade with the Levant, and, a growing source of wealth, with Algeria, but to discount the golden future that would dawn with the opening of the Suez Canal, a prospect that justified almost the most extravagant examples of oratory in the style of Marius. In 1853 the great sea-wall was at last completed at Cherbourg and the railway reached the new port in 1858. Brest dreamed of a day when it would cease to be a mere naval base and would rival Southampton; the new port of Saint-Nazaire was built at the mouth of the Loire, a little before there was trade to justify the investment, and Dunkirk, close to the booming northern coal-field, grew with startling speed.

From Marseilles the Messageries Maritimes began to spread its lines all over the Levant and at last the Compagnie Générale Trans-atlantique established a regular connection from Le Havre with New York and the West Indies, although handicapped by having sunk most of its capital in paddle steamers, just as the screw steamer was beginning to be effective.

The main begetters of this magical expansion were, for the moment, doubly favoured, by the Emperor and by the world of finance. A daughter of Mirès became the Princesse de Polignac; more important, a daughter of Isaac Péreire was successfully married into the great Protestant banking firm of Thurneyssen. But the euphoria of the great speculators was shortlived. The increasing indebtedness of the regime was marked and reproved as it began to lose its dictatorial character. It became necessary to cultivate the goodwill of the ortho-dox bankers. The Corps Législatif, if it was docile enough in matters of general policy, had, from the beginning, taken seriously its duties as the source of money. The embellishment of Paris was perhaps necessary; it was a hobby of the Emperor and a political insurance policy against a new revolt. But why should the rural taxpayer pay for the splendid new Rue Impériale in Lyons? The Louvre—that could be defended; but the expenditure in reconstructing the area round the new and vast Opera House that was to be one of the most characteristic monuments of the regime—why should the rural and small town taxpayer pay for what Guéroult called the 'home of venal love and effeminate arts'?

Then the completion of the main railway systems made the problem of freight rates of great importance. The abandonment of work on canals and rivers was repented of and there were heated demands for the control of railway rates. The Government was not willing to control, but it did bring pressure to bear to secure that rates were uniform and that something less than all that the traffic would bear was charged. The regions that still had no railways clamoured for them; but by 1860 all the really profitable lines had been allocated and most of them built. The Government had now to guarantee interest on lines running through poor and difficult areas like the

Massif Central, and allow the existing companies to separate the accounts of these new lines from those of the more profitable old lines. The guarantee of interest became a charge, not a mere support for the marketing of securities; and it would have been cheaper openly to subsidize the less and less profitable lines that were politically necessary. For the provision of railways was now one of the recognized methods of winning voters and rewarding or punishing Deputies. No mere plea for economy could be allowed to interfere with the rules of political economics. So in the Corrèze, it was mainly by the promise of governmental support for a railway that his formerly loyal voters were stolen away from the inconveniently Catholic Baron de Jouvenel.

But with all the political will in the world, not every village or small town could have its railway. So there were experiments with various types of light railways, one assumed to be particularly economical since it was believed to have been successful in Scotland. At increasing cost, France was unified. There was one very novel result of this achievement. The last famine in France was in 1855; henceforward a bad harvest, local or general, meant high prices but not a shortage of grain. It was not only a matter of railways; the steam-driven mills, detested by Alphonse Daudet's miller, made the grinding of the grain immune from the caprice of the winds. The much dreaded 'soudure' of the bad years was no longer a source of acute distress to the poor and of political alarm to the Government.

France was united in another way. The electric telegraph replaced the old semaphores. These had carried only Government messages; the electric telegraph carried private messages too. Morny was the Minister who pushed the system: that great stock gambler could gauge its possibilities. The new service paid handsomely; it gave the Government quick news and the possibility of telling its story with the speed of lightning. It competed with and complemented the rapidly extended postal services; far-seeing civil servants already advocated their union. France began to know a physical unity unprecedented in history and French began at last to conquer the *patois*. It was time, just time, for Mistral to give to the dying language of Provence its classical embodiment in *Mireille*.

This unification cost money as did the embellishment of Paris, the great Army, the brilliant foreign policy. And the possessing classes, which had welcomed the dictatorship with gratitude, were now not so frightened and so not so grateful, and were, in other ways, alienated from the regime. Rural deputies could say that they 'sent their sons to the Army, their money to the cities and we are up to our knees in mud'. Yet they did not want more 'routes impériales', planned from Paris and controlled by the haughty engineers of the Ponts et Chaussées. They wanted more local roads, run by local and not independent surveyors.

The embellishment of Paris did vastly increase wealth and it made business flourish. 'When building booms, everything booms', was the saying. The fervid Bonapartist Persigny believed that. He was, in a very crude way, a kind of Keynesian. Money borrowed for the re-making of Paris was a multiplier. Baron Haussmann thought that way too. With the profits of one improvement, he could pay for a new one. But the Conseil d'État reserved a great part of the profits for the fortunate proprietors; the increment might be unearned, but it was sacred. It was time, all the most solid elements in France thought, to call a halt. And the symbol of the halt was the replace-ment of Magne at the Ministry of Finance by Achille Fould, a Jewish banker, friend of the Rothschilds and representative of sound finance. He was the new Necker. From 1859 there was to be peace, balanced budgets; the Emperor was not to commit the country to expendi-ture and send the bills to the Corps Législatif. He was to be respectful, if not docile, to the old order, the great Protestant banks and the Rothschilds. He was to listen seriously to the head of the great house of Casimir-Périer (that meant Anzin as well as banking). And Casimir-Périer said and believed that liberty—that is, the control of the executive by the vigilance of the deputies—meant probity, eco-nomy, prudence.

It was a widespread illusion. The symbol of the revolution in the world of finance was the reception by James de Rothschild of the Emperor in 1862 at his great château of Ferrières. It was less a gracious compliment paid by a sovereign to a subject than a meeting of two sovereigns as at Tilsit. And as at Tilsit, Napoleon was the less secure of the two potentates. The visit was a public demonstration that the Emperor was regularizing his position. As is usual in such situations, there were sufferers. The first was Mirès who went down, was prosecuted, but triumphantly acquitted. The time of the Péreire brothers had not yet come. But their field was invaded. In 1863 and 1864 were founded the Crédit Lyonnais and the Société Générale, banks but not so called, banks enticing investors to buy stock as well as to deposit funds. Behind the first was a consortium of Lyons and Geneva bankers, behind the second was Rothschild. This was competition for the Crédit Mobilier and for its ally, the Crédit Foncier. The Crédit Foncier had, as one of its ostensible objects, the improvement of rural credit. But it failed to shake the hold of the local notaries who lent money to the man, not to the bits of land he owned. French landed property was too divided for it to be easy to organize credit on a national scale. So the Crédit Foncier had to retire from the rural field assigned to it and devote itself to bolstering up the great programme of urbanization, personified in prefects like Haussmann in Paris and Vaissé in Lyons.

If the 'tales of Haussmann' were the butt of opposition wit, the trade treaty of the Emperor evoked far more resentment. Napoleon III had, from the beginning of his reign, tried to break down the preposterously high tariffs, complicated by total prohibitions, that cut France off from the expanding world economy and, as the railway boom had revealed, greatly hampered her industrial development. But the Corps Législatif rebelled. The new Corps Législatif, elected in 1857, was no more docile. Indeed, in it appeared, for the first time, open opposition leaders like the young Émile Ollivier. If the Emperor was to have his free-trade dreams realized, he would have to ignore the Corps Législatif. He did. He negotiated, with Richard Cobden, the first of a series of commercial treaties that opened English and other markets to French wines, silks, fruits, flowers, perfumes, expensive textiles, and that, in return, abolished prohibitions, reduced tariffs, forced French industry to modernize itself. The manufacturers protested; their rancour was permanent; but France was forced into the modern world by Napoleon III and the Saint-Simonian, Michel Chevalier. The peasant was, for the moment, grateful. The pampered businessmen were unforgiving. And the cotton famine that the American Civil War produced brought great distress to textile industries in the process of conversion. To a Rouen businessman like Pouyer-Quertier, the Cobden Treaty was a crime worse than the *coup d'état*, Napoleon III more detestable than Gustave Flaubert; and, all over France, businessmen were converted to the need for parliamentary government to save them (and the French economy) from the horrors of competition. The Emperor had made new enemies and reinforced the contempt of M. Thiers. That contempt was deepened as the historian of the Consulate and the Empire saw Napoleon III dissipate his resources and those of France in enterprises more and more romantic.

v

The Empire *was* dispersing its forces in an alarming manner, spending its peasant soldiers and marines all over the globe. The laurels of 1859 were still fresh when French arms won further glory in China. Allied with Britain in what was coarsely called the 'Second Opium War', a French expeditionary force under General de Montauban stormed the Taku forts. The victorious general was made 'Comte de Palikao' and, with the aid of his Allies, burned down the Summer Palace as a lesson to the barbarous Chinese. After all, the palace was not worth serious respect from the emissaries of a civilization that had produced Pugin and Viollet-le-Duc, the Houses of Parliament and Pierrefonds. At the other end of the Chinese Empire, in a remote dependency of the satellite Empire of Annam, French sailors established a new colony in the nearly empty lands of Cochin-China, with the new Frenchified city of Saigon as the capital. Annam had been one of the most cherished fields of French missionary effort. The martyrs of Hué were famous all over the Catholic world, and even hardened 'reds' were prepared to respect the seminarists bound for that dangerous mission field, greeting them as St. Philip Neri had greeted the students of the English College, 'salvete flores martyrum'. The Spaniards from the Philippines who had shared in the enterprise were pushed on one side, and France got a new colony and a foothold in further Asia.

In a more traditional field of French enterprise, Napoleon III was active. The Christians of Syria and the Lebanon were enduring their traditional ordeal by massacre. The Turks were, or professed to be, impotent. Syria was doubly sacred ground. There were the memories of the crusades and of General Bonaparte, of Acre and of Mont-Thabor. Was not the ballad written by the Emperor's mother, Queen Hortense, 'En partant pour la Syrie', an official substitute for 'La Marseillaise'? So an expeditionary force was sent to Syria to restore order, under the vigilant gaze of Britain, determined to see that the expedition was not made the basis for a new colony. It was not, then.

But 'the great design' of the Empire was across the Atlantic. Among the numerous dreams that floated before the captive prince in Ham, was the project of an inter-oceanic canal and the redemption of Central America. The dream of Nicaragua was transferred to Mexico, then going through an even more violent revolutionary turmoil than usual. Why should not Napoleon III redeem this land of Latin culture and immense resources from anarchy? Mexico was in debt; Britain, Spain, France, all had legitimate claims and, in the fashion of the day, were ready to enforce them by arms. But an event extraneous to the bloody flux of Mexican politics tempted the Emperor. The United States was torn to pieces by civil war.

Like many other ill-informed spectators, Napoleon III assumed that the Union would never be restored. A Latin empire in Mexico would redress the overweening power of the 'Anglo-Saxons'. An emperor would be needed, and by choosing the brother of the Emperor of Austria some sop would be offered to the pride of Francis-Joseph. The scheme was hare-brained from the first. The Archduke Maximilian hesitated; he rightly doubted the authority of the adventurers offering him the crown. The French troops in Mexico discovered that the partisans of President Juarez, men like the young Porfirio Diaz, were formidable foes. The Foreign Legion won fresh fame; Mexico City was occupied; Maximilian was won over. (Even his very astute father-in-law, Leopold I of the Belgians, encouraged him in the adventure.)

The French officers serving in Mexico were in despair at their allies. A tough ranker officer, General Bazaine, won fame and a marshal's bâton. Maximilian established a Court, and tried to mitigate

the savagery of his partisans. But—and this was decisive—in the
United States the North was winning. Napoleon III rightly con-
sidered a Northern victory a defeat for him. But without English
support, he could not intervene. The English Government, equally
hostile to the North, did nothing—or nothing effective. In April
1865, when Lee surrendered at Appomattox, Maximilian was
doomed and Napoleon III was defeated. It took nearly two years to
organize the withdrawal, under the diplomatic pressure of Secretary
Seward and the military pressure of the presence of General Sheridan
on the Texas border, but it was done. The Emperor's protégé was
abandoned to his fate. By that time, his patron was hardly able to
maintain his own position.

After the establishment of the Kingdom of Italy, an Italy lacking
both Rome and Venice, Napoleon III was in a cleft stick. As far as
he had any one principle of foreign policy, it was to acquire Venetia
for Italy, to redeem the promise of 1859. This was not a French interest; it was the private interest of the old *carbonaro*. But as the Emperor of the French, Napoleon III could not give the Italians, or
permit them to take, what they wanted more than Venetia: Rome.
He could not win Italy to his side and he was bound to alienate
Austria, a power that had the same real interests as France, the maintenance of the *status quo*. It was not only Italy that had an interest in
upsetting the *status quo*. The Tsar smarted under the humiliations of
the Treaty of Paris. Only England was interested, now, in preserving
the fruits of victory. But French opinion was always liable to be
excited by the wrongs of Poland and, in 1863, a series of hopeless
outbreaks revealed the realities of Russian rule. The 'Liberator Tsar'
was not so unlike his father. National sentiment, personal sentiment
forced Napoleon III to try to 'do something for the Poles'. All he
did was to alienate the Tsar and acquire a cause of resentment against
an England which had been more than tepid. And the new authoritarian Prime Minister of Prussia, Herr von Bismarck, whom most
observers thought doomed with his stupid master, Wilhelm I, to
ignominious defeat at the hands of the Prussian Liberals, took the
opportunity to win the favour of the Tsar and to reveal one of the
bases of Prussian policy by offering to help to crush the Poles. But,
as yet, Bismarck was not thought formidable. Neither was Prussia.

Had not that clever weathercock, Edmond About, asked that France should help Prussia to become the Piedmont of Germany? The results of helping Piedmont to take over Italy had not been totally gratifying, and Prussia was not Piedmont. But Prussia was enlightened, cultured, Protestant, the enemy of reactionary and Catholic Austria. Enlightened opinion was for Prussia.

There was soon a chance to show sympathy with Prussia. In 1864 Prussia, allied by Bismarck's skill with Austria, made war on Denmark to 'liberate' Schleswig-Holstein. This move angered and alarmed England. But only the French Army could threaten the invaders, and Napoleon III had no desire to risk war for the pleasure of Palmerston and Russell. The victors quarrelled over the spoil and Herr von Bismarck set about winning the connivance of France in the approaching war with Austria. It should have been a difficult job but, fortunately for Bismarck, Napoleon III was what Napoleon I most detested: he was an 'ideologue'. He wanted to get Venice for Italy and he dreamed, vaguely, without much will behind the dreaming, of *something* to be gained for France in the struggle that was coming.

For it was assumed that there would be a long and exhausting war that would leave France the arbiter, unless Napoleon III had to step in to save Prussia. The most satisfactory solution would have been the peaceful cession of Venice by Austria, but since Austrian obstinacy forbade that, France could not desire a simple Austrian victory. Here the Emperor had on his side the most enlightened of subjects. What they feared was the victory of the veteran Austrian army, backed up by the armies of the German states, Hanover, Saxony, Bavaria, over a force that Lord Clyde (with all the authority of a Crimean veteran) had described as a first-rate militia. What could bookish generals like Moltke do against the veterans of Radetzky's school, the formidable soldiers of Magenta and Solferino?

All calculations were upset by the 'Six Weeks War'. If Nachod was a new Magenta (with von Verdy du Vernois, son of a gentleman of the household of the Comte d'Artois, as the new and bolder MacMahon), Sadowa was no Solferino, but a victory as complete as Wagram if not as Austerlitz. There was no arbiter's role for France. There was violent and heated discussion. Should France intervene to save Austria? The Army was not ready; neither were the bankers; neither was the public. The expeditionary force immobilized in Mexico was an excuse for inaction. Austria, easily victorious on sea and land over the new Kingdom of Italy, transferred Venetia to Napoleon III who transferred it to Victor Emmanuel II. For a moment, French opinion was dazzled, ready to believe that the Emperor's role in Europe was that of the disposer of the fruits of victory. But a sadder and a wiser judgement was expressed by Marshal Randan: 'It is France that has been beaten at Sadowa.' 'There are no faults left to commit', said M. Thiers.

It was an ominous prelude to the great exhibition of 1867. How different from the splendours of the Exhibition of 1855! Now the cynosure of all eyes was not a victorious Emperor of the French, but the victorious Count von Bismarck. And in the midst of the artificial gaiety and splendour of the exhibition came the noise of the rifle shots that ended the life of Maximilian, Emperor of Mexico. The 'great design' had failed, bloodily. The young painter, Manet, reconstructed the scene at Queretaro, but his picture was banned. It was even more dangerous than the 'Déjeuner sur l'Herbe' that had so shocked the moralists.

The censorship, the prudery of the Empire was one, but only one, of the reasons for its decline in public esteem. From the beginning, it had had against it the class that was to be called 'the intellectuals', the great literary *salons*, the Academies, the great periodicals like the *Revue des Deux-Mondes*, and the muzzled and resentful University. Few—and little esteemed—were the men of letters who, like Sainte-Beuve, 'rallied' to the Empire. The Emperor, it is true, was an intellectual himself. It was not merely the servility of courtiers that made plausible a suggestion that he should be made a member of the *Institut*. His interest in archaeology and philology was genuine. So was his interest in scientists like Claude Bernard and Deville (the inventor of aluminium). But his literary interests were limited. (He was to attribute the coming catastrophes to the reading of books like *Mademoiselle de Maupin*.) The Empress was becoming more and more pious (although it was not in her family tradition), and it was to her that the malicious attributed the prosecution of *Madame Bovary*. The favourite author of the Court was Octave Feuillet and it was a literary visitor to Compiègne who put his finger on a weakness of the imperial couple: 'They are very charming but they are foreigners.'

As far as the Empire had any links with the world of letters, they were provided by the *salon* of the Princess Mathilde. She had a genuine interest in the arts. (Her 'amant en titre' was the sculptor Nieuwerkerke.) In Paris and at Saint-Gratien, the men of letters were more at home than at Compiègne or the Tuileries. But even the Princess remembered, a little too often, that she was a Bonaparte or a Princess of Württemberg. There was a limit to her toleration of *frondeurs*. Sainte-Beuve overpassed it when, in his sordid old age, he turned against the Empire: 'You foolishly believe it is a fairy tale; it is a drawing-room. There are no more princesses.' So the Goncourts summed up their experience; it is the whole social lesson of Proust (who used the Princess Mathilde for part of the Duchesse de Guermantes).

The climate of opinion in these autumnal days was changing. The Prussian victory only added to the infatuation with German culture that had been the mark of the intellectuals since the young days of Ernest Renan and Edgar Quinet. Quinet was beginning to wonder whether he had not worshipped a false god. But his doubts were rare.

The change in the fame of Wagner was symptomatic. Although it was at a rehearsal of the Ninth Symphony by the Conservatoire orchestra that Wagner, in 1841, had had his Damascus conversion to serious music, he was little known and little liked when, in 1861, Princess Pauline de Metternich, wife of the Austrian Ambassador, induced the Emperor to sponsor a production of *Tannhaüser* at the Opera. The young gentlemen of the Jockey Club took a great interest in the Opera or, at least, in the *corps de ballet*—and *Tannhaüser* did not give enough opportunities to their protégées. To Republicans like Madame Adam, the patronage of this noisy German was proof of the imbecility of the Empire. It was asserted by the wits that *Tannhaüser* was produced as part of a secret bargain made at Villafranca. So the production was hooted down.

It was very different now. It was not an occasional poet like Baudelaire or an occasional politician like Wagner's brother-in-law, Émile Ollivier, who appreciated his genius. It was the advance guard of culture. And in 1868, the two great romantic schools were linked when Judith Gautier, daughter of Théo, future wife of Catulle Mendès, future mistress of Victor Hugo, went with Villiers de l'Isle Adam to Munich to see *Das Rheingold*. German, as Matthew Arnold noted, not English, was now the foreign language of ideas for the cultivated Frenchman. In German, the world's debate was carried on. And that debate was one that the Church and traditional values seemed destined to lose. Faith—even vague deism—was both hated and despised by the rising generation of 'the Schools'. The alliance between Pope and Emperor had not fostered faith.

VI

Faith was ebbing in more than religion. After the elections of 1863, the opposition in the Corps Législatif was open, numerous and talented. Thiers, Berryer returned to the battle. There were new combatants like Jules Favre and Jules Ferry. The Emperor had talked of the 'crowning of the edifice' and, step by step, he retreated from the autocratic position he had occupied. The control of the Press was relaxed. The Protestant world of high finance was represented by *Le Temps* which, in that slack age, was allowed to have as its London correspondent one of the most eminent and unreconcilable of the exiles, Louis Blanc. There were fewer and fewer exiles; Hugo refused all pardons; Ledru-Rollin was kept in an exile which prevented his making a fool of himself in France.

The Corps Législatif was given and took more and more power. It debated openly; it was given the right to 'interpellate' the Government, to put it on the defensive. The Catholics were often in opposition and there was a tacit or sometimes open alliance between friends of the Pope and friends of the Republic. Morny, now a Duke, presided over this slow return to the days of Louis-Philippe; but the spokesman of the Empire most in view was the able, honest, unscrupulous, industrious Auvergnat lawyer, Rouher. He understood how to win the peasants, how to make the official candidates popular with an unideological peasant public. When the Emperor visited the excavations at Gergovia, conducted by his favourite military archaeologist, Colonel Stoffel, he was accompanied by the two leading deputies of the Puy-de-Dôme, Morny and Rouher. And, on the plateau, the contrast between the old and the new order was made manifest: on one side the elegant, amiable but visibly superior, noble half-brother of the Emperor, grandson of Talleyrand; on the other the small-town lawyer, with his official uniform open at the neck, greeting the peasant voters by name and winning men where Morny only impressed them. The future was to men like Rouher, if not to Rouher.

The present was to him, for Morny died in 1865 and Rouher was now what was to be called by his enemies the 'vice-emperor', the Minister who defended the Emperor and the Empire in the Corps Législatif against the massed batteries of opposition talent. In that defence, Rouher was conscious that his master was not wholly behind him. Napoleon III was prematurely aged. It seemed unlikely that he would live to see his heir a grown man. If the regime was to be modified, it would have to be soon. And yet, modifications could only make things easier for the enemies of the Emperor and of such great servants of the Emperor as Haussmann. The Imperial Ministers who, like Zola's Eugène Rougon, had played with their heads on the 2nd of December, were not disposed to welcome eleventh-hour converts, notably M. Émile Ollivier.

For Ollivier was undoubtedly moving towards the Emperor who was, with many zigzags, moving towards him. Ollivier was no longer an intransigent enemy of the Empire as such. It could be overthrown only by violence, and France was tired of violence. Could she not be spared the price of a revolution or know the novel pleasure of a peaceful revolution? Ollivier thought she could, but on one condition. There must be an unadventurous foreign policy. The Prussian victory of 1866 must be accepted. That this victory had no attractive aspects for France was made evident in 1867 when Bismarck effectively vetoed a scheme of the King of the Netherlands to sell his Grand-Duchy of Luxemburg to France. All that France got was the establishment of an independent and defenceless state and the dismantling of the fortress. But fewer and fewer people cared. Even old Jacobins like Delescluze realized that the claim to the frontiers of

1814 was empty now. For one thing, Prussia was too formidable—and Bismarck had revealed that the German states, south of the Main, were linked by alliances with the 'North German Confederation', that is, Prussia.

It was, indeed, a question whether France could stand up to her formidable neighbour. The Prussian army was no longer laughed at as a first-class militia. It was copied. It was copied in armament. The result of Sadowa was attributed to the Prussian breechloading rifle, the 'needle gun'; so France was hastily provided with what was rightly claimed to be a much superior weapon, the 'chassepot'. The Emperor began experiments with the ancestor of the machine-gun; great if secret hopes were placed in the 'mitrailleuse'. Not enough attention was paid to the new breechloading artillery provided by Herr Krupp. Not all of the Prussian army had been provided with this weapon in 1866, so its importance was ignored, although Herr Krupp's firm was famous enough to be called on to provide the engines of the 'Nautilus' in Jules Verne's *Twenty Thousand Leagues under the Sea*. The Emperor, again, saw the importance of the innovation in artillery; there was a prototype of a French breechloading field gun in existence, but he had not the energy to insist on its adoption. Fuses were tinkered with, but that was all.

More important still, the great Prussian innovation of universal service was not, could not be adopted. The reforming War Minister, Marshal Niel, had to accept this fact. To abolish the lottery that sent some young men to the army and left others in peace was politically impossible. The peasant did not want equality of service; he wanted the chance of a 'good number' for his son. He had been accustomed, if he was prosperous, to buy a substitute for a son who drew a bad number, from a 'merchant of men'. He could even insure against a bad number. The Imperial Government improved on this system; it made itself the 'merchant of men'. It allowed the prosperous to buy exemption and, with their money, it paid lavish bonuses to old soldiers to get them to re-enlist. This system satisfied everybody. It left only the very poor to pay the blood tax and it gave the Empire a force of long-service mercenary soldiers, totally cut off from civil life, blindly loyal and officered chiefly by semi-literate, recklessly brave, unintelligent ranker officers of the type Zola was to depict in

La Débâcle. Such an army, however useful politically, had one great fault. It did not produce nearly enough soldiers to match the armies, composed for the most part of reservists, that Prussia could draw on.

Niel hoped for a real reform but he was opposed, thwarted, and died. He had hoped, for example, to make of the National Guard something like the Prussian Landwehr. The National Guard was not a serious military force. It might serve in civil war, and its obligations, slight as they were, were resented. (More than one French man of letters spent sulky days in the guard-house for neglecting them.) Niel wanted to create an effective auxiliary mobile National Guard in which young men who had drawn good numbers would get a serious military training. The Corps Législatif would have none of it. The National Guard, mobile or sedentary, remained a paper force. The only real improvement made was that military service was cut from eight years to five, and the soldier, at the end of his period of active service, was to spend six years in the reserves. It would be a long time before the reserves amounted to much, numerically, and no serious thought was given to their use. But public opinion was reassured by the news of Mentana. There Garibaldi, who had invaded the tiny Papal State, was easily defeated by a French force hastily sent to save Rome. The new Italian Government had got Napoleon III to evacuate Rome in return for a promise not to depose the Pope. They had not been able, perhaps had not been willing, to keep their word. So a French garrison was left in Rome, to the irritation of French anti-clericals and Italian patriots. And all Italians remembered, bitterly, the unfortunate way in which the news of Mentana had been conveyed: 'The chassepots worked wonders.' There was no love lost between the 'Latin sisters'.

As the authority and the will of the Emperor weakened, the hopes of his enemies revived. So did their ingenuity. A fund was started to erect a monument to Baudin, the 'representative of the people' killed on a barricade in 1851. No one marked him then, but he was a martyr now. Against the advice of the prudent Rouher, the organizers of the subscription were prosecuted. It was an error magnified into a disaster by the burning eloquence of one of the lawyers for the defence, a young barrister of Italian origin, Léon Gambetta. He was famous overnight. His fame was only one of the signs of the times. The relaxation of the Press laws produced newspapers very unlike *Le Temps*. An irresponsible and brilliant young nobleman, the Marquis Henri de Rochefort, changed his name simply to Rochefort, for the same reasons that, nineteen hundred years before, had turned a Claudius into Clodius. *La Lanterne* frightened the supporters of the Empire; it also frightened the readers of *Le Temps*. Indeed, the virulence of the Republican Press was such that timid enemies of the Empire accused it of fostering papers like *La Lanterne* to frighten the bourgeoisie. They were not frightened enough to prevent them, in the great towns, from allying themselves with Republicans, Legitimists, Catholics to oppose the Imperialist candidates in the elections of 1869. The candidates of the Empire got a working majority but only barely a majority of the votes. The timid remembered the last electoral triumph of Guizot. The Emperor read the signs of the times, too. At long last, he got rid of the faithful Ministers of the Empire, and in January 1870 Émile Ollivier formed the first Ministry of the 'Liberal Empire'.

It was apparently formed under the most promising auspices. Many of the bourgeoisie had been frightened by the character of the Republican and 'socialist' campaign of 1869. Most decidedly, they did not think the overthrow of the Empire worth the risk of a new 1848. They feared, rightly, that Paris was neither tamed nor secure against dangerous social doctrines. The Emperor had catered to the workers by amending the law against 'coalitions'. It was no longer an offence to organize a strike—and there had been some formidable strikes, as the President of the Corps Législatif, M. Eugène Schneider, of the great steel company of Le Creusot, had good reason to know. M. Thiers, still technically an Orléanist, blessed the Ministry of M. Ollivier, and one of the leading Orléanist intellectuals, Prévost-Paradol, consented to become Minister to Washington.

There were some shadows. While M. Ollivier was fairly confident of the support of the Emperor, he was conscious of the hostility of the Empress. The Corps Législatif had, after all, an Imperialist majority, returned by the docile peasants, and that majority had no fondness for Ollivier. Now that parliamentary government had been restored, parliamentary appetites were reviving. There were those who thought that M. Thiers might condescend to serve Napoleon III as he had Louis-Philippe; there were those who thought that Maître Gambetta would serve Napoleon IV if not Napoleon III. Then Ollivier was only Vice-President of the Council and did not secure complete command over his Ministers. This was a pity, for there were storm signals.

One was a mere though a great scandal. The worthless cousin of the Emperor, Prince Pierre Bonaparte, killed and possibly killed treacherously a journalist who called himself Victor Noir. Again men remembered the Duc de Praslin. The Prince was tried before a special court at Tours and acquitted; an attempt by the Blanquists to turn the day of Victor Noir's funeral into a revolution failed. But the dynasty was hurt. It was apparently strengthened by a bold move of the Emperor. He insisted on calling on the French people to approve the new order of things. This imperial intervention led to the resignation of the Foreign Minister, Daru, the cousin of M. de Stendhal and an ambitious defender of the purity of parliamentary government. Ollivier submitted and the French people were asked to approve of the liberalization of the Empire. It was a loaded question, for to vote 'No' was to imply, possibly, approval of the illiberal Empire. But the opposition advised its supporters to vote 'no' all the same. The result was a triumph for the Emperor. There were no more 'noes' than there had been in the plebiscites of 1851 and 1852. Most decidedly, France did not want a revolution. Some noted with gratification that 50,000 soldiers had voted 'no'. Others noted that only 350,000 soldiers had voted at all. But few were shocked by this revelation of the weakness of the French standing army. An era of peace was at hand. Out of many hundreds of candidates in 1869, only a score had not promised peace and a reduction of armaments. The annual contingent of conscripts was symbolically cut by 10,000.

It was this complacent world that was awakened by the news that Prince Leopold of Hohenzollern-Sigmaringen had been offered and had accepted the throne of Spain, left vacant by the deposition of Isabella the Amorous. No one doubted that the prime mover was not Marshal Prim, the current military saviour of Spain, but Count von Bismarck. It is often said that a man's testimony against himself can be safely believed. In his old age, Bismarck gave abundant testimony against himself, testimony that he had planned the Spanish candidacy and the war that followed. War was inevitable; it was desirable to get it over before France had really reformed her army and found allies. Perhaps Bismarck told the truth in his embittered retirement. Perhaps he only 'waved a match in front of the gas'. The war came, but it need not have come then except for French folly, and if it had not come then it might not have come at all. The Franco-German feud that poisoned Europe for two generations might have been avoided. Bismarck merely played with matches; the price of his game was terribly high, for Germany and for France.

A more competent and stronger Government than Ollivier's might have handled the situation calmly and successfully. But Ollivier did not think he could afford to be weak in face of the imperialist majority. Unfortunately, he had in the Duc de Gramont a lethally incompetent Foreign Minister, a 'grand seigneur' who united the mind and vocabulary of a M. de Norpois to the political fatuity of an Odilon Barrot. It was not certain that Prince Leopold on the throne of Spain was a threat; he was a very remote kinsman of the King of Prussia and a very close one of the Emperor of the French who had helped to put his brother, Charles, on the throne of the new 'Latin' state of Rumania. It was not likely that Leopold would stay long on the Spanish throne; and the place to make representations was Madrid, not Berlin, which falsely denied any knowledge of the plot. Accident played its part. The sagacious Lord Clarendon (falsely rumoured to be the father of the Empress Eugénie) had died; his successor, Lord Granville, was just learning his business and did not learn it quickly enough. The Catholic world was distracted by the meeting of the Vatican Council called to declare and define the infallibility of the Pope and there were many Frenchmen who thought this extravagance, as they saw it, more dangerous than the Hohenzollern candidacy. Italy would not fight on the French side as long as there was a French garrison in Rome; and Austria had reasonable doubts of French victory and was not going to do more than clinch a French victory when it came, if it came.

Everything suggested caution, discretion, playing down the issue. Gramont insisted on dramatizing it, making it a matter of life and death and on directly involving Prussia. Luck was on his side. For the old King of Prussia did not want war; neither did his Queen, a very close friend of the adroit French Ambassador, Count Benedetti. The King was on holiday at Bad Ems. He was persuaded to induce Prince Anton of Hohenzollern-Sigmaringen to withdraw his son's candidacy. It was a great triumph for France. Bismarck appeared not as a master diplomat, but as the patron of a timid Maximilian. But storms were loose in Paris. Nothing but a final renunciation would satisfy 'France'.

The greater part of France, peasant, Imperialist France, was highly pacific; so was the Emperor; so was not the Empress. Benedetti was asked to demand further assurances from the King. They were refused; Bismarck was able to represent the refusal as a direct affront to the Ambassador, that is, to France. In the Corps Législatif, where Thiers alone kept his head, there was turmoil. No one noticed that the King had, in fact, greeted Benedetti amicably when they met again. The streets were full of mobs, some of them officially inspired, shouting 'À Berlin' and singing the long-banned 'Marseillaise'. The first official document the Prussian Government received was the French declaration of war. The whole world put the blame for the rupture on France (as, until the last moment, it had blamed Bismarck). English sympathy went out at once to Prussia. American public opinion had never forgiven Napoleon III for the Mexican adventure. The Tsar was the admiring pupil of his uncle, the King of Prussia. 'We go to war with a light heart', said Ollivier. 'The Army is ready down to the last gaiter button', said Marshal Lebœuf, the Minister of War. Each phrase could be explained away; but they were not forgotten. France went to war, the world thought, in the spirit of Madame de Pompadour and of Cardinal de Bernis.

V

THE THIRD REPUBLIC

I

FEW wars between great powers have begun with the decision less in doubt. True, the world, bemused by French military renown, unwilling to believe that an army composed chiefly of civilians brought back from civil life, many of whose soldiers wore spectacles, could defeat the tough, long-service professionals of Napoleon III, expected, like Delane of *The Times*, an easy French victory. The Austrian military attaché in Paris knew better; but his pessimism was shared by few people—one of them being Napoleon III. His sad lucidity of soul did not desert him; he knew how inadequate the military reforms had been; for dynastic reasons, he was forced to take over the command of all the armies, and he knew himself totally unfitted, physically and intellectually, for high command. The effective command had been destined for Marshal Bazaine, crowned with the ambiguous laurels of Mexico and admired and trusted by the Republican opposition. The Marshal, deceived in his hopes, sulked.

God was, as usual, on the side of the big battalions. The German armies drew on their great pool of trained reservists; they had adopted, to their profit, the revolutionary idea of the nation in arms. The French reserves were a mere 60,000. And since the French plan of campaign called for the rushing of all troops to the frontier, the reservists had to run after their units in what was often a demoralizing wild-goose chase. Nor was inferiority in numbers made up for by intellectual virtues. All the bad lessons of the African wars had been faithfully learned, a contempt for the enemy, a blind reliance on improvisation. But some of the lessons of colonial war had been forgotten. Again and again, French units, from regiments to divisions, were disgracefully surprised. In peace time, there was no unit bigger than a regiment; corps, divisions, brigades came into existence only in time of war. Generals did not know each other and did not know their staffs or their subordinates. There was a most imperfect sense of collaboration. Corps lay inert, or marched with deadly slowness, when the sound of cannon showed that a battle was engaged. So MacMahon was defeated at Wörth and Frossard at Spicheren while neighbouring units lay passive or barely moved. No army was less like the army of Napoleon I than the army of Napoleon III.

By the beginning of the second week of the campaign, the French abandoned Alsace and were on the defensive in Lorraine. Napoleon III, deeply pessimistic, gave up the command to Bazaine on whose bewildered 'army of the Rhine' Moltke concentrated. Bazaine's befuddlement upset the plans of the excessively rational Moltke. His headlong subordinate, Steinmetz, plunged into the French rearguard, disastrously. A Davoût or a Masséna might have turned the tide; but all that Bazaine could think of was to try to hold the heights of Gravelotte-Mars-la-Tour outside Metz. Here he displayed all the courage of a promoted ranker. He commanded batteries and battalions, completely neglecting his duties as commander-in-chief. The Germans were sent forward in repeated desperate and bloodily repulsed assaults. The French 'chassepots' and the 'mitrailleuses', the primitive machine-guns that the French Army owed to Napoleon III, did deadly execution. But to no avail. The Krupp breechloading cannon completely outranged the French guns. Numbers and intelligent will told. Canrobert was driven out of his stronghold and Bazaine, on August 18, took refuge in Metz. From the point of view of the professional soldier, the war was over. Inside Metz lay the flower of the French Army, the Imperial Guard, three Marshals. The débris of MacMahon's 'army of Alsace' had been re-assembled at the camp of Châlons-sur-Marne. It was reinforced by some fresh troops scraped up from the depots, by admirably combative marines and by the 'Garde Mobile' of Paris. These citizen soldiers might have been of some use if fed into existing units; untrained, drunken, ill-disciplined, they were, as J.-K. Huysmans was to testify from his own experience, only a nuisance. They were sent back to Paris.

There was no hope of victory; only of prolonging resistance and avoïding a complete capitulation. The great French trump card was the entrenched camp of Paris. Could the Germans surround the immense perimeter? If they did, what troops would they have left over? The only sensible military policy was to withdraw MacMahon's army under the walls of Paris and hold out. But the Imperial regime could not bear the shock of such an open confession of defeat. The Empress forbade the Emperor to return to Paris. The news of the defeats had ended 'the Liberal Empire'. The Corps Législatif had overthrown the panic-stricken Ollivier. General de Montauban, made Comte de Palikao for his services in the Chinese war of 1860, became President of the Council and uncompromising Bonapartists filled the Ministries. One of them, Clement Duvernois, showed great energy in provisioning Paris and the French genius for improvisation showed results. A Blanquist attempt at revolt was suppressed; but only victory could save the Empire. The Republican opposition was as much astonished at the French defeats as were the Imperialists. They had gloomily expected the Empire to draw from its certain victory a new birth of power, and they had received the news that 'the armies of the Emperor are beaten' with mixed feelings. But they had no desire for revolution or responsibility. The Empire was allowed its last throw.

MacMahon's army, accompanied by the sick and despairing Emperor, set off to relieve Metz; its movements were faithfully reported in the Press. It was surrounded in the obsolete frontier fortress of Sedan where it was hopelessly outnumbered, crushed by a vastly superior artillery. It was less a battle than a massacre. The marines held Bazeilles heroically; the cavalry of Margueritte died in heroic but futile charges. ('O the brave fellows!' cried the old King of Prussia on the heights.) MacMahon was wounded. The Emperor refused to try to break his way out. On September 2, the last French army and the head of the French State surrendered.

Thus ended the Second Empire. There were futile attempts to provide for a legal transfer of power, but they broke down. The Empress-Regent was smuggled out of Paris by her American dentist, Dr. Evans. The Corps Législatif was invaded and disbanded; the Deputies of Paris formed a Provisional Government, 'the Government of National Defence'. So on September 4, the Third Republic was born, destined to die in a greater and more disgraceful catastrophe than Sedan.

It was a strange revolution, for Paris was *en fête*, apparently more full of joy at the fall of the Empire than of sorrow at the shame of France. To hundreds of thousands of the credulous, the word 'republic' was magical; in itself it promised peace or victory. Was it not against the Empire that Bismarck was making war? He would make peace with the innocent Republic but on the Republic's terms, terms too hastily announced by the new Minister of Foreign Affairs, Jules Favre, as 'not an inch of soil, not a stone of our fortresses'. If Bismarck refused the proud conditions of the Republic, then it was war and victory. All the legend of '93 sprang to life, the legend of the invincible Republic driving out the armies of the coalesced Kings by the mere energy of the Sovereign People. Meissonier, on his way to talk over the desperate situation with the deputy Cézanne, was astonished by the simple faith of the populace. But, he later reflected, only such a faith made resistance possible.

From a rational point of view the war was over. So thought Bismarck and Thiers, Moltke and Bazaine. So thought in their hearts some members of the Government of National Defence. So did not think young Léon Gambetta who, while his colleagues orated, seized the Ministry of the Interior. It was decisive for the policy of the new Government. For Gambetta believed in war, in success; alone among the phrase-makers of the new Government, he was a man of the real Jacobin temper. The preparations begun under the Empire continued. Paris was provisioned. The core of its garrison was provided by sailors and by Ducrot's corps that had not got as far as Sedan. General Trochu, the eminent critic of the Imperial Army, was made Military Governor and proved a most brilliant talker and phrase-maker. And the National Guard, overwhelmingly recruited from the poorer quarters, was armed and swollen in numbers to nearly 400,000 strong.

The Germans advanced carefully and methodically. Not until September 19 was Paris cut off. That day the first sortie failed ignominiously. That day, Jules Favre learned from Bismarck at Ferrières that his proud slogan had no meaning for the Chancellor. Moltke planned to be home by October; and in Metz Bazaine, maintaining the fiction of Imperial authority, made a few sorties for the record, but really prepared to 'restore order' when peace came. His Mexican experience had not been wasted; he thought like Santa Anna. Everybody reckoned without two forces, the pride, courage, baseless but potent faith of the French people, and the audacity of Léon Gambetta. The new Government had resolutely and irrelevantly imitated the Jacobin dictators of '93 and stayed in Paris. They sent a 'delegation' to Tours of elderly and reliable representatives of whom the most prominent was the eloquent and empty Crémieux. Only one of the newly constituted leaders, Gambetta, knew how to use the spirit of the nation. Gambetta escaped from Paris by balloon and arrived at Tours on October 9. From that moment, the direction of the war was in his hands.

A good deal had been done by the time he arrived. The arsenals were working overtime. Weapons of all kinds and merits were bought all over the western world. The 'Garde Mobile' was embodied, some units sent off to Paris, others made the nucleus of the new 'levée en masse' that was to repeat the miracle of 1793. To the astonishment and professional irritation of the Germans, the war was not over. Amateur armies sprang out of the ground. The two main German armies were pinned down by the sieges of Metz and Paris, and the world learned with astonishment that, at Coulmiers, a scratch army under d'Aurelle de Paladines had defeated Von der Tann and re-occupied Orléans. Had the victory come a day or two earlier, the Germans would have been forced to raise the siege of Paris; but Bazaine had decided that honour was satisfied and surrendered. The army of Prince Frederick Charles was now free for action in the field. It was not the only disaster befalling the French. No attempt had been made to estimate how long Paris could hold out. Its fall was thought to be imminent, so that Gambetta staked all on a rush on Paris, supported by a sortie of the garrison. After the fall of Metz, there was no need to hurry; there was every need to delay action till the new raw troops could be trained and armed. They now had generals, Faidherbe and Chanzy, very different from Bazaine and Frossard. Germany as well as France was feeling the strain, and there was always the danger of diplomatic intervention.

Thiers had gone on a tour of the European capitals. Everywhere, he was most flatteringly received. Like many Frenchmen, he placed too much hope in Russia. But however the rise of Prussia might disturb St. Petersburg and Vienna, no one would risk stepping be-

tween Bismarck and his prey. Victor Emmanuel took advantage of
the withdrawal of the French garrison to occupy Rome (September
20). Only Gladstone really felt the danger of the success of Bismarck
and Bismarckian methods, and he was nearly alone. English and
American opinion rejoiced in the victory of virtuous, progressive,
Protestant Germany. Bismarck had artfully released the reports of
his negotiations with Napoleon III for compensation, and thus
alarmed Britain for the safety of Belgium, threatened by the French.
The Russians prepared to take the not very serious risk of denoun-
cing the Treaty of Paris that had deprived them of a Black Sea fleet.
Thiers had nothing to offer and he had no hope of victory.

That hope still burned in Paris. If sorties failed, it was due to
treason, to incompetence, to the sloth of the reactionary provinces
that did not rush to the rescue of the 'city of light'. The news of the
fall of Metz, of the negotiations of Thiers was too much for the revolutionary elements in Paris. On October 31, the Hôtel-de-Ville and
many of the members of the Provisional Government were seized
by the revolutionaries. They were rescued and a plebiscite on
November 3 was a qualified vote of confidence in the Government.
But with Paris in such a temper, peace was impossible.

There were revolutionary outbreaks elsewhere—in Lyons, in
Marseilles. Professional trouble-makers like Bakunin, George Francis
Train, Cluseret, rejoiced in their opportunities. Everywhere, the
newly triumphant Republicans were digging themselves in, making
themselves the conspicuous instruments of the policy of war to the
end. The mass of the population that had voted in its millions for the
Empire was bewildered and increasingly defeatist. Old Dr. Clemenceau in La Vendée was convinced that the name 'Government of
National Defence' was a cause of the malaise. It hid the Republic.
The Government had proposed to hold elections to an Assembly
that alone could make peace. (If there was no such legitimate authority to negotiate with, Bismarck, it was feared, would negotiate with
the Emperor.) But Gambetta was insistent that there should be no
peace until victory was achieved. Victory was receding as winter
deepened. Paris was now near starvation. Chanzy at Le Mans,
Faidherbe at St. Quentin were heroically defeated; but they were
defeated. Bourbaki set off by train with a raw army to cut the Ger-

man communications in the east. Paris was bombarded, an outrage
that in those innocent days aroused protests not only among neutrals
but at the Prussian Court. All was over. Gambetta resisted in vain.
On January 26, Jules Favre accepted the Prussian terms. Bourbaki's
unfortunate army was chased into Switzerland. But before the last
agony, the world was notified that a great revolution had been con-
summated. In the 'Galerie des Glaces', erected by the pride of Louis
XIV, whose motto had been 'Nec pluribus impar', King Wilhelm
was proclaimed German Emperor. Dominance in Europe had passed
to Germany, as over two hundred years before it had passed to
France.

II

The armistice was a defeat for Paris even more than for France.
There were plenty of zealots in the city who still believed in the
magic of the Republic and there were others who agreed with
Gambetta that the Assembly, with which alone Bismarck would
make peace, must not include former Imperialist officials, Bismarck
would have none of it; the new Assembly must consist of those
whom the French people freely chose.

Their choice at first sight was startling. The new Assembly was
overwhelmingly Royalist and Catholic. To the credulous, it might
seem that France had at last repented of her sins, had turned both
from the usurping Empire and anti-Catholic Republic to the cause
of Church and King. The reality was very different. Everywhere,
the Republic was associated with war and defeat. The French people
voted for peace and, with the Imperial political personnel discredited
if not excluded, it turned to other natural leaders, above all to the
local gentry. The squires had fought well; one of the heroic names
of the war was that of the 'Chouan' general, Charette, with his
banner of the Sacred Heart. But the Royalists were now the peace
party. Voting by departments, for hastily composed lists, the mass
of the electors made sure of peace by voting for the lists that had
fewest notoriously Republican names. Where they could, they voted
for Thiers; he was returned in thirty-two departments. The true-

blue Republicans were only a hundred in a house of over seven hundred.

Before the election, the Republicans had preached the constituent power of the Assembly; now they declared, truly enough, that the only mandate the electors had given was for peace. The victors, who had not, except in a few instances, made any profession of political faith, claimed that the whole power of giving France new and reformed institutions lay with the Assembly which the people, in a possibly fleeting moment of wisdom, had chosen. But there were other things to be done first. Peace had to be made with Germany, peace involving the agonizing mutilation of the loss of Alsace-Lorraine. The deputies from the lost provinces protested in a moving scene. The Mayor of Strasbourg died of shock. But although Thiers saved the fortress of Belfort, Bismarck would make no further territorial concessions. The new provinces were his gift of joyous advent to the new Empire, a gift paid for at a terrible price, more than once, by France, by Germany, by Europe. The occupation of Paris was formal; but the east of France was to be held until the indemnity of £200,000,000 was paid, an immense sum by the standards of that age. Financially as well as territorially, the war had paid a handsome profit to the victors, for the indemnity was really a ransom.

The armistice, the terms of the treaty, the personality of the head of the new Government, Thiers, the man of the Rue Transnonain, the threat of a Royal Restoration were all salt rubbed in the wounds of Paris. There was, in fact, no immediate danger of a Royal Restoration. Thiers was theoretically a Royalist of the Orléanist stripe. He had had many harsh words to say of the bad habits of the Republic; he had kind words for the monarchists and even for the monarchy. But he insisted that first things must come first, and the National Assembly, meeting at Bordeaux, accepted what was called 'the pact of Bordeaux'. Until peace was made and the most terribly urgent business settled, there was to be no upsetting of the provisional regime, the rule of 'the Chief of the Executive Power'.

Its bitter business done at Bordeaux, the Assembly moved, but not to feared, hated Paris. It moved to Versailles where it proceeded to legislate for and against the sullen city at its door. To the majority of the Assembly, Paris was the curse of France. To the majority of

Parisians, the Assembly was a usurping group of squires, chosen by priest-ridden peasantry, representative of that rural France that had supported the Empire and failed to rescue Paris. It *was* largely a rural Assembly, and it failed to understand either the pride or the needs of Paris. The Paris National Guard was, to one faction, a permanent centre of disorder, of atheism, of socialism. To the majority of Parisians, it was the safeguard of the Republic, betrayed once, in danger of being betrayed again.

The Paris which drifted into revolt was not an industrial city of the modern proletarian type. As Sir John Clapham pointed out, it lacked the very basis of the new factory economy, power-driven machinery. There were true proletarians of the classical type in the railway yards; there were a few mass-production industries like the plate factories of the popular jeweller, Christophle. But Paris was a city of craftsmen, of shopkeepers, of servants, of officials, of clerks. All were affected by two stupid and unfeeling decisions of the Assembly—to end the moratorium on commercial bills passed in the last days of the Empire, and to end the suspension of house rents. Bills played a great part in the economic life even of minor businesses; few Parisians owned their flats or houses. Few but the rich had any funds either to pay their rent or to meet their other obligations. There was mass unemployment. As Millière foresaw, the situation of June 1848 had returned. But there were differences. The National Guard was more numerous, better armed, more combative. The Government was far weaker, dependent on very raw recruits and with a country too exhausted to display the enthusiasm for the restoration of order that had marked the rural National Guard in 1848. Tact, skill, sympathy were needed and were not at hand.

The National Guard of 1871 was better armed than that of 1848 in one very important way. It had its great artillery park on the top of the semi-rural hill of Montmartre. Thiers decided that it must be seized. The attempt failed and on March 18, the Government found itself defeated and believed itself forced to leave Paris. The great, heroic disaster of 'the Commune' began.

The Commune is more important as a legend than as an event, bloody and materially destructive as it was. It was erected by Marx in a brilliant pamphlet (*The Civil War in France*) into a symbol and

an example of what to do and what not to do. It provoked the execration of all right-thinking people and the more or less covert sympathies of the Left everywhere, sympathies that grew bolder and
more open as their expression became less dangerous. It was not a
proletarian and still less a Marxian revolt. The only leader who knew
anything of Marxism was the Hungarian Jew, Fränkel. It expressed
agonizing patriotic frustration and the illusions and despairs of the
old revolutionary tradition much more than any socialist or communist convictions. Marx had warned the French workers at the
time of the overthrow of the Empire that their business was 'not to
begin the past over again, but to build the future'. And certainly one
of the numerous and fatal errors of the Commune was its passion for
reviving the traditions of the Revolution.

The name 'Commune of Paris' had all the implications of the
great Commune of Paris that had overthrown Louis XVI. Since
there had been a 'Committee of Public Safety' in 1793, there must
be one in 1871. Since Hébert had published his *Père Duchesne* under
the old Commune, there must be a vulgar, obscene and tedious imitation of it under the new. There was no unified revolutionary doctrine. For some Danton was a hero; for others Robespierre; for
others Chaumette and Hébert. The ineffable Félix Pyat, the most
imbecile of the leaders, used Mignet's tepid *Histoire de la Révolution
Française* as a handbook. The sacred revolutionary institution of the
political club was revived; there was a 'Club des Folies Bergère', a
'Club du Collège de France'. (These very different institutions played
the part of the original Jacobins and Cordeliers in giving their names
to the politicians who used their premises.) There were political cafés
like La Corderie du Temple. There was endless talk and declamation
with messages from political painters like Courbet, Bohemian men
of letters like Jules Vallès, innocent well-wishers to mankind like
Beslay. There were Jacobin doctrinaires like Delescluze, disciples of
Blanqui like Vaillant (Blanqui was held as a hostage by the Government of Versailles). But there was no party, no doctrine, no plan of
campaign, military or political. Nor was there, at first, any very resolute revolutionary intention. Many left-wing deputies hoped to
arrange some kind of patched-up peace, to let tempers cool. Thiers
and the majority of the Assembly, but above all Thiers, were

determined that, once and for all, Paris should be taught a lesson. Thiers had always thought that the way to deal with a rebellious Paris was to besiege it and capture it in a great military operation. He was determined to try his recipe now. There was blood already between the Assembly and Paris, for the mob on Montmartre had murdered Generals Lecomte and Clément Thomas despite the efforts of the Mayor of Montmartre, the younger Dr. Clemenceau. Willy-nilly, 'the Commune' was forced to fight.

What was the Commune? It was represented by Thiers and his allies as a body of secret conspirators, an agency of that mysterious body 'the International', whose numbers, power, unity were fantastically exaggerated. The real authority of the 'Commune' was the delegates of 'the Republican Federation of the National Guard', a body that gave the misleading name of 'Fédérés' to the soldiers of the Commune. Not all of the National Guard accepted the authority of the 'Central Executive Committee'. The Ist and VIth arrondissements were no more revolutionary then than now. Many of the more prosperous Parisians had fled Paris at the beginning of the siege. Others had left it after the armistice. Paris was more a city of the poor than it had ever been. The expulsion of the 'Versaillais', as the agents of the legal Government were beginning to be called, created some of the same credulous enthusiasm that had marked the Fourth of September. The people of that classic hotbed of revolution, Belleville, were told, 'You are the admiration of the world and it is Belleville that will save Europe.' On March 26, a municipal council was elected which took the august name of 'the Commune of Paris', inspiring or terrifying according to taste. But the National Guard officers did not abdicate and there was never anything like the Jacobin, still less the Bolshevik unity of command.

Had the Commune advanced on Versailles at once, it might have driven out Thiers from his stronghold. But it had no revolutionary programme. It hoped (as Paris had hoped) that the provinces would come to its rescue; but apart from a few verbal demonstrations in the Midi, France lay passive. Bismarck hastened the return of enough soldiers of the old Army to give Thiers the means of crushing the revolt; a great sortie failed; its leaders were shot. There was more blood. Paris was again invested except in the section commanded by the scornful Germans. Inside Paris, dreams were the order of the day. Generals were appointed, defeated, deposed. The National Guard displayed very uneven zeal in guarding the walls. The key fortress of Mont-Valérien, hastily abandoned by the Versaillais, had been hastily re-occupied. There was no hope for the Commune. In vain it issued proclamations, organized patriotic demonstrations, abolished the union of Church and State, pursued with irrelevant zeal priests and nuns. Its only social legislation was the abolition of night work in bakeries. It respected the sacred autonomy of the Bank of France from which it borrowed money in due, bourgeois form. It was a pageant rather than a revolution.

But each day, the power of Versailles grew. As the end cast its shadow before, sinister figures like Raoul Rigault, disciple more of the Marquis de Sade than of Robespierre or Condorcet, came to the top. Hostages were seized—the liberal Archbishop of Paris, the President of the Court of Cassation. Treachery opened one of the gates, and slowly the avenging troops of Versailles entered Paris. They had much to avenge: Sedan and Metz as well as the atrocities freely attributed to the 'Communards'. There were legends of viragos with bottles of petrol—the 'petroleuses'—to inflame them. The maniacal elements of the Commune took command. A great part of Paris, the Tuileries, the Hôtel-de-Ville, the Cour des Comptes, went up in flames. In Basle, Burckhardt heard, with horror, that the Louvre had been destroyed. It was saved by its keeper, Héron de Villefosse; but it was by the light of the devastating fires set by the Communards that the victorious restorers of order worked. The hostages were slain. Archbishop Darboy died like his two immediate predecessors by violence. Paris was a see as dangerous as nineteenth-century Korea or medieval Canterbury.

Vengeance was exacted on a colossal scale. What was to be called 'the bloody week' was the bloodiest in the bloody history of Paris. At least 20,000 perished at the hands of the forces of order. Some leaders, like the upright Varlin, were shot after farcical courts martial; Delescluze, the last of the Jacobins, died, in the great tradition, on the barricades, girt with his tricolour sash. But most victims of the victors were shot out of hand. The final battue took place in the cemetery of Père Lachaise. There, before what was to be known as the 'mur des Fédérés', which became another of those shrines of bloody memory in which Paris is too rich, the Commune died.

Thiers had won; he had tamed Paris. Never again did it decide the fate of France. The respectable world rejoiced, although Matthew Arnold knew too well what Thiers stood for to find his victory heart-warming. The fine ladies of Versailles, who had seen Paris burning from the terraces, screamed for more blood. The execution squads were busy. 'Blood was on the grass like dew.' The last word was to a boy of genius who had escaped from the doomed city. The triumph of the frightened bourgeoisie made Rimbaud vomit:

> 'O cœurs de saleté, bouches épouvantables,
> Fonctionnez plus fort, bouches de puanteurs,
> Un vin, pour ces torpeurs ignobles, sur ces tables!
> Vos ventres sont fondus de hontes, vainqueurs.'

The Commune was a folly; some of its leaders were criminals. But the greatest crime of its authors (of whom Thiers was one) was in making final that alienation of the workers of Paris from the official organization of the French State which the days of June 1848 had begun. The 'bloody week' of May 1871 was a wound that, if at times it seemed closed, was never really healed.

III

It was a natural assumption of the Royalist majority that the crushing of the Commune left the way free for the establishment of the monarchy. Had not the horrors of Paris shown what the Republic really meant? But many timid souls read the lesson the other way. The bloody week, the long tale of executions and exile that followed showed (as the June days had shown in 1848) that the Republic could repress, with far more vigour, not to say savagery, than could King or Emperor. There was little to be feared from the Republic of M. Thiers. No one was more firmly convinced of this than Thiers himself. His reputation was immense and almost up to his own opinion of his deserts. After a long and frustrating political career, justice was being done at last. He had liquidated the follies of the Empire and of Gambetta's Republic; he had made peace; he was preparing to 'liberate the territory'; he had tamed Paris. The 'red' spectre was laid. Why should he abandon power, responsibility, for the chance of service to a King—and to what King?

There was one throne; there were three claimants. True, Napoleon III was out of the question. No open Bonapartists had been elected outside Corsica, although there were fellow-travellers in such regions as the two Charentes. But of the two Royal candidates, one, the less suitable, had all the advantages that come from faith, his faith and the faith of his followers. The Comte de Paris, grandson and heir of Louis-Philippe, was the kind of King that Thiers might, *might* have accepted. He was intelligent; widely travelled (he had written a good book on the American Civil War, which he had observed at close hand). He suited the great bankers and financiers with whom Thiers was so closely linked. But he did not believe, nobody did believe, that he had a right to be King. He was a candidate, not a claimant. This was so obvious that he was soon not even a candidate. He and his princely kin submitted to the Comte de Chambord. What was for the Orléans Princes an implicit bargain—they would accept the Comte de Chambord as King for his lifetime if the Comte de Paris were recognized as his heir—was, for the Comte de Chambord, a due if delayed submission of rebellious princes to their rightful sovereign and the head of their House. He forgave them, forgave them their own sins and the more serious sins of their father, the usurper, and their grandfather, the regicide. To the most devoted supporters of the Comte de Chambord, this was a great deal, almost too much. The Comtesse de Chambord was ugly, stupid, without charm, speaking atrocious French. She had only one thing to endear her to her husband's most devoted partisans: she, like them, detested the House of Orléans more than the House of Bonaparte. Next in the list of high malefactors were the great nobles like Duc Albert de Broglie, grandson of Madame de Staël and of Benjamin Constant and son of Duc Victor who had been an agent in the overthrow of Charles X. They detested that other duke, Decazes, whose name recalled the 'captivity' of Louis XVIII, and that other, the Duc d'Audiffret-Pasquier, whose name recalled the great lawyer who had served all regimes at such profit to himself. These were 'Whigs'. France did not like Whigs; the Legitimists detested them.

In the crisis that ran from 1871 to 1873, the chief role was played by the Pretender; but a great role was played by the Pretender's party, by the men he really trusted. The Legitimists paid for their long exile from power and its responsibilities. They had sulked in their châteaux and their hôtels in stagnant provincial towns for more than a generation. The elections of 1871 were as much a miracle as the Restoration of 1814, and the Legitimists were as ill-prepared as the émigrés. In all but physical fact, they *had* been émigrés. A few of their spokesmen, like the great lawyer and orator, Berryer, had been assimilated to the Orléanists; a few had gone over to Napoleon III. But the representative Legitimists were the 'chevaux-légers', the 'guardees', the brave, fanatical, innocent gentry who brought to the politics of 1871 not so much the spirit of the old regime as the spirit of the League. They wanted the triumph of the Church as much as of the King. They detested those heirs of the 'Politiques', the Orléanists.

The Pretender agreed with them. He was less irresponsible than his partisans, less bent on punishment, more ready to be a father, if a severe and authoritarian father, of his people. He was willing to make some concessions to the spirit of the age, in effect to renew the Charter, although the political solution he really favoured was the dictatorial constitution of the first ten years of Napoleon III. But the long exile of the Comte de Chambord had not weakened his belief in the Divine Right he embodied, or his detestation of the principles of the Revolution to which the Comte de Paris had been dedicated by his father. In exile at Frohsdorf, he was as much removed from the world as his kinsman, Ludwig II of Bavaria, in Neuschwanstein. He dwelt in Axel's Castle, a child of the romantic movement. The Assembly had repealed the laws exiling the princes; the Comte de Chambord passed through Paris, visited his great castle and returned to exile. He made no attempt to discuss his projects with the leaders of any of the Royalist factions. He saw only the courtiers of the extreme Royalist obedience. His return was not a reconnaissance; it was a pilgrimage to the sinful city and nation. And it was now known that there was one thing on which the Prince threatened to be adamant: he would insist on the white flag under which his grand-father had gone into exile. And everybody, even the most devoted Legitimists, knew that France and the tricolour were far more insep-arable than France and her rightful King.

This conviction was reinforced by the fear that France was again quitting the path of wisdom. In July 1871, over a great part of France, elections were held to fill vacancies in the Assembly. Some members had died; some had resigned; the Deputies who had been elected for more than one seat had to be replaced in the departments they had abandoned. The results were a shock to the majority, a delight and a ground of confident hope to the Republicans. If all the seats in the departments where there were by-elections had been con-tested, it seemed likely that 350 Republicans would have been returned. The new Republicans, like the war hero, Admiral Jaurès, in the Tarn, were not dangerous 'reds', but they were Republicans. Equally full of menace for the future was the kind of campaign the Republicans waged. Royalist candidates were accused of being in favour of the restoration of the tithe; even the legend of the 'droit du seigneur' was revived in most explicit forms. The distinctions between parties and candidates were not necessarily very clear in their verbal expression. But a voter knew that a candidate who came out for 'God, Order, Liberty' in that order was a Monarchist while the supporter of 'Religion, Order, and Liberty' was a Republican. Most voters were Republicans. It was the ending of an illusion, like the shock of the Hundred Days. France was hostile to the old regime and identified the monarchy with it. It was in vain to protest against the legendary character of the popular picture of the monarchy. A traditional institution against which the most lively traditions of the country worked, was not a stabilizing institution. The white flag, for millions, symbolized all the real and legendary abuses from which France had been delivered.

If this legend was the chief cause of the discomfiture of the Royalists, there were secondary causes. The Deputies elected, to their own surprise, in February 1871, had taken the election as a sign of divine intervention or a recognition of their natural right to rule. They tended to treat their voters as vassals. They neglected all the arts of winning support in which the Second Empire had excelled.

Their militant Catholicism and social exclusiveness alienated the Orléanist bourgeoisie and accelerated its natural drift to Republicanism. To many of the Royalists, the 'captivity' of the Pope since September 20, 1870, was as great a disaster as the defeat of France, the loss of the Papal States by Pius IX as great a catastrophe as the loss of Alsace-Lorraine by France. A proposal to build a basilica to the Sacred Heart on Montmartre, was transformed by ingenious Republican propaganda, aided by indiscreet zealots, into a proposal to expiate the sins of France by the erection of a church. An attempt to raise revenue by increasing the tax on cartridges awakened suspicions that the squires still resented the claims of the peasants to shoot game—and the memory of the game laws, as much as anything else, made the old regime odious in rural memories.

Even the Legitimists realized that the temporary deal of the 'pact of Bordeaux' was not enough of a governmental system for France and that until the Comte de Chambord had decided to accept the inevitable, Thiers must be given a more secure basis of authority, if only to prevent the formal establishment of the Republic. So Thiers was named 'President of the Republic', given the right to address the Assembly, to appoint Ministers—all under the reserved powers of the Assembly which had the last word and was determined to keep it, and not to dissolve itself until it had given France permanent institutions, that is, until it had restored the King.

Meantime it had a great deal to do. The Assembly, if it had the faults of the Restoration, had some of the virtues. It was industrious, honest, patriotic, often fairly enlightened. It was, indeed, a great deal more enlightened than was Thiers. He was as much a devotee of high tariffs as ever, and tried to overthrow the low tariff policy of the Empire, running up against the treaties of commerce of Napoleon III—and the most-favoured-nation clause inserted in the peace treaty by the victorious Germans. He bitterly and successfully opposed an income tax which had many supporters. He managed to prevent a blind imitation of the Prussian military system. Despite the lesson of 1870, he did not believe in short-service armies and, nominally, service was to be for five years—with many adjustments: the bourgeoisie would serve only for one. But there were to be no Frenchmen exempt from the Army except the clergy.

The great triumph of Thiers was the exploitation of French credit to pay off the German indemnity before it was due, and thus to accelerate the 'liberation of the territory'. Europe was impressed and Germany alarmed by the apparently miraculous recovery of the French economy. It was remarkable, inspiring, but the readiness of the peasant and the shopkeeper to invest their savings in Government securities, if it proved the foolishness of the extreme critics of imperial financial policy, suggested something unhealthy in the economy. Balzac's dislike of mere hoarding in place of investment was still timely. But few reflected in these terms. Thiers was triumphant, admired by Europe as well as by France; and Thiers, at last, had definitely declared for the Republic. Then Napoleon III died; 'Napoleon IV' was a far greater danger than his father had been, a danger to the King and to the Republic, for Bonapartism was reviving. The Empire was already 'the good old times'. The Assembly tied the President's hands: he could address the Assembly only after giving twenty-four hours' notice, and there was no debate. He was being reduced to the rank of a constitutional king. And, sign of the times, an extreme Republican, Barodet, defeated in Paris Thiers's own candidate, Charles de Rémusat. Thiers no longer was a guarantee against the 'red republic'. The Right must act, and it had a leader, Duc Albert de Broglie, returned from the London Embassy. Thiers, to his astonishment, was overthrown. Marshal MacMahon was elected President, but, as everyone knew, only until the King came into his own again.

The attempted restoration of 1873 was undertaken under much less favourable omens than it would have been had the Assembly acted on its beliefs in 1871. The Republic was now in possession; it was 'the government that divides us the least'; and an exhausted people might reasonably protest against upsetting a system that had brought about, or presided over, so miraculous a recovery. The fiction of a popular mandate to bring back the King was intolerably thin by 1873. Then Bismarck, at war with the Church in Germany, would not welcome the restoration of so pious a monarch as 'Henri V', any more than he would have welcomed the restoration of an Emperor, 'Napoleon IV', trained by Eugénie. No one in France loved Bismarck, but all feared him and few wished to anger or alarm him by intemperate support for Pius IX. Henri V might give that support.

Yet the preparations for the restoration were pushed ahead. Pious ladies embroidered flags; harness for the royal joyous entry was made. Imperialist soldiers (there were plenty) and officials (there were many) promised obedience if not active collaboration. All was ready but the Pretender. He was, if possible, more set in his ways than in 1871. He had his right and his divine commission to rule and save France. He had no desire to be a figurehead such as, he rightly thought, the Orléanist 'Burgraves' destined him to be. The flag was not only the sacred emblem left him by Charles X, it was the symbol of the kind of King he would be. That was exactly what the fomenters of the restoration feared. They sent the eloquent Chesnelong to argue. The King was not accustomed to being argued with. Chesnelong failed but kept his failure quiet. The Pretender, with disastrous candour, announced his decision. The flag would be discussed between himself and the Army—after the restoration. That ended all hope. As MacMahon was supposed to have said, 'The chassepots would go off of themselves'. There was nothing to do but swallow the most bitter chagrin and save something from the wreck. The Legitimists could not blame the King; they blamed the Orléanists; but a majority was found to vote 'the Septennate': MacMahon was to be President for seven years. Who knew?—in seven years the Comte de Chambord might be dead.

At last, the Comte de Chambord acted. He came to Versailles in a well-kept incognito. He waited for the President to call on him; the President refused. All dreams were vain; 'Henri V' returned to his enchanted castle. He had been given the name of his great ancestor as a symbol, but no man could have been less like the Henri IV of 'Paris is worth a mass' than Henri V. The France he wanted to rule not only did not exist, it never had existed. The kingship he was offered had no meaning for him, the Paris he had glimpsed was odious. So, like the lover in the old song, he said to his tempters,

> 'Reprenez votre Paris,
> J'aime mieux ma mie au gué
> J'aime mieux ma mie.'

IV

For nearly two years after the failure of the autumn restoration of 1873, France 'entered the Republic backwards', as Gambetta's paper, the *République Française*, put it. The monarchist majority could not quite bring itself to swallow the odious word, so much worse than the thing. The failure of the restoration had made relations between the two wings of the Royalist party worse than ever. Forbidden by their principles to blame their King, the Legitimists blamed their allies. And many natural Constitutional Monarchists, seeing the cause as lost, became moderate Republicans, 'Centre Left' instead of 'Centre Right'. The task was put off; but two forces were at work that imposed some respect for reality. The Radicals, the rising left wing of the Republicans, threatened to make a republic that was much more dangerous than that of M. Thiers. And the Empire was not dead. Both Royalists and Republicans discovered this to their horror. Districts like the Nièvre that had voted 'Republican' in protest against the danger of Henri V, the tithe, the game laws, voted now for openly Bonapartist candidates. The double danger drove the centres together. In January 1875, by one vote out of a total of seven hundred and five, the Wallon amendment was carried. 'The President of the Republic is elected by a plurality of votes cast by the Senate and the Chamber of Deputies united in a National Assembly.' The word was swallowed. The rest was comparatively easy.

The 'Constitution of 1875' was the vaguest, least doctrinaire, least systematic, longest-lived of all the constitutions that France had hopefully adopted since the States General met in 1789. It was also the least hopefully adopted. Some of its sponsors hoped for no more than the regularization of the existing system of loosely organized parliamentary supremacy; others hoped that the new Senate would avert the dangers of single chamber government such as had ruined the Second Republic; others, many others, saw in the distribution of powers between a President and two houses the pattern of a constitutional monarchy. Death aiding, the Comte de Paris could step into the place held by the Marshal Duc de Magenta without difficulty and with only a change of title, not of function. For sovereignty was to lie in the Chamber of Deputies elected by universal male suffrage. None could avoid this necessity. The Senate elected by 'colleges' representing mainly the communes of France (the smallest commune in a department casting the same vote as the largest city) would be a stronghold of rural sagacity. The Senate would have in its seventy-five life members chosen, in the first instance, by the dying Assembly, thereafter by co-option, 'the illustrations' of French life to give splendour to the upper house. Nothing would be too clearly defined. Nothing was.

But the dying Assembly displayed, in its agonies, the weaknesses that had frustrated its greatest designs. The extreme Right took their revenge on the Orléanists. In a conspiracy with the Left, they elected to the life senatorships their own most fanatical members; the Left elected its oldest, wordiest, most superannuated ornaments. The life Senators were, from the first, a joke as well as an anomaly. As everyone expected, there was a large Republican majority in the new Chamber, a narrow monarchist majority in the Senate (it would have been large but for the childishly rancorous trick of the 'chevaux-légers'). The Marshal remained in office to hold the fort, like the Malakoff.

The new Chamber was not a dangerously Republican body. The new Prime Minister, Jules Simon, was a professional philosopher of Jewish origin but no fanatic. Good sense would have suggested giving the new regime a trial. But the Royalists of all schools were embittered by the ungrateful folly of the people. The Republicans would dig themselves in. That must be prevented. So the Marshal was induced to dismiss his Ministry and the Duc de Broglie formed the Ministry of May 16 (a date so celebrated that Proust used it as the basis of his chronology). Broglie had to dissolve Parliament, and the 'making' of the elections of 1877 was given to a Bonapartist, Fortou. All the weapons of the worst period of the personal rule of Napoleon III were used, with no Emperor to use them for. Serious and conservative voters were astonished to see the son of Victor de Broglie in the role of Jules de Polignac. Thiers saw, in this folly, the chance for revenge. Death took him before his hopes were fulfilled. But despite the parading of MacMahon round the country (dissipating the prestige of that honest if dull soldier, exploiting, in vain, his rank and ambiguous glory), despite Fortou, 'Republican discipline' triumphed. No Deputy, not even Prince Napoleon, was opposed by a Republican candidate if he had voted against the Broglie Ministry. It was 1830 over again: the Government was beaten. There were some foolish enough to wish to carry the imitation of Charles X further, to impose 'order' by force. But it was too late for that. In a fit of ill-calculated anger, the Right had thrown away what assets remained to it. It had been a great triumph to get the un-republican right of dissolution, an open imitation of English and Monarchist practice, into the constitutional laws, even safeguarded by the necessity of getting the consent of the Senate for its use. This last weapon had been rashly used; it was never, in the life of the Third Republic, to be used again. And the Presidency was weakened and discredited by the use of MacMahon. Not all the bills were presented at once. 1878 was the year of the great exhibition that was to show the world that 'Paris was herself again'. MacMahon presided over the festivities with the grace of a great nobleman. But in January 1879, he was asked to accept the retirement of some generals. He refused. 'He must give in or get out', said Gambetta. He got out. He was succeeded by Jules Grévy who, in 1848, had opposed the creation of the office of President of the Republic. Grévy was a grave, avaricious, discreet and sly country lawyer. He was very different from MacMahon. What was more important, he was very different from Gambetta. The full life of the Third Republic had begun.

That life was to be marked by a grave distrust of leadership; by the assertion, by the Chamber of Deputies, of a detailed and incessant control of executive action as well as policy; and by the failure to develop an adequately organized party system that would translate the popular will into a coherent programme and a unified execution of it. The successful impediment imposed by the new President to the accession to power of Gambetta was the first sign of the new order. For Gambetta, since the death of Thiers, was by far the most famous, popular, attractive of the Republican leaders. He had been the main organizer of victory in the fight against the Ministry of May 16. To the outside world, to Bismarck for instance, he incarnated the new Republican Republic. He had lived down the hostility bred by his war policy; that was now an advantageous legend, not a handicap. His excessively Bohemian private life was now better ordered. He was the friend of the Prince of Wales, of Sir Charles Dilke, of Sir Henry Campbell-Bannerman. 'His trousers now met his waistcoat', as it was put. He had his mistress, Léonie Léon, but he had quitted the Latin Quarter. He was (as he always had been) temperamentally a man of government. It was not in jest that men said that he would have been a Minister of Napoleon IV if the Empire had lasted.

This evolution, it is true, had cost Gambetta some support on the Left. There were still literally minded voters who clung to the Belleville programme of 1869, separation of Church and State, abolition of a standing army, single chamber government. To them, Gambetta was a renegade, and in a famous meeting he had been shouted down and had rashly told his interrupters to go back to their dens. But Gambetta did appeal to what he called 'the new levels' of society, to the patriotic, anti-clerical, mildly progressive petty bourgeoisie. And he had a doctrine of government for them, the doctrine of a unified 'Republican' party with a programme and a leader. The leader was, of course, himself, the programme one of the restoration of the power and prestige of France; of discretion on the question of the lost provinces—'always think of them, never talk of them'; of the assertion of French rights in all regions of the world and, internally, of the assertion of the rights of the French State over the great agglomerations of capital, notably over the railway companies whose bargains with the Second Empire were coming up for renewal. Only a strong State, with a secure executive, could negotiate on equal terms with the great corporations, so much more potent than the religious orders of Radical oratory. The model that dazzled Gambetta was not any of the great ancestors of the Revolution; it was Gladstone. And round him he had what would now be called his 'brains trust' and then were called his 'marshals'—Waldeck-Rousseau, Joseph Reinach and others who had tied their fortunes to his. He hoped, by an appeal to the voters, to acquire a position that would impose him on the President and on the Parliament. And to do that, it was necessary to abandon the single-member electoral districts that the Right had created in the vain belief that their local influence would offset the ideological programmes of the Left. In these districts, dominated by local interests and local personalities, France saw herself, said Gambetta, as 'in a broken mirror'. Only if all the deputies of a department were elected on a common list could national issues be presented to the nation and a national programme be adopted.

M. Grévy had no desire to facilitate this programme. His only claim to fame had been his defence of complete parliamentary sovereignty, his opposition to any strong executive. He arrived in the Elysée full of gratitude to himself, and his self-esteem grew with each year that he passed there. The conspicuous fact that Gambetta, holding no office but that of President of the Chamber of Deputies, could eclipse the President of the Republic on public occasions was, in itself, justification for keeping him from the premiership. This resolution was not confined to Grévy. Jules Ferry, Georges Clemenceau were not disposed to accept the leadership of Gambetta, and many Deputies were reluctant to abandon their own interpretation of their mandate to any party leadership. The Republicans did not, in fact, need to unite in a disciplined party, since the Republic was not in danger. The Right was demoralized and divided. The Comte de Chambord lived on to divide the Royalists; the death of the Prince Imperial, in Zululand in 1879, removed the only really formidable Pretender. For Prince Napoleon, anti-clerical, 'Republican', scandalously separated from his Italian wife, was no bond of union for the Imperialists and their hopes were centred on his son, Prince Victor. With each Monarchist party hating the other, with Pretenders divided and inactive, the Republicans could afford the luxury of division. Like the Pope of the story who attained the papacy, 'they had attained the Republic and proposed to enjoy it'. They had no liking for the strenuous and authoritarian regime of the Gambetta plan.

The representative politician of the new order was not Gambetta, but his wartime collaborator, Charles de Freycinet. No man was less doctrinaire than this deferential, evasive, and highly intelligent engineer. He was not known as 'the white mouse' for nothing. He had been ready to serve the Empire as a member of the Corps Législatif and although he belonged to that increasingly important social and political force, 'la haute société protestante' (the Protestant upper class), he had persuaded the credulous Dom Guéranger that he was seriously thinking of becoming a Catholic. Under Gambetta, he had in 1870 and 1871 displayed great administrative abilities. He was again and again to be called on to take high office when it was important (to the politicians) that nothing should be done. He had imitators in plenty, good easy men who would upset no apple carts.

There were of course more positive characters in the new ruling class than Freycinet. There was Waddington, a man of ability and of probity. But he suffered from being classed as an Englishman (he had been to Rugby) and from a notable lack of bonhomie. There was Jules Ferry, dour, firm but lacking in popular appeal. There was Georges Clemenceau, most ruthless of debaters, most formidable of duellists, but regarded as a mere 'Rupert of debate', neither wishing nor caring to discipline himself to attain office.

And there was the Chamber. Not every Republican deputy thought of himself as a Minister, but most did. There were ambitious provincial lawyers who knew that it did not hurt to be a deputy; there were spokesmen for great interests like the eminent Protestant economist, Léon Say, who represented orthodox political economy, and the Rothschilds. There were an increasing number of what were to be called 'intellectuals', young products of the École Normale Supérieure who found the life of action at the tribune, or in a ministry, more attractive than the educational mission for which they had been trained. There were plain adventurers, political Rastignacs who found that the Chamber led to golden opportunities.

In the last years of the Empire, the Republican party had, like the Republican party in the United States in its early days, been 'the party of moral ideas'. Like Montesquieu, Republicans believed, many of them sincerely, that virtue was the mark of a republic. Like the father of Anatole France's Monsieur Bergeret, they believed that 'the Republic was justice'. They; or the French people, were soon to learn like Monsieur Bergeret that it was not justice, 'c'est la facilité'. It was the possibility of adjustment, if you had the proper credentials. And those credentials were above all political. The

Republic owed justice to all, it was said, but favours only to its friends. So it got more and more friends. The Royalist reliance on local influence told for less and less in competition with the political influence of the Prefect and of his master, the Deputy, who could make and unmake Prefects. And, except in the west and parts of the south, the power of the old 'notables', Catholics, Royalists, declined.

At first sight, the division between the naturally conservative elements, between the lay, anti-clerical Republican rich and the Catholic, Royalist or Imperialist rich, should have favoured radical economic legislation. It did not work that way, for allied with the verbal enemies of the rich were many rich who were sound on the clerical question. Until the Church was reduced to submission or even reduced to complete impotence, the French peasant, the French worker could be induced to vote for soundly 'Republican' candidates, often Jews or Protestants. Had the rich been united in one conservative party, the poor might have united against them. Then in all sections of the new political class, there was at work the secret, unifying, bewildering force of Masonry, above all the militantly atheistic Masonry of the Grand Orient. Deputies otherwise obscure, Blatin in one generation, Laferre in the next, were potent in the Chamber, since they directed the masonic vote, and that was powerful in all parties but those of the extreme Right. The decisions of the 'convent' of the Grand Orient were often more important than those of party congresses or of the open debates and votes of the Chamber. And in the lodges, rich and not so rich, Jew and Gentile, met in a fraternity that made public doctrinal differences unimportant. What was largely legend in the case of the 'Congregation', was largely fact in the case of the 'Grand Orient'. And because the power was real, was great, it was exaggerated in the popular imagination and so increased.

So was the resentment of the important and frustrated Right which saw in the Republic, not a form of government, but a system in which adventurers of recent immigrant origin like Gambetta, rich, clannish Protestants, more and more aggressive Jews (many of them recklessly outrageous in their attacks on the Church) combined to re-make France in their odious image. This was to be done above all by the creation of a 'Republican' system of education or, as the

Right saw it, an atheistic and mendacious system paid for by the right-thinking—to their undoing and the undoing of France.

As usual, the Right was so convinced of its own virtues, so ready to see an explanation of its weakness in the sins of its enemies, that it did not note where the strength of the Left really lay. One source of that strength was the almost universal conviction that the superiority of German education was a main cause of German victory and of the increasingly visible disparity between the power of France and of the new German Empire. Whether 'the Prussian schoolmaster' who had triumphed at Sedan was Clausewitz or the humbler teachers who had produced the highly literate Prussian soldier, was a matter of debate. But the low literacy of rural France was a handicap, especially since so much of the land was in the hands of peasants, doomed by their illiteracy to slavish routine. Education must be made universal and compulsory, and if so, it would have to be 'lay'.

The Church had now to pay for the favours it had got from the Empire. The nuns and the brothers who had staffed so many schools could not work as individuals; and most communes, if they liked nuns (they were cheap), did not like brothers. The village school-master would have to be a layman. It was almost certain that he would be an anti-clerical layman. He had often been that in the past, but he had been forced to outward conformity by the odious clerical pressure that gave Flaubert the materials for one of the most effec-tive scenes in *Bouvard et Pécuchet*. Only if the curé had been willing to meet the 'instituteur' halfway would peace have been possible. But the curé's principles and pride forbade any accommodation. The Right was only too correct in its fears; a general system of free edu-cation would put a 'Republican' in a position of influence in nearly every village in France. If the State schools were free, while the Church had to charge for its private schools, the faith of the tepid would be severely tried. So the Right wriggled and dodged and complained of the cost of what most Frenchmen thought a neces-sary implementation of democratic equality and a necessity of national revival. There was pinned on the Right the odious appella-tion of 'enemies of the schools'.

In this bitter conflict, France wasted, for generations, passion, faith, hate, thought that might have been better employed. The absolute 'laicity' of the schools was the mark of the Republican; the duty of the State to aid Catholic schools was the main mark of the Right (especially as Monarchists' hopes grew fainter and fainter). Officially, the new schools were to be neutral. But not only is a school system which ignores God not neutral in the eyes of parents for whom God is the final cause of human endeavour, neutrality was a difficult concept to put into practice. The history of France was not the same to a Huguenot or a Vendéan. The Massacre of St. Bartholomew and the Massacres of September were differently appraised according to one's sympathies with the victims. The great question of the Revolution could not be dealt with neutrally. And for the village schoolmaster and the writers of his textbooks, French history really began in 1789. Here was the turning point in world as well as in French history.

This was a debate carried on at a much higher level in 'the University'. But refinements were not for the products of the normal schools set up in each department to produce good Republican teachers. These institutions were no more homes of free inquiry than were the diocesan seminaries. Indeed, many of the new schoolmasters were types which, a generation before, would have entered seminaries. For each the career of priest and then of schoolmaster was a promotion, and a promotion for the family as well as the individual. In the first generation, at any rate, the schoolmasters were grateful to the Republic. They were, it is true, badly paid, despite the bitter and revealing complaints of the Right. They had usually to eke out their pay by acting as secretary to the Mayor, which threw them into politics. And as little as commoner priests of the old regime could they hope for serious promotion. They were commanded from above by inspectors and rectors chosen from 'the University', the unified corporation of secondary and university teachers. The primary teachers were, at best, non-commissioned officers in the Republican educational army. Or rather, they were parish priests and curates in the new established Church, for the Republic now paid two rival establishments: one of them it harassed and humiliated; the other it favoured and cherished, up to the point of really serious expenditure. Tabernacle was set up against tabernacle in every village in France.

Things were not so simple at a higher educational level. As more and more of the peasantry drifted away from the Church, more and more of the bourgeoisie drifted back. More and more bourgeois families sent their sons to schools run by the religious orders. In a once Republican city like Lyons, the stagnation of the lycée and the increasing prosperity of the Church schools was a subject of scandal to the University. The bourgeoisie was being divided into two groups receiving different and opposed educations, not united in a common secular religion of Republican patriotism. To some leaders of the University, to permit this was to betray the Republic. Lintilhac had no more use for toleration than had Veuillot in the other camp. But it would have been going beyond the grounds of political prudence openly to suppress the Church schools. So the Minister whose name was to be associated with the policy of the lay state, Jules Ferry, made the accustomed gesture. By administrative action he expelled the Jesuits. He was also the author of the system of free, lay, compulsory education, and by his refusal to go through the, to him, meaningless ceremony of a religious marriage, he had further offended Catholic faith and bourgeois convention. He had also shown the special meaning given to freedom by Republicans, by suspending the famous Catholic philosophy professor of the École Normale, Ollé-Laprune, who had protested against the Minister's policy. The expulsion of the Jesuits was mainly a gesture, perhaps more important for its revelation of the innocence of the Right, who thought the mass of the people of Paris would be impressed by the escorting of the Jesuits from their house by respectable gentlemen in tall hats. They liked the Jesuits little and their pupils less. And possibly not all pupils of Church schools were devoted admirers of their masters even if, like Daudet's Numa Roumestan, they paraded their devotion in public.

Not all pupils of the State schools were necessarily devoted to their masters, either. It was by reaction against State teaching that the young Maurice Barrès found a doctrine and the brilliant boy, Paul Claudel, who had received prizes from the hands of Renan, was converted in Notre-Dame. Nothing, indeed, could exceed the rigorous orthodoxy of Republican agnosticism. Renan distilled his sceptical unction. The noble 'atheist' Littré was elected to the French Academy, an election that drove Bishop Dupanloup (who had put up with so many less worthy colleagues) to resign. The group that used the aged Victor Hugo as a mascot were even more anxious to conceal from the public his continuing belief in God than his continuing pursuit of women.

Yet, despite the Republican triumph, the intellectual state of the Church was healthier than it had been for generations. The National Assembly had permitted the creation of Catholic universities and one of these, the Paris Institut Catholique, had at last begun to do what had vainly been attempted before, to give to France a Catholic institution of higher learning fit to be compared with Louvain or the German Catholic faculties. The death of Pius IX, the accession of the politic Leo XIII made things easier, the more that the new Pope most severely rebuked the most famous representative of the reactionary politics and scholarship of Solesmes, Cardinal Pitra. The young Duchesne was a Church historian of a very different school, and the official philosophy and history of the Republic soon suffered the fate of all official doctrines in France: its teachers were suspect and its doctrines unfashionable. At last, the social complacency of French Catholicism was shaken; German social reformers like Bishop von Keteler were gingerly followed as German scholars like Bishop Hefele and Father Denifle were more boldly imitated. There was a revival of interest in scholastic philosophy and in original apologists like Newman. There was even an interest in the success of the American Church, which owed nothing to the State and yet grew so fast. The experience of Archbishop Ireland of St. Paul seemed more relevant to the needs of the age than the time-tested and bankrupt practices of Cardinal Pie. At any rate, to the irritation of the zealots of laicity, the Church showed no signs of death. And since it was obviously living, there were good Republicans who began to wonder if war to the knife between the Church and the Republic was necessary and wise—especially in face of the revival of socialism, the rehabilitation of the Commune.

The tide had certainly turned since 1871. Toleration, then defence, of the Commune became a necessary attitude for a candidate in the great cities, above all Paris. Amnesties brought back from exile socialist theorists like Jules Guesde and firebrands like Rochefort. Marxian doctrine was, at last, beginning to be known, although a serialized translation of *Das Kapital* found few readers. But a digest of the main teachings had more success and older French doctrines, like those of Proudhon, gave ground before the new German doctrine whose prestige was increased by the growth in wealth, numbers and discipline, if not in power, of the German Social Democratic party, now formally Marxian. True, the master in London found the French Socialists with their political preoccupations, their obsession with their out-of-date Revolution, their lack of doctrinal seriousness, almost too much for his scanty patience. But if winning over of the French workers was no longer so important as it had been, if in Socialism, as in so many other things, hegemony had passed the Rhine, it was worth watering the Marxian wine a little to gain an entry into France. Socialism, dead in 1871, persecuted by the use of martial law under the 'moral order' of the National Assembly, was reviving and competing with Radicalism for the allegiance of the Paris worker. Cheap concessions had already been made to him. The Parliament returned from Versailles; July 14 was made a national holiday; the 'Marseillaise' was made the national anthem. But the workers asked for more; they were beginning to howl down old-fashioned Radicals like Clemenceau, as they had howled down Gambetta.

He, at least, was now immune. Grévy had not finally been able to prevent him from becoming Prime Minister, but the 'great Ministry' that had been so much talked of was wrecked by the refusal of Ferry and the other Republican leaders to join it. The Gambetta Ministry was full of men with important futures, but no very impressive present. Gambetta's Finance Minister, Allain-Targé, had staked his policy on dealing firmly with the railway companies. But the time for dealing firmly with them was past. Perhaps a really 'great Ministry', supported by a united Chamber, might have done so, but not the weak team that was all that Gambetta could assemble. The tides of business had turned against the Republic.

The discovery that France was not ruined by the war, that French credit was excellent, had enabled the Republic to reconstruct and to expand, to restore the Army, to fortify the eastern frontier, to begin a new educational system and to finish the Opera. The great world depression that began in 1873 was slow to affect France where the needs of reconstruction, the great borrowings needed to pay off Germany, stimulated the economy, while the victor suffered the pangs of a speculative boom and slump. The old taxes of the Napoleonic system proved surprisingly elastic, the horrid resource of the income tax that so alarmed M. Thiers proved unnecessary. But this happy state did not continue. Like all of Europe, France suffered from bad harvests and the necessity for expensive imports of grains. One of the two main branches of French agriculture was suffering more and more from disease and competition. Mildew had done great damage to the vines under the Empire, phylloxera had made its appearance. But it was under the Republic that phylloxera did most damage, ruining whole departments and important social groups. In vain M. Pasteur experimented. Not until the new world was called in to redress the balance of the old, until all French vines were grafted on American stocks, was the plague stopped. And there was the other plague of importations of cheap Italian and Spanish wines (the day of massive importations from Algeria had not yet come).

The agricultural crisis, common to the whole western world, was less serious in France, where there were so many subsistence farmers, than in England, America, or Prussia, but it was serious. It hurt the big proprietor more than the small peasant (who raised few cash crops) and it aggravated his sense of grievance against the Republic. He was further aggrieved by the failure of the Union Générale, the Catholic bank that was to free French business and agriculture from Jewish and Protestant domination. Creditors were aggrieved and fearful. The Republic no longer knew surpluses, only deficits. It had to borrow, and borrowers find it hard to dictate terms to lenders. The Gambetta Ministry fell after an inglorious three months. Allain-Targé's successor was Léon Say who had announced his terms: no loans, no nationalization of the railways. Only a few scraps of unprofitable lines in the south-west were nationalized, becoming the nucleus of the State railway system, but with no entry to Paris, no connection with the great ports. The principle was accepted; the State would take over insolvent lines but would be allowed to pay for the new lines wanted by deputies and voters. All the cream had been allocated by the Second Empire. The Third Republic had given away the milk. 'The era of dangers is at an end; the era of difficulties has begun', said Gambetta. He was to say no more, for, on December 1, 1881, Gambetta died, after a mysterious accident in which his mistress played a strange role. With Gambetta went the only Republican leader who appealed to the dramatic sense of the people. Such leaders were neither liked nor needed by the managers of the new political system who assumed that their tastes were general. They might well do so. The elections of 1881 had not merely repulsed the Right, they had reduced it to a handful of representatives of faithful conservative departments. The Republic could allow herself any liberties she chose, adopt any policy or none. Freycinet came back.

It fell to him to decide what to do in Egypt and he decided, characteristically, to do too little but not absolutely nothing. The Khedive of Egypt, nominally a feudatory of the Turkish Empire, was facing the financial problems left him by his lavish father, Ismail. Egypt was hopelessly in debt and the chief creditors were the investors of Britain and France. Britain, in addition, had an extra interest in Egypt. By far the greater part of the shipping passing through the Suez Canal was British and, since Disraeli's bold coup, the purchase of the Khedive's shares, she was the biggest single shareholder in the canal company. On the other hand, the canal was a French creation and the Canal Company a French corporation. French sentimental and traditional interests, recalling more Napoleon than St. Louis, were important, and France, like Britain, had an interest in forcing Egypt to pay her debts, threatened by a nationalist revolt. But the Chamber refused to let Freycinet send any troops; he resigned, and the task and profits of restoring Egypt to order and obedience fell to Britain. It was a great defeat for a country cautiously re-entering the world of high politics.

Immediately after the war of 1870, extreme caution was the French policy accepted by all parties. The conquests of Francis Garnier in Annam were renounced; the chance to buy the Khedive's shares was neglected. The only, and that mainly mythical triumph of the epoch was the prevention of a German invasion in 1875. According to the legend, Bismarck planned to strike down a renascent France but was prevented by the veto of Russia instigated by the astute Decazes. Bismarck had rattled the sabre; he had had no intention of launching a preventive war. But many Frenchmen began to think of Russian aid as a guarantee against a new invasion, as some began to think of it as a means of recovering the lost provinces. At the Berlin Congress of 1878, Bismarck made it plain that he would not oppose the French occupation of Tunis. Border incidents duly occurred; the Regency was invaded and easily subdued; the chief opposition came not from the Bey or the Tunisians, but from the Italians who protested in vain, sulked—and joined the Germans and Austrians in the Triple Alliance.

The acquisition of Tunis was the first toe put in the water. It was followed by the conquest of Tonkin. Rivière followed where Garnier had led. This time there was no falling back. Rivière was killed, but the Government of Jules Ferry pushed on. The war was deeply unpopular; it gave the Radicals a campaign cry; it gave the Right a chance to avenge itself on the author of the lay school system; it involved an undeclared war with China; it obviously gratified Bismarck who saw French effort directed from Europe halfway round the globe. News of a military repulse brought down Ferry; but the war was over and what was to be, for two generations, the greatest of French colonies, Indo-China, was founded.

It was not the sole achievement of the Government of the 'Opportunists'. They were so called because they claimed only to introduce reforms when they were opportune—which was seldom. The term was used abusively by the Right and by the Radicals; yet Opportunist practice, if not its absence of doctrines, suited the mass of consciously Republican voters. The constitution of 1875 was amended, but in no radical way. The life Senators were abolished; but the rights of the existing life Senators scrupulously preserved. The Colleges electing the Senators were weighted a little in favour of the biggish towns. The cities could now elect their Mayors. A divorce law accepted the realities of Republican morals and had the advantage of infuriating the Catholics. They were equally angered—and others were appalled—by the bold step of encouraging the higher education of girls and putting it into lay hands. There were plenty of sound Republican voters who would no more have thought of freeing their daughters from the bonds of Catholic doctrine and morals than of submitting their sons to them. But female students began to frequent the Sorbonne; there were lycées for girls and normal schools for female school teachers. The lead in the movement for this alarming emancipation of women was taken by Jews and Protestants, and this aroused fears and scabrous curiosity to be gratified by Colette's *Claudine à l'École*, read with the same type of curiosity as the fine ladies of the Directory had read *La Religieuse*. The Opportunists had, they thought, deserved well of the Republic. But the elections of 1885 seemed to show that nearly half the French voters cared nothing for the Republic. The parties of the Right, reduced to despicable fragments in 1881, had sweeping triumphs. Only 'Republican discipline', the rallying of all Republicans round the strongest candidate, saved the day, that and most shameless administrative pressure. The Republic was saved—just.

The next four years were to be one political crisis after another in which the Republic nearly foundered. There was, first of all, the handicap of mere duration. The Republic was approaching the period at which all previous regimes since 1789 had gone under. The old, credulous belief in the Republic as a reign of virtue and of prosperity was dead. 'How fine the Republic was—under the Empire', said the café philosopher in Forain's cartoon. The Republican personnel was fat with office and had lost its old charm for the young. Alsace-Lorraine had not been recovered and did not seem likely to be. French strength was being wasted in remote colonial wars. France was isolated (perhaps because she was a republic in a monarchical Europe). The Comte de Chambord was dead at last. Above all, bad times had set in. Agricultural depression had come at last. So had a long-drawn-out economic crisis affecting all the western world. The merely political slogans had no meaning to the unemployed worker or discontented and impoverished peasant, especially in the wine-exporting areas. The war against the Church was all very well, but it filled no bellies.

The Republic was unfortunate in another way. Grévy had been re-elected, and Grévy was an excessively good family man. Some of his family did him no credit, notably his son-in-law, Daniel Wilson. Wilson, despite his name, was of good Jacobin ancestry, but he had cast himself as a Republican Morny rather than as Saint-Just. He needed a great deal of money for his amusements and ambitions and it became known that the Elysée (where he lived) was a good place to approach for favours. At last the scandal, mainly one of the sale of dècorations, broke and Wilson was found out. Grévy had now to pay for the sins of his son-in-law and for his fatuous vanity and sordid greed. A strike of politicians forced the President to resign. The third President, like his two predecessors, had been forced out of office. The obvious successor was Ferry; but Radicals, Catholics, the merely envious, the ambitious combined against him. Sadi Carnot was chosen, a distinguished engineer but chosen because he was the son of a patriarch of the Republic and the grandson of the 'organizer of victory'. The Presidency was further weakened. It was no time to weaken it, for the whole constitutional system was in danger. The French people had found a successor to Gambetta, General Boulanger.

v

General Boulanger was, as the event showed, so empty that his success cast a most depressing light on the state of the political system. He was handsome, physically brave, mendacious, politically timid. He had been pushed on by the Radicals, above all by Clemenceau. As Minister of War, he had introduced some minor but obvious reforms like painting the sentry-boxes red, white, and blue. He had improved the conditions of service of the rank-and-file and he managed, on his black horse Tunis, to incarnate for the mass of simple people the pride of the Army and the hope of revenge. For if practical politicians had reconciled themselves to the loss of Alsace, knew that it could be recovered only at the cost of a general European war, the man in the street did not know this. If it was not to restore the lost provinces, for what end did France bear the ever greater burden of a military effort that was, in proportion to her resources, greater than that of any country in Europe? So balladmongers and less simple people saw in Boulanger a way to use the universal discontent with the mediocre and shady Republic. The Right, defeated at the moment of victory in 1885, needed Boulanger. So did all sorts of adventurers, deceived in their hopes for advancement; so did honest and passionate young men disgusted by the drab and sterile political life of the regime. The Royalists had the additional grievance that the Princes had been deprived of their commands in the Army, and the head of the House of France, the Comte de Paris, had been for ever debarred from living on French soil (so had Prince Napoleon, but no one cared).

The Boulanger movement was a perfect cave of Adullam. It provided a home and a hope for passionate Republicans like Paul Déroulède, head of the 'League of Patriots' who wanted a strong executive to avenge 1870, an alliance with Russia and a joint war on Bismarck's Germany. It was financed by the rich and passionately Royalist Duchesse d'Uzès who hoped General Boulanger would play General Monk. If Boulanger was so tempted, he was more tempted to play the part for the Bonapartists and he paid a secret visit to Prince Napoleon in his Swiss exile. There were 'Socialists' anxious to overthrow the corrupt parliamentary system, old Communards like the journalistic demagogue Rochefort, devout Catholics and ardent 'priest-eaters'. The heterogeneous character of the troops under Boulanger's command accounted for much of the early success of the General and for his final failure. He could not transfer his own fantastic and irrational popularity to his allies; he could not impose mutual trust on clericals and anti-clericals. He inspired deep distrust in those who knew him well, including the old Orléanist high command. But in exile the Comte de Paris smiled on the adventurer, and the movement, in its higher ranks, took on more and more the character of preparation for a Royalist *coup d'état*. The General won by-election after by-election. The new system of voting by departments (the 'scrutin de liste') made each by-election a plebiscite. Nothing had been seen like it since the days of Prince Louis Bonaparte. The supreme test came: Boulanger became a candidate for Paris. Vast sums of money were poured out on both sides. Dillon, Boulanger's manager, imported some of the latest American methods and on January 27, 1889, Boulanger was overwhelmingly elected Deputy for Paris or mandated by Paris to 'sweep the rascals out'. He did not march on the Elysée where panic reigned; he spent the night with his mistress. The adventure was over. The Government got its courage back; Boulanger fled; his chief allies were arrested and the movement collapsed. The chief killed himself on his mistress's grave in Brussels, and the centenary of the great Revolution was not greeted by a new revolt, by the taking of the parliamentary Bastille.

More than Boulanger was beaten. The Right threw away most of its remaining assets on this preposterous adventurer. The Royalist party had been both strengthened and weakened by the death of the Comte de Chambord in 1883. Weakened, for the old, fanatical Royalists bitterly resented having to give allegiance to the Orléanist claimant, strengthened because the Comte de Paris was not tied to the archaic doctrines of the Comte de Chambord. But he was now smirched by his association with Boulanger. Another casualty of the Boulangist episode was the revolutionary tradition of Paris. For the last time, Paris had exploded in one of its crises of Jacobinical passion. Nothing had happened. Never again was naïve patriotism to unite Parisians of all classes. A score of able leaders (some of them honest) were exiled from public life. Republican complacency was restored. 1889 could be duly celebrated. There was a good deal to celebrate. The Republic had created, was creating an Empire. Indo-China, if not yet totally subdued, was obviously soon to be so. The foundations had been laid for the conquest of the great island of Madagascar, although a few years would elapse before the feminine dynasty of the Hova Queens would be ended. Tunis, as a protectorate, was almost as completely under French control as Algeria which, divided into three departments, was governed as part of France by the Ministries in Paris, the Governor-General reduced to being a letter-box. The Berlin treaties of 1884 had given a great part of tropical Africa to France to rule and a series of colonial wars was extending French power to Timbuktu, to the Congo basin and towards the Nile. In Egypt, British control was growing daily more complete, but France as a creditor had a power of being a nuisance that was vigorously used.

French credit was good; the savings of the peasants brought out to pay for the war of 1870 supplied the Paris market with an abundance of cheap money, regarded covetously by the poor powers of Europe, notably by the great, nearly bankrupt Empire of Russia. There was an increasingly felt and resented depression in agricultural prices. But, almost unnoticed, the application of the Gilchrist-Thomas process to the iron ores of Lorraine was turning that poor province (what the Germans had left of it) into one of the treasure houses of a steel-hungry world.

VI

Paris was herself again. The great works begun by the Second Empire had been continued though some, like the Boulevard Haussmann, were not to be completed for another generation. The exhibition of 1878 had left the atrocious Trocadéro to sixty years of life. And the exhibition that was to commemorate the centenary of the Revolution gave Paris a monument that was far more bitterly attacked than the Trocadéro, since it was completely untraditional. But the Eiffel Tower, in less than a decade, became a great traditional monument, as much an emblem of Paris as the towers of Notre-Dame. On Montmartre, the great, vaguely Moslem basilica of the Sacré-Cœur moved slowly to completion—and beside it, the anti-clerical Republic put a statute of the Chevalier de la Barre, martyred victim of the Church that Voltaire had condemned as infamous. Even more than under the Second Empire, Paris was the world's playground. The village of Montmartre became a centre of gaiety, though there were placid bourgeois streets within a stone's throw of the sinful Place Pigalle. Nearly all economic levels were catered for. There were cheap versions of the 'tournée des grands ducs' that attracted tens of thousands of English, Americans, Germans. There were cheap restaurants as well as Maxim's, the most famous or notorious restaurant in the world. The Prince of Wales, the King of the Netherlands, Polish and German Princes, as well as the traditional Russian Grand Dukes, spent lavishly; and, even more than under the Second Empire, Paris was the delight of women. Here Henry Adams took his Bostonian bride, convinced that even for a Boston woman Greek was not enough.

True, there was in the opinion of old Parisians something missing. There was no Court. The splendours of the Court of the Second Empire might be sneered at in Schönbrunn and Balmoral, but they

were impressive all the same. Madame Grévy was no substitute for
the Empress Eugénie. Indeed, the head of Paris society, as far as it
had one, was the Comte de Paris. There were few who, like Charles
Swann, dined both with President Grévy and the Pretender. One
reason for the expulsion of the Pretenders was the resentment of the
Republican politicians like Clemenceau at their successful social pretensions. With the expulsion, Paris society dissolved into worlds
knowing as little of each other as Oriane de Guermantes did of
Madame Verdurin. There were Royalist *salons*; Republican *salons*
like that of Madame Straus who had been Madame Bizet; the great
salon of the Princess Mathilde, where something of the atmosphere
of the world of Sainte-Beuve remained. There were great 'cocottes'
like Laure Hayman; but although journalists talked of 'tout Paris'
there was no one Paris. The decline in world importance of the
French State was felt. Foreign sovereigns no longer came respectfully
to see and be seen. There was no popular rejoicing that could equal,
in the memories of the veteran boulevardier, the return of the army
of Italy in 1859. More than the Comtesse de Brionne (who had been
Hortense Schneider) could ask, like another countess:

> 'Dove sono i bei momenti
> Di dolcezza e di piacer?'

But there was another Paris of even greater reputation than the
Paris of Napoleon III: the Paris of the arts, of music, medicine,
science, scholarship. Some of the internationally most famous 'illustrations' of Paris, Meissonier, Carolus Duran, Bouguereau, were, it
is true, regarded with irony by the young. Matisse and Rouault
moved from the orthodox studios to the more original *atelier* of
Gustave Moreau. In the English-speaking world, Gustave Doré was
the French artist most generally revered, although Millet and Rosa
Bonheur were runners-up in the esteem of the uncritical. Students
from all over the world and, notably from the United States, came
to study architecture at the Beaux Arts, and from Tokio to San
Francisco the teachers of that academy might have asked proudly,
'Quae regio in terris nostri non plena laboris?'

Below the official surface, there were great stirrings. It was no
longer fashionable to sneer at the 'Impressionists'. Renoir, Monet,

Manet were on the way to being classics, although Cézanne found no buyers as he had firmly refused to take the advice of his school-fellow, Zola, to paint like Ary Scheffer. But the collapse of the monopoly of the Salon, the rise of private galleries, freed the painter and sculptor from official tyranny. Prudent buyers from Glasgow and Philadelphia were beginning to pick up bargains, and the sculptor Rodin was beginning to acquire a position rather like that of Victor Hugo, immensely popular but too great for the most innovating critics to dare totally to despise.

It was, perhaps, in music that the change in taste was most remarkable. Gone were the days when Wagner was a joke. He was now more like a god. You had to be a Wagnerian or, like Elémir Bourges, pretend to be one. *La Revue Wagnérienne* spread the gospel, and the pilgrimage to Bayreuth became obligatory. Even Madame Swann saw that, and to go into raptures over the 'Tetralogy' (*The Ring*) was made necessary by fashion. France herself gave to the operatic repertoire of the world two immensely popular pieces, Gounod's *Faust* and Bizet's *Carmen*: the second, ill-received at first, was soon seen to be a masterpiece. Saint-Saëns, Fauré, Debussy catered for very different tastes from those of the Second Empire. Paris, if not a musical capital on the scale of Berlin, was at any rate ahead of London and socially, if not musically, Garnier's vast opera house, so Second Empire in spirit, was one of the glories of the Third Republic.

In other fields, Paris had moved to new heights. The seriousness and soberness that the catastrophe of 1870 had produced, even in politicians, survived in other *milieux*. What was loosely called 'the Sorbonne' had recovered its ancient glories and could look Berlin in the face, the more that the official mediocrity of Bismarck's *Reich* was one of the paradoxes of victory that most angered Nietzsche and rejoiced Frenchmen. The parallel of Athens and Sparta was remembered. The prestige of Pasteur was now world-wide; Charcot at Nancy and then at Paris laid the foundations of psychological medicine, even if to-day he is remembered only as the ancestor of Freud. In physics, Becquerel was laying foundations on which the two Curies were soon to erect so great a structure. The great Paris medical school improved its reputation (although Brown-Séquard had been an exile of the Commune). And in philology and history, all the lessons of the Germans had been learned and their instruction bettered. Most startling triumph of all, the Collège de France produced in Bergson a philosopher who could both delight fine ladies and impress professionals. Here was dispensed the honey of Hymettus, not the undigested and indigestible, if possibly nourishing raw meat of Bonn and Berlin. France and the Republic had much to be proud of in 1889. The fillip given to national pride was needed, for the great abscess of Panama was about to burst.

VII

Among the reputations that had survived the *débâcle* of 1870 none was greater than that of Ferdinand de Lesseps. The Suez Canal was a triumph of French faith as well as of French engineering. So when de Lesseps appealed for funds to build an inter-oceanic canal across the Isthmus of Panama, there was a renewed outburst of faith. Born in the year of Austerlitz (1805), he was as remarkable an old man as Victor Hugo. (He married a second wife, at sixty-four, and had twelve children by her.) He was not an engineer, but a visionary, a promoter, and he made two mistakes that a more technically qualified promoter might have avoided. He greatly under-estimated the cost of the canal, and asked for too little money to begin with when the faith of the small investor was unlimited. So he had to borrow on increasingly onerous terms, and the equity of the original investors was overlaid by a series of mortgages. Then he insisted on a sea-level canal in the mountainous and unstable isthmus, a heroic solution that the United States has not yet dared to adopt. The solution was too heroic and had to be abandoned, but too late for the lock canal to be finished. Then the whole project was threatened and, perhaps, doomed by the complete lack of tropical medicine at that time. Labourers died of yellow fever by the thousand, engineers by the hundred. The great technical schools of Paris suffered greater losses than in a war. Soon the news from Panama became bad and, if it were widely known, the faith on which the whole enterprise was based would fail. In Paris, as in all other cities at that time, most financial journalism was a form of paid advertising, and the cost of sweetening the Press grew and grew. So did the cost of sweetening the politicians whose aid in suppressing critical reports and in getting legislation permitting further loans had an increasingly high price.

Keeping the company afloat was the business of a very international figure, a Jewish immigrant, the Baron de Reinach (a German subject by birth, he was an Italian baron and a French citizen); his nephews were Gambetta's disciple, Joseph Reinach, and the rising if credulous archaeologist, Salomon. Baron de Reinach was not the only agent of the campaign to save the Panama Canal or make something substantial out of the wreck. There was Cornélius Herz, born more or less accidentally in France, but an American citizen by naturalization. There was Arton, another mysterious Jewish adventurer of a lower type. On the payroll were such eminent Gentile journalists as Émile de Girardin, whose hands had been in every pocket since the days of Louis-Philippe; the Jewish Arthur Meyer, soon to be a spectacular if not impressive convert to Catholicism; and, indirectly, there was Georges Clemenceau, for the hammer of the Opportunists and the idol of the stern and unbending Radicals ran his paper *Justice* on money supplied by Cornélius Herz. But these were only a few of the beneficiaries of the company. Every section of the Chamber had its share of pensioners of Panama. Nobody who had anything to lose would throw the first stones.

They were thrown by a pamphleteer of great talent, Édouard Drumont whose lengthy tract, *La France Juive*, may claim the dubious honour of being the first great explosion of modern anti-Semitism. He had fired more or less at random in the book. He had been firing more or less at random in his newly founded paper, *La Libre Parole*. But now he could draw a bead and he did. He brought down Panama; he brought down the Baron de Reinach (who committed suicide); he brought down Cornélius Herz, although that cheerful knave took comfortable refuge in Eastbourne. He brought down Clemenceau, and if the collapse of Panama had occurred before the collapse of Boulangism, he could have brought down the Republic. Bitterly the Right reflected on its bad luck (it might have reflected more profitably on its bad judgement). It was the Boulangists who

had survived the disaster—Delahaye, the young Maurice Barrès—
who pushed the attack home. Politicians like Floquet, Rouvier,
Loubet equivocated. It was too late; something had to be done. So
de Lesseps was prosecuted and convicted; the politicians were prosecuted and acquitted (all but one who was foolish enough to confess).
The Republic had saved its own. But at a great cost. The conviction
was general that to expect financial probity from a deputy was as
foolish as to expect conjugal fidelity from a stationmaster's wife. The
conviction was widespread that justice was blind where the politicians and friends of politicians were concerned. The conviction was
general that France was the victim of international crooks, most of
them Jews battening on a country whose chosen rulers were in their
pay. Underneath the glittering political and social world of Paris was
a vast accumulation of sewer gas. Only an incident was needed to
cause an explosion.

The washing of the dirty linen of Panama, if it came too late to
impose a change of regime, did cause a partial renewal of the political personnel of the Republic. Some of those implicated vanished
from political life for good; others, like Rouvier and Clemenceau,
had to work their passage and that took time—and an occasion. The
elections, when they came, benefited the Socialists, and they, too,
had new leaders, not romantics like the poet Clovis Hugues or doctrinaires like Jules Guesde, but the brilliant 'Normalien' Jean Jaurès
who returned to the Chamber as a Socialist, and the rising young
lawyer, Alexandre Millerand. It was Millerand who found the for-
mula. In his famous speech at Saint-Mandé he preached the ending
of exploitation, by parliamentary not by revolutionary means; and,
before these two stars, minor performers like Brousse and Allemane
were relegated to the wings. Socialism was now an important, growing and alarming political force. More alarming, on the short view,
was anarchism. 'Propaganda by the deed' had replaced the pacific
anarchist teachings of the disciples of Proudhon. The wave of action
mounted to the height of a bomb-throwing in the Chamber and the
assassination of the President of the Republic at Lyons: another President had been removed from office.

In a moment of panic, the members of the Senate and the Chamber
fell back on an historic name, on Casimir-Périer, grandson of the

Prime Minister who had saved the infant monarchy of Louis-Philippe in 1832. He was to save the Republic. But he was vulnerable. He was not only a member of the very uppermost layers of the *grande bourgeoisie* (his hyphenated name showed that); he was connected with such noble houses as Audiffret-Pasquier and Ségur; and, most important of all, he was a director of the Anzin Company, the citadel of French industrial capitalism. The Socialists, the Anarchists, the Boulangists descended on him. A bloody strike gave them their chance. His Ministers neither could nor would protect him. In a moment of fury, he resigned. Another presidential term ended untimely. His successor, Félix Faure, was not born to the bourgeois purple. Félix Faure was a tanner, decidedly a self-made man. But no President of the Republic carried out the court ritual of the Republic with such aplomb and conviction. The presidential shoots at Rambouillet and Marly; the race meetings at Longchamps; the dinners and receptions at the Elysée were presided over to the manner born. When the Queen-Regent of Spain made him a Knight of the Golden Fleece, Faure received the decoration with all the unsurprised graciousness of one Bourbon accepting a formal but expected compliment from another. If the Elysée was still not smart, it was no longer dowdy. And it was Félix Faure who visited the Tsar and saw him, standing bareheaded while the illegal 'Marseillaise' was played, give proof to Europe that the Republic had emerged from isolation.

The Franco-Russian alliance was a long time aborning. Credulous patriots like Déroulède had placed great hopes in the hostility of the Tsar Alexander III to Germany. Others placed more hope in the fall of Bismarck which ended his ingenious juggling act. Germany, having openly to choose between Austria and Russia, chose Austria. The rash closing of the German money market to Russia and a tariff war forced the bankrupt autocracy to look elsewhere for help and a political alignment with France was the price of admission to the Paris money market. It was slowly and reluctantly paid. But the deal was made. Part of the price on the French side was the persecution of Russian political refugees. The French police worked hand in hand with the police of the Tsar and the 'scoundrelly laws', passed at the height of the Anarchist panic, were used to lock up Prince Kropotkin who found French prisons harder to escape from than St. Peter and St. Paul. The Republic was willing to pay a price for what seemed to most, though not to all, Frenchmen a great good: at worst a guarantee against invasion, at best a way to the recovery of Alsace-Lorraine. This was some compensation for Panama.

There were others. French agriculture was in a bad way; like all European agriculture it had suffered from the competition of the American prairies, of Russia, and was rightly fearful of worse to come from Canada, Australia, Argentina. The small peasant proprietor, producing little for the market, could weather the storm, but the large proprietors suffered from the fall in the value of land, the fall, less but noticeable, in the value of rents, from the feeling that the free trade policy of the Empire was out-of-date, that instead of complaining of the privileged position of the manufacturing interests, the remedy was to join them in a common demand for the sweeping away of the last fragments of the liberal policy of the Empire.

This was the doctrine preached by Pouyer-Quertier and by the 'Society of French Farmers' (Société des Agriculteurs de France) founded in 1867. This society represented the big proprietors (by English standards an ambiguous term since, in 1882, there were less than 1,000 properties of over 1,000 acres). The Society, although it piously professed to have no politics, was, in fact, Catholic and Royalist. Its chief was the Marquis de Dampierre and its enemies called it 'the league of Marquises for dear bread'. Many of its members cherished the perennial illusion that, given a lead, rural France would rally to its natural leaders, look to 'the château as a star', as one of them hopefully put it. Leave mere politics to the Freemasons; group all agricultural interests under their natural leaders.

This policy ran aground on several different reefs. The Republicans saw the trap and under Gambetta's leadership founded in 1880 the 'Society for the Encouragement of Agriculture'. There were now two lobbies. The original society, while anxious to call on the State to increase prices, had a horror of any other intervention. There was to be no interference between owner and tenant, between owner and sharecropper. 'Tenant's right is landlord's wrong', Palmerston had said. The Marquis de Dampierre and his friends were in entire agreement with Palmerston. Still less was there to be any interference with the wage contracts. Already there were hundreds of thousands of foreign farm labourers in France; they were not to be protected against Frenchmen and so French farm labourers (whose drifting away from the soil caused so much patriotic headshaking) were not to be protected either. There was, for example, to be no workmen's compensation for injuries for them. But both lobbies could combine to make a deal with industry. As the commercial treaties fell in, the pressure for high tariffs grew. They were defended by naïve bullionist doctrines, startling in their crudity even for French economic argument. The case for enabling French industry and agriculture to contract out of the modern world was put with much ingenuity by Professor Cauwès of the Faculty of Law in Paris and the whole transaction found its promoter in Jules Méline. The result was the Méline tariff of 1892. As in the fabrication of all scientific tariffs, the legislation ended as a series of bargains in which everybody was promised protection or an offsetting subsidy. It is hard to say what industries or sections of agriculture gained. French costs were pushed up; so were the costs in the Empire, but the peasant, it was proudly and possibly truly asserted, was given fresh confidence, his exodus from the soil slowed up. He was honoured, too, for Méline founded the 'Order of Agricultural Merit' and the deputy who had powerful political friends had a cheap reward to give his partisans. The Republic, so it was thought, had deserved well of the countryside; and the dreams of M. de Dampierre and his friends, of a restoration of the political power of the gentry, were made even more absurd.

VIII

Whatever illusions the rural nobility cherished, one observer was exempt from them. Pope Leo XIII had waited to see whether the Republic would weather the Boulangist storm. It had done so and the Pope decided that the time had come to cut the Church free from the Royalist wreck. In his disbelief in the future of the monarchy, *any* monarchy, the Pope was of the opinion of most of the French bishops. But they neither dared avow their opinion nor act on it. The

Royalists were their friends; from their purses came the funds for the education of recruits to the clergy, for the schools that the Church ran in rivalry with the State, for convents, hospitals, monasteries, for the great French missionary effort. If the Church made peace with the Republic, would the pious donors who had united Pope and King in their hopes and prayers continue to give? It was doubtful.

Yet the bishop whom the Pope chose to announce the new policy of the acceptance of the Republic, of 'le Ralliement', more than any other needed the funds of the pious. Cardinal Lavigerie, Archbishop of Algiers and Carthage, was in the eyes of the world the most eminent of French prelates. After the occupation of Tunis, he had begun to restore the glories of the see of Carthage. He had founded schools, orphanages, hospitals; he had founded the White Fathers to war against slavery in the name of Christ. He ranked with Father Damien in the eyes of that Catholic world which saw, in the mission field, its greatest duty and opportunity. He was also a leader, bold, authoritarian, realist, full of ill-concealed contempt for his timid episcopal colleagues. He obeyed, called for the acceptance of the Republic, and, as he had foreseen, was assailed and subjected to an economic boycott by the furious Royalists. It was not that they were much more confident of the return of the King than he was. The old Legitimists were sulky at the thought of giving allegiance to a Prince of the detested House of Orléans, and the Comte de Paris did little to placate them. The political resources of the Royalists dwindled every year. Hardly any candidates dared admit, any longer, that they were Royalists. But pride, passion, devotion were involved. The Republic was a beast. To accept it was to admit not only defeat, but by implication, folly, folly in 1830, folly in 1873, folly in 1875. The whole rickety Republican structure might, must collapse. To recognize it was to give it the support that might save it (again, the illusion of the political importance of the approval or disapproval of the nobility played its part). Better to practise the policy of extremes, 'la politique du pire', vote for the extreme candidates on either side, make the Pope's dream of a centre party, Republican but not anticlerical, impossible.

By what right did the Pope condemn them for being uncompromising and unrealistic? Were they any more blind than he was, ignoring the fact that a united Italy, with the capital in Rome, had come to stay? These passions were strong enough to prevent immediate success for the Pope's policy. But great forces were on its side. The bourgeoisie, Right Centre and Left Centre, was frightened, frightened of Socialism, frightened of Anarchism. Could it afford to be divided by the dead issue of Church and State? The pretensions of the nobility were a nuisance. They had still not accepted the social equality of all the rich. Many a wealthy man was kept anti-clerical and sentimentally 'Left' by aristocratic snobbery. Many would not imitate M. Legrandin and pass, surreptitiously, into the nobility. Even in the Church, the prejudices of the nobility were resented. Few became secular priests. For a time only one bishop, Monseigneur de Cabrières, was of aristocratic origin, and the peace of the Carmel of Lisieux was disturbed by the aristocratic pretensions of the Superior.

On the Republican side, men like Spuller, Gambetta's disciple but of South German origin and so baffled and dismayed by French intransigence, wanted a 'new spirit'. Let the Catholics accept the conquests of the lay state and there could be union in defence of the social order. The violence of Radical anti-clericalism frightened many unbelieving bourgeois, who were even more frightened by the Radical project of the infamous income tax. The same spirit of realism that had led so many great nobles to marry very rich bourgeois brides (even Americans like Miss Gould and Miss Singer), which had led them to join the boards of great companies, would, in no short time, lead them to weaken the sentimental and social ties that united them to the exile of Twickenham, the more that the next heir, the Duc d'Orléans, was notoriously unstable and fantastical. It was a prospect to frighten the older Republican politicians who saw so many hitherto harmless colleagues in Parliament become suddenly rivals for ministerial portfolios. It was still more alarming to the zealots of the extreme Right and the extreme Left. For one, the thought of a Republic on good terms with the Church was incredible; for the other, it was odious, for if the Republic did not fight the Church how could it be a Republic?

The 'Anglo-Saxon' critics of France were wrong. France was a deeply religious country, divided into two groups of passionately opposed believers, believers in the God of St. Louis and in the God of Voltaire. It would be more accurate to say the 'Anti-God' of Voltaire, for his vague deism was now suspect. The Republic had no need of any God, not even the God of the deists, not even the God of Victor Cousin. It had its own philosophy, provided by the new and inferior Victor Cousin, the Radical philosopher-politician Léon Bourgeois, whose doctrine of 'solidarity' was designed to quench the thirst for the absolute, for social justice—that is, for God or economic equality—that tormented so many Frenchmen. But wise men did not put much hope in M. Bourgeois. The possessors should unite. After all, the Catholics, as a group and as individuals, had so much to lose! They detested the income tax as much as anybody! And, despite the irregularity of their position, the religious orders flourished: Trappists, Benedictines, Carthusians, Carmelites, Dominicans, Franciscans; new orders like the Assumptionists, old ones like the Jesuits (for they had quietly returned). Wise men would ask no questions, raise no storms. The time for a new Edict of Nantes was at hand, this time with the Church as a beneficiary.

It seemed too good to be true; it was. On October 29, 1894, the vigilant *Libre Parole* announced that a traitor had been arrested. It was soon able to announce, with gratification, that the traitor was a Jew, as was to be expected, but that every patriot must be vigilant, the traitor must not escape as the men of Panama had escaped.

'The Affair' is, in one sense, simple. Dreyfus, an Alsatian like nearly all the original figures in the case, was a brilliant, promising and unpopular officer. He would have been unpopular even if he had been a Gentile. There was a traitor offering to sell information (none of it of the highest importance) to the German military attaché who, unknown to his Ambassador, had more than one spy on his payroll. It will never be fully known what lay behind the discovery of the 'bordereau', the list of secrets offered to Schwartzkoppen. The head of 'the Statistical Service of the Second Bureau', the counter-espionage division of the General Staff, was Sandherr, an Alsatian suffering from general paralysis of the insane, a complaint not yet known to be syphilitic but known to be disastrous for the judgement. His deputy was Commandant Henry, a barely literate ranker, given a job for which he was totally unsuited by General de Miribel.

There was also the Commandant du Paty de Clam, featherheaded and inventive. Between them, by giving the court martial secret documents concealed from the defence, they secured the condemnation of Dreyfus, who was sentenced to perpetual imprisonment on Devil's Island off the coast of French Guiana. The case was closed. There was some bitter criticism, from the Left, of the fact that a rich officer traitor had had his life spared. But the Republic had shown, what badly needed to be shown, that justice could occasionally be done.

Everybody but the family of the condemned man was anxious to have the whole distressing episode forgotten. The Foreign Office had been rightly alarmed that the implication of the German Embassy would be an irritant in Franco-German relations and the Ambassador, who knew nothing of the activities of his attaché, did, in fact, protest. But that was all. No one was less anxious to re-open the affair than French Jews. Reinach, Herz, Arton, now Dreyfus! The small, rich, unpopular, nervous community of the Paris Jews wanted nothing better than silence. They were not to get it. For Dreyfus was not the traitor, who was still at large and at work.

Few historical negatives are better established than the innocence of Alfred Dreyfus. There are still Frenchmen who believe, or say they believe, in his guilt, but there are Englishmen who believe the world is flat and there were to be plenty of distinguished Frenchmen to believe in Stalinist history and science. The real mystery of the Dreyfus case is twofold. Was there more than one traitor and, more important, why did the leaders of the French Army march steadily to ruin when fate (more kind than they deserved) gave them more than one opportunity to break off the battle? The first question may never be solved. The 'bordereau' was the work of the Commandant Walsin-Esterhazy, a rascal ruined by debt, with expensive tastes, fit for anything. He was a cheap scoundrel, everything was false about him, even, it is likely, the name. He continued to betray; the successor to Sandherr, Colonel Picquart, caught him, and the 'bordereau' was in his writing. This was the first chance given to the 'great chiefs' of the French Army. It was not taken. Boisdeffre, Gonse, Pellieux, all were either fools or knaves, all were blinded by religious and party passion to considerations of reason or even of justice.

General Mercier, the War Minister who did not take the prudent advice of the Foreign Minister, Gabriel Hanotaux, and hush-up the whole affair, was able, desperately ambitious and very politically minded. When the storm rose, he fell back on a legend, of an historic night spent with the President of the Republic, Casimir-Périer, in fear of a German ultimatum if the connivance of the Kaiser in the subornation of Dreyfus was not concealed. In the more extravagant versions of this story, Mercier had a photographic copy of either the 'bordereau', annotated in the handwriting of Wilhelm II, or of a letter from the Emperor to Dreyfus. Formally intelligent men believed this nonsense. If the Affair had any villain almost worthy of its importance, it was Mercier. He lied like Boulanger, but coldly, firmly, impressively.

'Truth will out, even in an affidavit', as the English judge put it, and more and more people began to suspect that Dreyfus was innocent, more and more to suspect that the traitor was the odious Esterhazy. Yet the fiction that 'there is no Dreyfus case' was maintained by the politicians and by 'the Army', an ambiguous term used to mean the higher officers.

In the long agony of the Affair, it is to be noted that any Government would have had to face a storm if it had re-opened the case, and no French Government was strong enough to face a storm on what was, at first, a minor issue. Again and again, the chance to deal effectively with the case was sacrificed to the apparently greater need of holding a parliamentary majority together. The prolongation of the Affair was one of the prices paid for the merits, such as they were, of the French parliamentary system. The role of the Army was more important. If the High Command had displayed any good sense or good faith, even a weak Government might have dared to do justice. But in refusing to re-open the Dreyfus case, the Army was giving way, disastrously, to very human passions.

The generals, the officers, the non-commissioned officers were all conscious that their position in the national hierarchy was not what it had been. Never had the French Army been more dear to the French people than on the morrow of the catastrophe. The legend of 'the National Defence', of the untrained, badly armed, ragged 'Mobiles' standing up to the ever-victorious Germans, was glorious enough

and some compensation for the fate of the brave but incompetent
Imperial Army. To restore the military power of France was the
main purpose of the National Assembly. Not even the restoration of
the King was so dear to the Royalists, while to the Republicans the
Third Republic must revive the glories of the First. The servitudes of
the military revival were willingly accepted. France was now the
most heavily taxed country in Europe, but no money spent on the
Army was grudged. The eastern frontier was covered with a great
fortress chain by the engineer Séré de Rivière; the great gunner, de
Bange, provided a new artillery; then came the first smokeless
powder and the first magazine rifles. France was a leader in the armament race. Nor was this all. Military service, formally but not really
for five years, was reduced to three and the clergy were forced 'to put
a knapsack on their backs'; but the three years' service was a reality,
not a fiction, as the five years' service, insisted on by Thiers, had often
been. There was no exemption for the bourgeoisie, which began to
know military service at first hand, although 'educated' men normally served one year. It had been thought that this common experience would breed national unity. At first it may have done so, but
as the years passed, as the hope of a war for the lost provinces faded,
military service became an increasingly resented burden for the educated classes, not only the time of service but the periods spent in
training in the reserves. A rich young man could often, it is true, live
out of barracks, feed much better than his officers, have his own servant, undergo few more severe hardships than Proust makes 'Marcel'
suffer at Doncières. But there were many clever young men with no
money for whom their period of service, the necessary submission to
military authority and to the hardships of barrack life, was intolerable. The village schoolmaster was no longer uniformly a priest of
the old religion of patriotism, he was more and more the convert of
the new religion of Socialism which averred with the mouth of Marx
and Engels that the workers of the world had nothing to lose but
their chains. Boulangism showed that the old nationalist tradition was
still strong, but Boulangism failed, to the profit of Socialism.

The arts followed the same course. The simple-minded might still
be moved by the patriotic pictures of Detaille and de Neuville, but
the painters most admired by the sophisticated left military glory on

one side (Manet's picture of the execution of Maximilian was about the nearest any of them got). The greatest of all had set a bad example, for Paul Cézanne had successfully and, with an easy conscience, dodged military service in the war of 1870. In literature it was the same story. Zola, in his own and the world's estimation, was the greatest living French writer but his *La Débâcle* was very different from Paul Déroulède's *Chants du Soldat*; so was the collection of short stories he assembled, the *Soirées de Medan*. The one masterpiece it contained, Maupassant's 'Boule de Suif', although a war story, was not a patriotic story. More and more writers agreed (though they might not have admitted it) with Rémy de Gourmont who boasted that he would not sacrifice the tip of the finger that he used to knock off the ash of his cigarette to recover Alsace-Lorraine. And there were hostile anti-militarist books, exposing the drabness and corruption of Army life. In the most famous of them, the *Sous-Offs* of Lucien Descaves, it was notable that all the most disagreeable characters were either Alsatians or Germans passing as Alsatians. Even more ominous in a country where ridicule kills, the comic genius of George Courteline was employed to make the Army funny and ridiculous.

Not only the Army but the Frenchness of France seemed to be under attack. It was not only that Wagner was still a god (only a few heretics like the young Gide found him a bore as well), but all the old literary standards were submerged. There was the vogue for the Russians, Tolstoi, Dostoievski; for Nietzsche, for Strindberg and Ibsen. In vain Edmond de Goncourt grumbled about this craze for 'gleanings of a northern shore'. The makers of advanced literary taste were above patriotism; Lugné-Poë who produced Ibsen was serious, respectable, while the Comédie Française was regarded as being little better than the Salon.

In this world, the simple ideas, loyalties, passions of the officers were laughed at. Moreover, many officers were cut off from the new governing and administrative class by their origin. The Army, the Navy and, to a much less degree, the diplomatic service were the only remaining public employments in which a young man of Catholic and Royalist origins was not fatally handicapped in competition with Protestants, free-thinkers—and Jews. If not quite barred from the civil service and the University, he was certainly not welcomed.

In 'the Army' was the last citadel of French values and French virtues. The representative officer was one who quite probably had
suffered through his family in the crash of the Union Générale or of
Panama or both, who had been a pupil in a Jesuit or other Catholic
school. Of course there were many Freethinking and Protestant
officers, even a few Jewish officers, although only one of them had
been allowed to enter the sacred citadel of the Army, the General
Staff; and he was Alfred Dreyfus. But the tone of the Army was
Catholic; 'Republican officers' like General André felt themselves
snubbed, at any rate knew that their wives were snubbed. It was
rumoured that the Jesuit, Père du Lac, controlled promotions, an
illusion that the foolish priest did not dispel. In practice, the Minister
of War had no control over promotions; the high command of the
Army recruited itself. The Army was suspicious and suspect. It was
certainly not 'Republican'; it did not dwell with pride on Hoche or
Marceau; its heroes were more likely to be Turenne and, of course,
the Emperor.

The prestige of the Revolution was under attack, too. The Socialist
critics of the complacent official historiography were Jacobins, even
criticizing Robespierre for not going far enough. For them Thermidor was a crime, not a deliverance. On the other side, there were
bitter critics of the whole revolutionary and Republican ideology,
not in the old romantic, Catholic manner, but in what claimed to be
the application of modern science. Chief of these was Taine. But he
had many disciples like the sociological novelist Paul Bourget, like
a much better writer, the Boulangist and Nationalist deputy, Maurice
Barrès. The Sorbonne might think that Aulard had refuted Taine,
but Aulard himself was under fire as being too favourable to Danton.
France, so thought some, the Republic, so thought others, was in
danger from the spirit of the age. For this possibly inevitable conflict, the case of Captain Dreyfus provided an excuse.

His ghost still walked. Great public figures were now involved.
Scheurer-Kestner, most eminent of the exiled Alsatians, took up the
case of his fellow exile. There were more and more rumours and,
in desperation, Henry produced a document that would have been
conclusive if it had been genuine, but he had forged it—incompetently—and, when arrested, conveniently committed suicide. For

some this was the light at last. But the 'friends of the Army', the men who were calling themselves 'Nationalists', closed ranks. A hitherto unknown Provençal poet, Charles Maurras, declared that Henry was a martyr to be defended and avenged. Esterhazy was tried and acquitted in face of all the evidence. Zola, who had issued a pompous and vainglorious protest (remembered only for the title *J'Accuse* given to it by Clemenceau) was convicted and took refuge in England. Picquart, who had first seen the light, was imprisoned—and the last of the Panamists, including the ineffable Arton, were tried and acquitted. One Jew at least should pay for his people!

There were other blows to account for the frenzy. The exclusion of France from any share in the control of Egypt was more and more resented, as English control became more and more firm. There were bickerings and more than bickerings with England over the boundaries of Indo-China and Siam. Hanotaux decided on a bold counterstroke. Captain Marchand was sent to march across Africa to join hands with the King of Abyssinia, recently victorious over the Italians, and, with Abyssinian aid, to bar the English advance up the Nile. Marchand's march was an astonishing feat, worthy of a countryman of La Salle, but as he reached the Nile, the Sirdar Kitchener destroyed the Dervish armies of the Khalifa at Omdurman and moved on to encounter Marchand. They met at Fashoda. The issue was simple: support of Marchand meant war with England, a war that France could not win. With bitterness but good sense, the new Foreign Minister, Delcassé, surrendered. The whole Nile valley was left to 'Anglo-Egyptian' control. English comments on French justice were not made any more palatable by this humiliation.

The re-opening of the case was now almost inevitable. It was made quite inevitable by the sudden death of Félix Faure, in circumstances which were highly unedifying, recalling the death of Marshal Saxe and other heroes of the alcove. More serious from the point of view of the anti-Dreyfusards, they had relied on the adroit President to hold off the more powerful attacks that were being delivered on the fortress of the legal accomplished fact, 'la chose jugée'. The new President had been slightly soiled (as had so many others) by Panama. But Émile Loubet was safe and a 'Republican'. He had none of the social or political ambitions of Faure—and he was destined to be the first President of the Third Republic not to leave the Elysée by way of death or resignation under pressure. His position was strengthened by the comic and ineffective attempt at a *coup d'état* led by Paul Déroulède who tried to get the general commanding the funeral escort to march on the Elysée. A brutal assault on the President at Auteuil races, brought out the 'people' of Paris less in support of Loubet than in hatred of his enemies. It was belatedly discovered that the Paris workers hated Jesuits more than Jews.

Dreyfus was brought back; there was a new court martial at Rennes which, by a miracle of inconsequence, convicted Dreyfus by a majority but with 'extenuating circumstances'. But the two dissenters were the two most respected members of the court. The new Prime Minister decided it was time to finish all this nonsense. Dreyfus was pardoned (his acceptance of his pardon angered those who had found him useful as a martyr). Monsieur Waldeck-Rousseau had no use for such tactics. He had been one of Gambetta's young men; he was the leader of the Paris bar; he was a stout Republican Breton. In his Government, he had taken the precaution of including the leader of the Socialists, Alexandre Millerand, and General the Marquis de Gallifet. Gallifet was one of the few leading generals who had not discredited themselves in the Affair. He had been a hero in 1870 after being an adornment of the Court of Napoleon III or, more accurately, of Eugénie, and he was for the friends of the Commune, *the* man of blood. But he and possibly he alone could control the Army, as Millerand could, possibly, secure the adherence of the Socialist workers to the cause of 'Republican defence'. The main business of the Government, thought its chief, was to restore the power of the State. Troublesome priests, soldiers, officials must be taught their place. There must be no possibility of a renewal of the scandalous insubordination that had nearly wrecked the State. The Assumptionists, whose foolish Superior had been the most virulent and credulous enemy of revision, were expelled. The same fate was destined for the Jesuits who, if fairly discreet in Paris, had been very indiscreet in Rome. The elections of 1902 had to be 'made'. They were. Although the victory in terms of votes was not overwhelming, the Republican majority in the new Chamber was more than adequate.

There was nothing remarkable in the defeat of the 'Nationalists'. The old Royalist parties were in total decay; the Affair had wrecked the 'Ralliement'. The leaders of the Nationalists were journalists and men of letters, not practical politicians. The Dreyfusards had the lion's share of men of letters and men of science. Anatole France, Émile Boutroux, the young Painlevé, most of the lights of the University were members of 'the League of the Rights of Man'. But the political war was led by Waldeck-Rousseau and Clemenceau. The fact that most of the Nationalist leaders were journalists meant, also, that they were competitors for the same audience. Drumont's *Libre Parole*, Rochefort's *Lanterne*, the Assumptionists' *La Croix* all catered for the adherence and the subscriptions of much the same audience. The 'League of the French Nation' ('Ligue de la Patrie Française'), the reply to the League of the Rights of Man, had a mild literary critic at its head, Jules Lemaître. He had sound opinions but he had no doctrine. He had a very rich mistress who financed the League; but there were those who thought that the vulnerable past of the Comtesse de Loynes handicapped Lemaître. (That past was impressive: one of the first lovers of Madame de Loynes was Flaubert.) The violence of the Dreyfusard attacks on the Army drove some normally Republican but conservative areas like Normandy over to the Right. But, faced with a choice between the 'friends of the Army' and the 'friends of the Republic', the French voter sensibly came down on the side of the Republic or, at any rate, against the spokesman for a cause so ambiguous and so ill-defended as the Army.

The follies of the conservative attempt to use Boulanger were repeated, in a far more indefensible form, in the Dreyfus crisis. Catholics like the great scholar, Paul Viollet, who tried to plead for justice were ostracized. Demange, the courageous Catholic lawyer who had been Dreyfus's first counsel, was regarded as a traitor. The Duc d'Orléans multiplied the follies of his father by embracing Esterhazy. The Duc de Broglie lived long enough to approve of this new 'Sixteenth of May'. The scoundrels and liars, Esterhazy, Henry, Mercier, involved, in their merited disgrace, better men and valuable institutions. It was possibly unjust, but Charlemagne hanged Ganelon's innocent companions as well as Ganelon for

'Ki hume traist sei occit e altroi.'

The right side won, but it was a victory not wholly pure. It enabled some men of ability, like Clemenceau, to return to politics and he was undoubtedly moved by a passion for justice as well as by ambition. It created a totally false impression (to be made ludicrous by the 'treason of the learned' on a great scale, forty years later) that professors, above all professors of the natural sciences, are above the battle, are moved only by scientific passion for truth, by human passion for justice. The servility of the Stalinists was to be baser and more general than the hardboiled and public indifference to 'justice' of a man like Bourget. The Church deservedly suffered from its tolerance of deeply un-Christian vices, and its opponents got, automatically, an often totally undeserved reputation for virtue.

For the Church had now to pay. It was Waldeck-Rousseau's intention to settle, once for all, the question of the position of religious orders. Some were to be banned, like the Assumptionists and Jesuits. Others were to be allowed to apply for authorization. But Waldeck-Rousseau retired and his successor was no man for half-measures. Émile Combes was one of the most representative figures of the Third Republic. He was, like so many other politicians, a doctor by training and he had all the naïve confidence in science of Flaubert's pharmacist, Homais. But he had been a doctor of divinity before he became a doctor of medicine. He was proud of his theological knowledge, delighted to score off unlearned Catholics. 'Nourri dans le sérail, j'en connais les détours' was his motto. He was determined to pursue 'the clericals' down into their tunnels. He refused all authorizations, save for orders preparing for the foreign missions and for some nursing orders. Waldeck-Rousseau protested but in vain. Again, Frenchmen and Frenchwomen in 1903 began to go into exile, in Germany, England, the United States. Combes was delighted. He had promised his electors that the confiscation of the property of the orders would produce a thousand million francs (£40,000,000). The 'milliard des congrégations' proved rather volatile. At any rate, most of it never reached the lay charities for which it was designed. The liquidation of the orders proved more like a minor Panama than a great and beneficent act of policy.

But Combes was content with the enemies he had made. As Prime Minister, he was concerned only with the war on the Church. Not

St. Louis, not Philip II sacrificed more to religion than Combes. He
left Delcassé at the Foreign Office to pursue his own policy which
involved a serious risk of war; he allowed André at the War Office
to demoralize the Army; he was indifferent to all financial policy
that could not be translated into theological terms. He was defended
and protected by that light of the University, Jean Jaurès, who was
Vice-President of the Chamber and leading spirit in the 'délégation
des Gauches' that acted as a steering committee for the Republican
majority. The Chamber was re-organized and, for the first time since
the constitutional laws of 1875 went into effect, it had a set of standing committees for each great department (hitherto the only standing committee had been for finance). This improved the efficiency
of the legislature, but it also provided in the Chairmen of the committees rivals to the Ministers, and in the 'Reporters' of important
bills future Ministers, possibly more interested in their own careers
than in the stability of the executive. Combes did not care. Having
got rid of the orders, he prepared to await with complacency the
reply of the Pope. The new Pope (St. Pius X) was not a diplomat
like Leo XIII. He was a zealous parish priest of the type that had
read and followed Veuillot in France. He detested the Republic. A
series of incidents took place, notably a protest against the visit of
the President of the Republic to the King of Italy in Rome. Relations
were broken off; the end of the Concordat was in sight.

Loubet's visit to Rome had not been as important as his visit to
London, where he returned the visit of King Edward VII. Few
figures had been better known to the Parisians than the Prince of
Wales, but a visit as King was a very different thing from a visit
incognito to Maxim's. King Edward had never lost his early love for
Paris. The city, tormented by the Dreyfus affair, had yet managed to
put on an impressive show in the exhibition of 1900 which gave the
city two expensive buildings, the Grand and the Petit Palais, as
permanent adornments or eyesores. It was undergoing the revolution brought about by the new underground railways, although the
system was not allowed to pass the fortifications of Louis-Philippe.
But the visit, in 1903, of the King of England was the first real royal
visit the Republic had had since the chilly and formal appearance of
Nicholas II to open the Pont Alexandre III and thus underline the

reality of the Franco-Russian alliance. The visit of King Edward, greeted at first with hostility and ribaldry, was destined to underline something equally important, the settlement of the many Anglo-French disputes and the formation of something not quite an alliance called (with a reminiscence of Louis-Philippe and Victoria) the 'Entente Cordiale'. The King came; he won the hearts of the Parisians, and a policy on which he had no real influence benefited by his personal popularity.

IX

The 'Entente Cordiale'—the series of agreements concluded in 1904 —was one of the signs of the coming storm. The generation-long Bismarckian peace was coming to an end. The Tsar had, for a moment, frightened his French ally by proposing general disarmament; but the first Hague Conference fizzled out in pious resolutions. The political and military agreements between France and Russia were tightened. The original alliance was to last only as long as the Triple Alliance—which had the disadvantage that the dissolution of Austria-Hungary on the death of Francis-Joseph might precipitate a great crisis, just as both alliances lapsed. This danger was averted. Delcassé could count that a success. Another was the semi-detachment of Italy from her allies, the work in great part of the astute Ambassador in Rome. Camille Barère was a former Communard, and the grandson of the Jacobin stigmatized by Macaulay. His whole career was a proof of how completely a revolutionary youth could be put into the past. But the settlement with England was a greater triumph than either. Delcassé had learned the lesson of Fashoda. An aggressive colonial policy both alienated England and, as a necessary consequence, put France at the mercy of Germany. Delcassé decided to liquidate all past quarrels, in Siam, the Gambia, Newfoundland, the Pacific islands; but, above all, he decided to cut French losses in Egypt, recognize Britain's special interests in return for recognition of France's special interests in Morocco. There was one important difference between Delcassé's position and the position of Lord Lansdowne who was leading Britain away from Lord Salisbury's 'splendid isolation'. Britain *did* control Egypt while all France got in Morocco was an option offered by one of the possible clients for the interesting and profitable task of reforming the decadent Sherifian empire. Spain was bought off; Germany was ignored.

It was a mistake, for the winning of England was only a partial offset against the disastrous weakening of Russia. Without any consultation with her ally Russia plunged into war with Japan (which, since 1902, was the ally of Britain). The war was a series of humiliating disasters, reducing Russia to military impotence in Europe, to near bankruptcy, and to the imminent danger of revolution. It had always been the view of critics of the Russian alliance that it would serve Russian far more than French interests. The very role of debtor strengthened the Russian hand, for the French had to throw good money after what threatened to be bad. They had to give scandalously unneutral aid and comfort to the Russian Baltic fleet, zigzagging round the world to disaster in the Pacific. And the feeble Tsar was being sedulously courted by his cousin, Wilhelm II. If the Germans insisted on a showdown, there could be no better time for them. France had no effective ally on land and her military establishment was in danger of being wrecked in the campaign for revenge on the high command and the anti-Dreyfusard officers. Combes had a soul above or beside foreign policy. He gave Delcassé a dangerously free hand. He also gave his Defence Ministers a free hand, but he took more real interest in their robust methods of republicanizing the services. As usual, few cared about the Navy: though much less Republican than the Army, it had not been directly involved in the Affair. The Naval Minister encouraged the dockyard workers to demand better pay and better conditions. New warships were given Republican and unmilitary names like Ernest Renan and Edgar Quinet, two famous enemies of the Church to which most of the officers belonged. The 'Socialist' town council of Brest imposed a heavy local tax on cosmetics, as a workers' leader was offended by the perfumes that the officers' wives left trailing behind them. None of this mattered, since the Navy did not matter. The Army was something very different—as Combes and General André, the War Minister, discovered.

Promotions in the Army were now under the effectual control of the Minister of War. The days when it paid to be a friend of the Jesuits were over. It was necessary to make sure that the protégés of the proscribed Society did not get back into the High Command. The purge was entrusted to that coy body, the Freemasons of the Grand Orient. Their headquarters in the Rue Cadet replaced the notorious Jesuit school in the Rue des Postes. Officers of all ranks were encouraged to inform on their comrades: that one went to mass; that other sent his children to a Church school; that other made irreverent remarks about the Ministers of the Republic. These titbits were collected and collated and sent to Paris. The informants ranged from the commander of an army corps to lieutenants. And every Republican officer knew that the elimination of Catholic officers lightened the promotion lists. There was thus a great temptation to join the ranks of those 'who private dirt in public spirit throw', especially as the throwing could be done in private. On such information, André based his two registers, 'Corinth' and 'Carthage'. Those whose names were entered under Carthage were doomed to early retirement. There was nothing of Sarastro about the Masons of the Grand Orient. No love could redeem the sinner.

It is always a mistake to underpay for especially dirty work and an employé turned over the secret files, the 'fiches de délation', to the Right, who produced them to a disgusted Chamber. Combes saw nothing odd in this method of republicanizing the Army; André could only lament that he had been betrayed. But the Army was still cherished. The thought of going into battle under officers half of whom might well suspect the other half of the basest treachery, was alarming. The storm rose. The representative of the conscience of the 'haute société Protestante', a hereditary leader of the Huguenots, Francis de Pressensé, defended the Minister. There were more Jesuits than those that wore the cassock! So did that rising political mathematician, Paul Painlevé. But it took Athene to descend and cover André with the aegis. Jean Jaurès, the incarnation of the Republican conscience, like Desaix at Marengo, rallied the shattered ranks. As his former disciple and now bitter critic, Charles Péguy, put it, what had begun in 'mystique' ended in 'politique'. Even Jaurès could not save André—or Combes. The old, if not venerable, War Minister was slapped in the face by Syveton, a Nationalist Deputy, who then committed suicide in face of a great sexual scandal. Both André and Combes had to go. The Cour de Cassation finally quashed the original conviction of Dreyfus, who was now rehabilitated, not merely pardoned. The Affair ended as squalidly as it had begun. Perhaps, as Andrew Marvell said of the English Civil War, 'the cause was too good to have been fought for'. Yet the cause was good. In a good as well as a bad sense, the Affair could have taken place only in France. In a bad because of the deep divisions of the country, in a good because so many passionately cared for justice, justice for Dreyfus, justice for the Catholic officers. It was one of the 'gesta Dei per Francos', as squalid and heroic as other crusades.

The 'Dreyfusian revolution', like earlier revolutions, renewed or purged the political personnel. It brought back Rouvier and Clemenceau. It further depressed the old Right; it at last made the Radicals the governing party. Their one brief period of office under the philosophical politician, Léon Bourgeois, had foundered on the rock of the Senate. But that sagacious body was becoming Radical, of course with a difference, and it was more and more common for a Prime Minister to be a Senator. As a Senator, he had only a limited electorate to placate; he was elected for nine years and so saw out two legislatures whose term was four years and, freed from the daily chores of a Deputy, the Senator had more time to reflect or to administer. The life of a Deputy was full; the life of a Minister who was also a Deputy was too full. He had to act as a kind of consul for his voters, get jobs, decorations, promotions, grants, tax adjustments. This left little time for ideological politics except of the vaguest kind. The Church and State issue, evoking passion, easily comprehensible, involving no really difficult administrative problems, had been the very meat of French politics. It was in danger of being withdrawn from the political menu.

For Church and State were separated at last. Since the Concordat of 1802 had been a treaty between sovereign powers, it would have been more decorous to denounce it after negotiation. But it was necessary to break the bonds of Rome dramatically—and Pius X was not one with whom it was easy to negotiate. The terms offered to the clergy of France, not to the Pope, were not as rigorous as the more fanatical priest-eaters wanted. There was no question of taking away the churches from the priests, turning Notre-Dame again into a Temple of Reason (it was too large and public to serve as the holy hall of the Grand Orient). But it was possible to expel the clergy from seminaries like Saint Sulpice, to expel the Irish and Scottish levites from their colleges, bishops from their palaces. It was possible to give the clergy four years' notice of their discharge from State service, while preserving pension rights. 'Nothing will help us now but sanctity', said the Archbishop of Paris. But how was the Church to provide for the service of God?

The solution proposed was an ingenious one. There was to be created in each parish 'a religious corporation' ('association cultuelle'). It would administer the church buildings, raise funds, pay the priest, deal with the State. It would be elected. The French bishops saw possibilities in this scheme, despite its flavour of the Civil Constitution of the Clergy. But the rigorous Pope and his rigorous Spanish-Irish Secretary of State, Merry del Val, condemned it. The bishops submitted. There was something in the Pope's decision that could not be written off simply as Italian vicarious heroism. In most French parishes, there was no majority of believers so the German parallel did not apply. And there was possibly some danger of schism, a great danger of unedifying squabbles between parish priest and *association*. Unless divine service was to be suspended, the State would have to try again. It did through the subtle and supple mind and words of Aristide Briand, the 'Reporter' of the Law of Separation.

The deal was as unsymmetrical as the constitutional laws of 1875. No questions were settled; but religious life went on. There was only one danger. The State decided to take an inventory of the property in the churches. (Some had, for example, reliquaries of very great value.) It was not made sufficiently clear that there was no intention of seizing, for secular purposes, the sacred vessels. Zealots resisted the emissaries of the Republican Athalie; lives were lost; the inventories were called off. There was a truce.

X

There was a more important truce. The Russo-Japanese war had undermined the diplomatic position of France, but Delcassé pushed ahead. He had bought off Spain, but not a more formidable competitor for rights in Morocco. On March 31, 1905, Wilhelm II landed at Tangier. He had opposed this bold staking of a claim, insisted on by his Chancellor Bülow. But if Germany was to have a showdown, the time was now. The Russo-Japanese war was coming to an end. More than Sadowa, Mukden and Tsushima were to be defeats for France. The Kaiser had not yet detached his cousin, the Tsar, from his French ally; but there were serious hopes. It was the Tsar's throne that was now threatened, not his diplomatic position. Had Delcassé's policy, the denial to Germany of any right to intervene in Morocco, been maintained, there might well have been war, deeply unpopular and certainly disastrous war. Had Wilhelm II been a Bismarck or a Frederick the Great, there might well have been war and completely victorious war.

Rouvier, the new Prime Minister, rightly dismissed Delcassé despite the frenzied protests of the Nationalist Press. It was a French humiliation, but not the preliminary to a real German success. At the international conference held at Algeciras, Germany learned that the Entente would not break down under pressure; learned, again, that Italy was a very unreliable ally; and might have learned from his officious support of the Franco-British position that the President of the United States, Theodore Roosevelt, was a dangerous enemy. He was a dangerous enemy in another way, for by arranging peace between Japan and Russia, he made possible the staving off of the revolution in Russia. France also helped, for it was French loans that enabled the Autocracy to defy the new Russian parliament, the Duma, and crush the revolution. The Russian Ministers, if not the Tsar, learned their lesson. France was necessary and France learned, again, the immense power of a really great debtor whose bankruptcy cannot be permitted.

Rouvier went; he was succeeded by a phantom Minister, Sarrien, but the real leader of the new Ministry was Clemenceau, becoming a Minister for the first time after forty-five years in Parliament. He was not long content to be Mayor of the Palace; he became Prime Minister, beginning a long tenure of power that defied the rules of the parliamentary game.

The re-organization of the committee system of the Chamber had increased its power over legislation and administration. Eminent civil servants knew that Ministers came and went but that committee Chairmen stayed. They knew that a 'Reporter' of a great bill like Briand's was a coming man, and they knew that promotion came to men whom the rulers, open and covert, of the parliamentary Republic approved of.

Cabinets had to be formed of leaders of groups who could command loyalty or hope. But they were based on neither political nor personal loyalty. A great personality, like Clemenceau, could dominate, rule by fear if not affection, but Clemenceau was a political sport. Even he had to be constantly in the breech. The right of 'interpellation' made it possible for small groups of Deputies to put ambiguous and embarrassing, often purely rhetorical questions to a Minister or to the Ministry which could be answered only at the certain risk of alienating indispensable support. If an attack failed, another could be mounted with a slightly different combination of forces, and another, till the weak spot was found or the Minister lowered his guard. Then came the *coup de grâce*, the new Ministry, the distribution of the spoil of political war. Almost always, some of the defeated Ministers joined the victors. There was no ministerial solidarity. This had the advantage that there was more continuity of administrative policy than the long and depressing list of Cabinets overthrown would suggest. Thus Delcassé at the Foreign Office and later Leygues at the Ministry of Marine had tenures of office that an English Minister might have envied. But the price paid, in the temptation to prefer one's own safety to the survival of the ministerial group, was high.

Representative of the new politicians were Aristide Briand and Joseph Caillaux. Briand had begun his life as the legal spokesman for the extreme Left. He had preached the general strike and was the hope of the zealots who felt that they had been betrayed, by Millerand in one way and by Jaurès in another. Jaurès, it is true, had been brought to heel.

The Second International of Socialist parties which was to make national animosities meaningless had decided that constituent parties must not support bourgeois Ministries, accept office, play the bourgeois game. This was the policy of the strongest of Socialist parties, the German Social Democrats, admired by Jaurès, trusted by Lenin. True, unlike the French party, it was not tempted to accept office. Under Wilhelm II no effort was made to seduce its virtuous leaders. It laid down the law to the French, who submitted and became the 'French Section of the Second International', shortened into 'S.F.I.O.' (Section Française de l'Internationale Ouvrière). Jaurès submitted to Bebel. But France was not, in fact, Germany. The Socialists were not excluded from the normal political life of the country. Where there's a will, there's a way, and Socialist leader after Socialist leader left the S.F.I.O. and founded or joined a Socialist splinter group. Chief of these fugitives from German displine was Briand, too supple to admire discipline for discipline's sake. Remarkably free from pedantry (or, as his enemies would have put it, from formal education), he had none of the reverence of Jaurès for the German masters. 'Briand', it was to be said, 'knows nothing and understands everything.' He understood the strength, weakness and possibilities of the French political system.

So, in another way, did Joseph Caillaux. His origin was very different from that of Briand. He was the son, not of an inn-keeper, but of a Minister of the Sixteenth of May. Far from being indifferently educated, he had been an 'Inspector of Finance', a member of the most exclusive and prestige-laden section of the French bureaucracy. Briand could charm anybody and hated nobody but Joseph Caillaux. Caillaux disdained to charm anyone near his own level. Even the faithful Radical voters admired rather than liked him. But he liked himself. He affected the haughty superiority of a 'grand seigneur' and, at any rate, attained the complacency and arrogance of a 'Farmer-General' of the old regime. He could have borne with equanimity the ordeal of the Satrap in *Zadig*. He profoundly agreed:

> '. . . combien, Monseigneur
> Doit être content de lui-même.'

But he had great abilities as well as great arrogance. His official experience made him one of the few leaders on the Left who could discuss public finance on equal terms with the spokesmen of the great banks and great private companies. He, if anybody, could organize the system of income tax so long preached. And he was known to be preparing or, at any rate, to be preparing to prepare an income tax law. He was the rising hope of the Radicals. And he was complete master of his own electoral fief at Mamers in the Sarthe where, not so long ago, the La Rochefoucauld family had reigned unopposed.

There was another politician who, like Briand and Caillaux, represented a new generation. Raymond Poincaré was a leader of the Paris bar, the pupil of Waldeck-Rousseau who had gone farthest and whose training made him a sound defender of 'laicity'. He was less famous than his cousin, Henri, the great mathematician, but he had a clear if limited mind and prodigious powers of work. He was the kind of leader the disorientated Right was looking for. The defeat of 1902 had been followed by the worse defeat of 1906. The old leaders were discredited and the ending of the Church quarrel made it easier for the various conservative sections to unite.

The separation of the Church from the State was final. All that remained to be fought over was the degree of generosity with which the clergy were to be treated. Were they to be harassed or handled gently? Were the religious orders to be hunted down in the spirit of Louvois, were sisters who had been nuns and were living together to be forced to separate? Was the public exercise of the traditional processional rites to be prohibited or harassed? Were pilgrimages to be made easy or difficult? Of course, in so profitable an enterprise as the great shrine at Lourdes, the stoutest anti-clericals in the Basses-Pyrenées knew on what side their bread was buttered; but there were doubtful instances. Were the brothers, not wearing their habits, at a loss in their enforced 'freedom', whom Pierre Emmanuel has described, to be regarded as an illegally revived congregation, their schools closed? It was difficult to keep alive the registers of the new emigration, to prevent a large class of Frenchmen and Frenchwomen from exercising a right granted to all other French citizens, the right, under State control, to teach. It was all very well for the zealots of the University to demand a monopoly of all teaching. France was not a country which took kindly to totalitarian solutions, and the University was now the object of the hostility provoked by all established churches. All that wise Catholics hoped for, or wise anti-clericals wanted, was a certain amount of amiable discretion in the administration of the law. That might alarm M. Combes, but the day of M. Combes was over.

So was the day of the old Royalist party. It was eaten away on one side by indifference and incredulity among the new generations, on the other by a rigorous Royalist doctrine which was a new political Ultramontanism facing a dying Gallicanism. No one believed in the restoration of the monarchy by any regular political means. Even Bonapartism was stronger than Royalism in many regions, and only where the gentry was economically dominant was there even a pretence of faith and devotion to the lost cause. But the slow spread of industry ate away at the gentry's rule all over France; the network of good roads, of railways, the universality of military service broke down old habits. The acquisition of the Western Railway by the State not only gave the State railways, for the first time, an entrance to Paris at the Gare St. Lazare; it deprived the local conservative forces of a mass of useful patronage. The clergy noticed this. In some regions, still dependent on social classes that had accepted neither the House of Orléans nor the 'Ralliement', they had to be silent. But in regions where the clergy were strong, the gentry weak, the local representatives of the Church did rally to the Republic. A Breton rector who, if his parish was a pilgrimage centre, was nearly as well off as an Irish parish priest, was not to be patronized by a poverty-striken laird of long pedigree. And the young priests were tired of the old ideas, of the illusions that had led to so many catastrophes. They read not La Libre Parole, but Le Sillon, in which Marc Sangnier preached a socialism that was not based on an aristocratic leadership from above in the manner of the Comte de Mun or the Marquis de la Tour du Pin, but on a fraternal reconciliation between democracy and Christianity. Sangnier was denounced to Rome and, of course, condemned by Pius X. Unlike Lamennais, he submitted in good faith. But the furrow had been ploughed, the seed sown.

If Le Sillon was a portent for the future, the Action Française was one for the present. It sprang out of the Affair; its originators were young teachers of the University who resented the assumption of righteousness and scientific infallibility made by the 'Intellectuals' on the other side. But the movement became significant of more than a flash of anger only when it was joined by Charles Maurras, the most ingenious, radical and effective enemy of the Dreyfusards. For him, the explanation of the Affair was simple. France had been taken over by a syndicate of 'the four nations', Freemasons, Protestants, Jews, and 'Métèques', imperfectly assimilated foreigners to whom the other three nations had treacherously given the right of entry to the City. Real France, Catholic France, would be betrayed and plundered until it fell back on the traditional remedy of putting the control of the State into the hands of the heir of 'the forty Kings who, in a thousand years, made France'. Maurras boasted that his Royalism was not traditional; it was based on a positivist view of politics. As a disciple of Comte, Maurras accepted the final and ineluctable fact of the nation-state as the political supreme good. Objectivity showed that France had waxed with the Monarchy, waned with the Republic. Only the restoration of the King, not as a parliamentary figurehead, could save France from sliding downhill, farther and faster. Q.E.D.

To the Action Française drifted the defeated of the Affair, the defeated of Boulangism, the former clients of Drumont and Rochefort, the enemies of modernist doctrines, the Legitimists who had no true King (they became more friendly at each quarrel between the neo-monarchists and the Pretender). But there came others: young men bored with the Republican ideology, with the official philosophy, history, prophecies of the University. The clever young man who did not turn Socialist joined the Action Française. If he did neither, he was classed as a mere job-hunter, a courtier.

Against the triumphant and respectable Republic, there was bound to be a reaction. It was a misfortune that a polemical writer of genius harnessed this reaction, in the name of scientific objectivity, to a totally dead cause, the restoration of the French Monarchy. To this cause, many able, brave, devoted and generous men and women gave themselves. The organization founded to sell the newspaper (also called L'Action Française) when it became a daily, the 'King's Hawkers' (les Camelots du Roi'), fought rival political bands, organized riots and demonstrations, was destined to have many and formidable disciples in Paris, Rome, Munich, Prague. The cult of violence, of the 'coup de force' was launched. Maurras was far from being a man of action. The irrelevance of his practical doctrine was seen by the sceptical and intelligent Maurice Barrès, but his influence was great. So was the influence of his lively disciple, Léon Daudet, the jovial, highly cultivated, mendacious, talented, brutal son of Alphonse Daudet, and, for a time, husband of Hugo's granddaughter. Daudet was as scurrilous as Rochefort or Drumont or Eugène Mayer. His very talents, his mischievous sense of humour, his wide and genuine literary culture, charmed the young and won them to a political movement where hate triumphed over love. Everything that had been done since 1789, or nearly everything, was wrong and rotten.

This conviction, in a different form, was general among the young, especially among the 'Intellectuals'. It was almost necessary for self-respect for a young man who graduated from the École Normale to be a 'Socialist'. The Alsatian librarian, Lucien Herr, made it his business and duty to indoctrinate the young Normaliens. And when he failed, as with Edouard Herriot, it was a kind of scandal. Herr knew a good deal about Germany and German Socialism; so in a literary sense did Jaurès. Marxism was beginning to tell, especially in historiography, and Marxism tinged the great co-operative work that Jaurès edited, the *Histoire Socialiste*, which re-told the history of modern France in a spirit far removed from the simple Jacobinism of the great official historian, Aulard. But by a fault in the organization of French higher education, the École Normale and its pupils were cut off from one important source of Marxism, from a close study of the classical economists. Economics was taught in France in the Faculties of Law and in the independent 'École Libre des Sciences Politiques'.

These schools recruited many of their pupils from social backgrounds different from those which supplied the École Normale. To the Normalien, objective economic doctrines, statistics, comparative studies of the economies of France, Germany, England, the United States were weapons of reaction. Philosophical or even merely rhetorical reflections on justice, on the true meaning of the French Revolution, were substitutes for the mastery of a difficult and discouraging technique. When all the world came to Paris to study history, pathology, painting, philosophy, physics, no one came to study economics. That was better taught in England, Austria, Sweden, Italy, Belgium, the United States. And a hunger and thirst for justice was not enough.

The triumph of the Intellectuals in the Affair was taken too seriously by them. From that great spiritual triumph (as they saw it and, in seeing it thus, they were not wholly wrong) should have come, would come, a reconstruction of French society and of French culture. They would, like their Russian spiritual ancestors, 'go to the people', bring to them the culture they were starving for, the culture denied them by the Church and the bourgeois State. So were founded the 'Universities for the people' ('les universités populaires'). The idea, like the name, was magniloquent. The 'Universities' were lecture courses given by young university teachers or men of letters, occasionally lit up by a visit from a great star of the movement like Anatole France. But the Paris worker soon tired of the literary and rhetorical culture that he was offered. There was no solid sub-structure like that provided by the Workers' Educational Association in England or, in another way, by the *Popular Science Monthly* in the United States.

The workers wanted something they could use, a doctrine of action. They got one, from the propagandists for 'direct action', for what was to be called 'syndicalism'. The Republic had, in 1884, extended the liberties grudgingly granted to the workers by the Second Empire. But the French State was suspect when bearing gifts; the militant leaders of the new unions were reluctant to register, to give an account of their organizations. They sometimes took advantage of the hospitality offered by the vaguely 'Socialist' municipalities to house their 'Labour Exchanges' in the Town Halls; but they were suspicious of such aid, and it could be and often was suddenly withdrawn.

Then, despite the tolerance of the Republic, the French worker was not good, docile material for trade unions on English lines. He had no Nonconformist tradition of freely giving to good causes for his own salvation in this world or the next. He had no German sense of discipline. Unions sprang up, died away, were reduced to handfuls of zealots who, knowing that they were a small minority, could not hope for results from continued mass action. They needed a doctrine of quick action and quick results. They got it in the theories of Pelloutier and in the theories of the Anarchists. 'Direct action' meant, first of all, industrial action as apart from vain trust in venal politicians; then it meant violence, the revolutionary seizure of power in one moment of popular wrath, canalized by a small revolutionary party (the legacy of Blanqui to the French revolutionary movement —and to Lenin). It also meant the day-to-day hardening of the will to revolt in petty acts of obstruction and destruction. 'Sabotage' (a new word given to the world) was added to such weapons as 'boycottage'. When the workers had been thus conditioned to revolutionary action, the prophecy of the 'Internationale' would come true. It would be the final struggle, 'la lutte finale', the 'Day' of French revolutionary mythology. The weapon would not be the barricade, the seizure of the Hôtel-de-Ville by an armed band; it would be the general strike that, by paralysing bourgeois society, would end the bourgeois order.

This doctrine found its apologist in a bourgeois engineer, full of contempt for his own class, over-estimating the will and energy of the workers. Georges Sorel was a prophet, an apologist for violence, but no more a man of action than Marx had been. His conversation was as exciting as his writing and he was one of the most important visitors to the shop where Charles Péguy produced the *Cahiers de la Quinzaine*, the organ of protest against *all* the established orders, the official Church which hid true Catholicism, the École Normale which hid true culture behind empty formulas, the empty orators of whom the greatest was Jaurès, who lulled the workers asleep by a base parody of Christianity.

Péguy was something that the Intellectuals had not bargained for; a Normalien who did not try to stay the course, a Socialist who despised the regular Socialists, a poet who protested, in prose and poetry, against mere literature. He drew to him very different types, men who would have haunted Mallarmé's conversation parties twenty years before, men who would have believed all that Lucien Herr told them ten years before, men who would have read Drumont and Barrès, perhaps even Maurras. The Dreyfusards disillusioned by the way their blow for justice had been cashed in by some belated converts; Catholics who hated the respectable and sterile religion of Paul

Bourget and Ferdinand Brunetière, of the congregations of the Madeleine and Saint-Philippe-du-Roule; enemies of the new orthodoxy of the Sorbonne: all read Péguy. His ancestor was, of course, Proudhon. Like Proudhon, he was unclassifiable; he accepted Catholicism but did not submit to the Church; he made a pilgrimage to Chartres but kept away from the sacraments. He was a prophet and a sign of the times. He had followed Verlaine's advice, he had taken eloquence and wrung its neck. He was loved, admired, resented, feared, an ex-disciple more deadly for the reputation of Jaurès than a dozen friendly enemies like Barrès. Péguy was a sign of strange times; he did not believe in progress; he saw war coming; he prepared for it by taking his duties as a reserve officer seriously, not merely as the most convenient way of discharging his imposed military obligations.

There were other signs of the times. The Church seemed to thrive. For one thing, as prudent Republicans had foreseen, with the ending of the Concordat the State lost all control. It no longer appointed bishops. Pius X was now in command of the Church of France to a degree undreamed of by Pius IX. A bishop, a parish priest, so the Council of State ruled, was the bishop, the parish priest that the Pope recognized. There was no danger of schism. When the bold Abbé Loisy was condemned for his modernist theories, there was less disturbance than when Lamennais or Père Hyacinthe had rebelled. The great Monseigneur Duchesne gave outward assent to the new fundamentalism. There was no place for a Renan to-day. Indeed, his brilliant grandson, Ernest Psichari, submitted to the Church, following the brilliant young biologist, Jacques Maritain, who was the grandson of Jules Favre. And if churches were filled with the most atrocious iconography, the 'bondieuserie' of the Place Saint-Sulpice, yet in the year of the great exile of the monks, Georges Rouault was converted.

'Bondieuserie' was not dead. It had now its own saint, the young Thérèse Martin of the Carmel of Lisieux, whose posthumous autobiography, *L'Histoire d'une âme*, was soon a best-seller of the whole Catholic world, not only of France. Within less than a generation, 'the Little Flower' was to be canonized and to eclipse, in popular esteem, her great patron, St. Theresa of Avila, and the basilica at Lisieux was to rival Lourdes.

There were other new devotions. More than it had ever been since the thirteenth century, Paris was the school of Europe. 'The School of Paris' dominated all art fashions. In 1900, Cézanne got his first public recognition at the Exhibition and Pablo Picasso paid his first visit to the city where he was to succeed Cézanne. He was only one of many immigrants. They came from Spain like himself and like Mirò, from Italy like Modigliani, from Russia like Chagall. Paris was a school of poets as well as of painters. The teaching, the example of Baudelaire, of Verlaine, of Rimbaud, of Mallarmé, was treasured all over the western world. Men came to school to France, more as they had done in the time of Brunetto Latini or Dante, than as they had in the time of Louis XIV or Voltaire. Some strangers wrote in French as had Brunetto. It was, so Mr. Edmund Wilson tells us, the half-American, Francis Vielé-Griffin, who 'broke the alexandrine'. It was not only to be secretary to Rodin that Rilke came to Paris. The dead and, in his time, little-known Jules Laforgue was the symbol of liberation for Mr. T. S. Eliot. The accolade of Paris was still sought. The coming of the Russians, Diaghileff, Benois, Nijinsky, Stravinsky, was a homage to Paris. The 'barbaric yawp' of the *Sacre du Printemps*, although it was received with violent abuse, was less like the first Paris performance of *Tannhaüser* than it was like the first night of *Hernani*.

There were other signs of new times. The internal combustion engine was a German invention, but it was France that gave it the warmest and most competent welcome. It opened a new life to an idle boy at the Lycée Condorcet. Louis Renault became a famous racing-car driver and founded (with a capital of 60,000 francs) what was to be the great Renault factory at Billancourt. The comparative excellence of French roads made the motor-car more useful than it could possibly be in the United States or even in England. For the people, the great invention was the bicycle. It was a liberating force and bicycle-racing became the first great popular sport. It was not the only one. Rugby football was acclimatized in the south (Lourdes became almost as famous for its fifteen as for its miracles). Association became popular in the north. The famous Paris Rugby team, the Racing Club de France, showed in its name the aristocratic character of the sport, but it soon ceased to be exclusive. Boxing was not unknown in France, but it had been a form of exercise in a gymnasium. (Villiers de l'Isle Adam made a miserable living as a sparring partner.) Now it became a spectator sport; it provided a good living for mediocre American and British boxers, then it began to produce its French stars. In a few years' time, the young Georges Carpentier was one of the most famous of Frenchmen. The aeroplane, like the motor-car, was not a French invention. But it appealed to the individuality of the national character. Frenchmen became pioneer pilots, inventing bold new techniques like 'looping the loop' and, in 1909, ominous date, Louis Blériot had flown the English Channel. Britain was no longer an island.

The new forms of life upset the mental habits of the old political and intellectual world. The University, although it preached Hellenism, was really medieval in its indifference to what the Greeks treasured under the name 'gymnastic'. Sport made heroes of young men whom the University classed as dunces. (In Renault, it helped to make a millionaire as well.) The new cult of physical excellence was thought of as reactionary. A Normalien faced with a class of louts knew it to be possible that among them was a potential national hero. Even if there was some comfort in the thought that fame in sport was 'a garland briefer than a girl's', it was real while it lasted. Soon the most famous Frenchwoman was a tennis star, Suzanne Lenglen. The time was to come when Normale would have a celebrated Rugby team, but that time was not yet. There was a transvaluation of values that so representative and upright a member of the University as Charles Seignobos deplored.

In this new world, the Prime Minister was, for different reasons, rather lost. For Clemenceau the Republic meant 'justice', equality before the law, keeping the Church and the High Command of the Army in their places. It meant a strong France in a world of great powers. It meant a more equitable system of taxation. But demands like that for the 'abolition of the salariat' were meaningless to Clemenceau. The sonorous rhetoric of Jaurès was offensive. The S.F.I.O., the new Socialist party, was bound by its statutes to independence of other parties; but even had it been possible to make an offer of collaboration to Clemenceau, the offer would not have been accepted. As he said, he was 'on the other side of the barricades'. He was now 'the chief French cop'. The Republic, he thought, had deserved well of all Frenchmen, including the industrial workers of whom he knew so little, who were so different from the craftsmen and little shopkeepers he had known when he combined the practice of medicine with the practice of politics in Montmartre. The senator from the Var, in the pre-industrial south, did not know, did not need to know anything of the life of Billancourt or Lens. Yet it was in the south that one of the great crises of the Ministry came.

The Midi had recovered from the great disaster of the phylloxera. But the new vineyards and the new wine-growers were not quite like the old. Many small men had been ruined beyond recovery. (It took money to pay for the new American stocks.) The consumption of wine had risen; its quality had fallen. The tariff war with Italy had been caused chiefly by the pressure of the small wine-growers to keep out the cheap Italian wines that were mixed with the domestic pro- duct to produce 'vin ordinaire'. Now the wine was flooding in from the new, vast, modernized vineyards of Algeria. The labour force of the southern vineyards was in the main nomadic and partly foreign. In 1907 the explosion came. There were riots, and the local regi- ment, the 17th, refused to fire on the mob. Its Republican virtue was celebrated in a famous ballad (written by a former Boulangist poet), but Clemenceau was not amused. The leader of the revolt, Marcellin Albert, was ingeniously discredited but the class war had entered Arcady. It was endemic elsewhere. There were strikes and riots in the industrial north; there were also deaths. The militant workers were embittered. What had the Republic done for them?

It had done a good deal, but not for them. It had reduced military service to two years, equally enforced on everyone. It had actually had some success in creating effective institutions for rural credit, succeeding where the Second Empire had failed. (The Crédit Foncier had concentrated on town property; the Crédit Agricole had ended by being one of the chief bankers of bankrupt Egypt.) It had spent more money, more effectually, on agricultural education as well as on rural schools. It had even relaxed the rules of French grammar for harassed schoolchildren. More important, it had, in 1896, at last begun to carry out the reform that Napoleon III had seen the necessity of, but had lacked the will-power to impose. It had created sixteen regional universities out of the disconnected bundles of 'Faculties'. This gave life to the moribund Faculties of Letters and created local institutions which could receive gifts and subsidies, attract local support, evoke local pride. The old tradition died hard. In 1904, the Dean of the Faculty of Sciences at Clermont-Ferrand boasted that 'Clermont is one of the cities where the public lecture guards its prestige and is not sacrificed to lectures of pure teaching utility.' But M. Julien was fighting a losing battle. And it was one of the greatest of the new (or, in this instance, revived) Universities that produced the theorist whose doctrines sapped the authority of the Jacobin state. In preaching the autonomy of the public services, their right and duty to establish their own standards, M. Duguit of the University of Bordeaux was in the spirit of the times.

The theories of the general strike, of the sterility of merely political action, of the servile character of mere State Socialism were in great favour. What did the workers, as a class, gain by the nationalization of the railways? In the Post Office, the State was a notoriously bad employer, more hostile to trade unions than many private employers. The political action of the Socialist party was concentrated on issues like 'laicity' or on foreign policy. The most eloquent orators of the workers' movement changed their tune when they became leading members of the bar (like Viviani) or Ministers or potential Ministers like Briand. While the Socialists were uniting in the S.F.I.O., the workers were uniting in the General Workers' Federation, the 'Confederation-Générale du Travail', the 'C.G.T.' In the 'Charter of Amiens', of 1904, it was most firmly laid down that the C.G.T. had no political aims or affiliations. It was not to be the industrial arm of any political party, not even of the Socialist party.

That this was the only salvation of the workers was the conviction of the militant Victor Griffuelhes and of his lieutenant and successor, the young Léon Jouhaux. The first test of the theory, a postal strike, failed. But the great day when the workers could impose their will by their own independent action was still in the future. The duty or opportunity of dealing with it fell to Briand. Clemenceau had outstayed his welcome; his arrogance irritated more and more Deputies; he was overthrown. There were to be no more long-lived Ministries for nearly ten years. The 'time of troubles' had begun. Briand was threatened with a railway strike; he countered by calling up the strikers as reservists. The strike collapsed. The State was not just an association like so many others; it had unsuspected reserves of power. That was one lesson learned. It was not the only one. The 'treason' of Briand was bitterly resented; his revolutionary past remembered. 'There is more in common', wrote Robert de Jouvenel, 'between two Deputies, one of whom is a revolutionary, than between two revolutionaries, one of whom is a Deputy.' So the non-deputies noted.

The political system, as it existed, served the now triumphant Radicals. Elections were by single-member constituencies which suited them admirably. A Radical Deputy was not tied to any precise doctrines; he could and did build up a local position. He gave away minor jobs, did minor favours. He was usually a Mayor or a leading member of the Council (the 'conseil-général') of the Department. It was a rash Prefect or Sub-Prefect who quarrelled with him. He often got elected, especially in the south, by a bold use of alcohol, if not money, backed up by the support of the Prefect. And it was a rule of French politics that infringements of electoral law were never committed by candidates of parties that made up the majority. Against this system, the Socialists, the Right, the splinter groups of men like Briand coalesced. The single-member constituency was a 'stagnant pool'. There was truth in the charge even if the majority did not want to trouble stagnant waters. But the whole French political system was stirred up, from the outside, by the danger of war.

XI

The Algeciras settlement had settled little. Morocco remained anarchical and there was some plausibility in the theory advanced by Jaurès that it would have been wiser for France to deal with the tribes on the Algerian border rather than with the Sultan whose authority was a fiction. But it was necessary to have an authority with whom a treaty could be made, so that this fiction could be used in dealing with foreign powers, notably with Germany. The authority of the Sultan had to be created by France so that France could rule in his name. Further disturbances broke out; Fez was occupied; the end of Moroccan independence was in sight. Again, Germany protested. A gunboat was sent to Agadir (a move calculated to alarm the British Admiralty) and war seemed in sight. But Britain stood by a hesitant France and a compromise with Germany was worked out. In return for accepting the special position of France in Morocco, Germany was ceded the greater part of the French Congo.

In fact, if not in form, the deal was the work of Caillaux and to the Nationalists the deal was near treason. For French national and Nationalist feeling was recovering from the blow of the Affair. A series of shocks to the stability of the European state system made the chance of war more real. Austria annexed Bosnia, a blow to 'Russian' prestige. Italy attacked Tripoli, an invitation to the Balkan states to attack Turkey in Europe. The appointment of Mr. Winston Churchill to be First Lord of the Admiralty showed how seriously the British Government took the danger. Elaborate plans were made to dispatch a British force of six divisions to France in the event of war. The French fleet was concentrated in the Mediterranean, that the British might concentrate in the North Sea. The Balkan wars came. The Bulgarian, Serbian, Greek armies trained and armed by French officers and French firms (an aspect of the power of the Paris money market) easily defeated the Turks, armed by Krupps and trained by Germans. French confidence in the Army was fortified. A new commander-in-chief, Joseph-César Joffre, was appointed and he began to re-cast the plan of campaign in an offensive form.

It was the doctrine of the new teachers at the War College, men like Colonel de Grandmaison, that the offensive at any cost was the way to victory, the bayonet a better weapon than the rifle or the machine-gun. It was a 'myth' like Sorel's doctrine of the general strike. Will was all that mattered; contours, cover, the power of new weapons were all ignored. It was, in the worst sense of the term, a very French doctrine, rhetorical, verbal, above serious calculation of material conditions and possibilities. It was a far remove from the more critical doctrine of the offensive preached by the soldier Clemenceau had made head of the War School, although he was a zealous Catholic with a Jesuit brother; but Foch was sent off to command the 20th Army Corps at Nancy.

Germany responded by a special war contribution, by an increase in the peacetime establishment. The only possible answer, said the French High Command, was to increase the term of military service to three years. It was a profoundly unpopular measure. That it could even be discussed was a sign of the times; so was the election of Raymond Poincaré as President of the Republic. He was a politician of much more weight and force of character than Faure, Loubet or Fallières. And he defeated, in secret ballot, the candidate of the Left. Never again, as long as the Third Republic existed, would the Left manage to elect its candidate; he was always betrayed by the more and more conservative Radicals of the Senate. But the Radicals of the Chamber and of the electoral committees were more loyal than ever to Caillaux. And he had a powerful ally in Jaurès, whose desperate campaign for peace was the noblest effort of his life. Ignoring the boiling pot of nationalist passion in eastern Europe, Jaurès insisted, rightly, that there was no quarrel over the Congo or the Bagdad railway or concessions in Morocco that could not be settled by bargaining. He was held up by the reviving Nationalists, above all in the *Action Française*, to execration as an agent of Germany. His brilliant and paradoxical lieutenant, Marcel Sembat, admitted the justice of the Royalist charges against the Republic. It could not, except by betraying itself, prepare adequately for war. Maurras was right; only the monarchy could do that. Well, then, 'Let's have a King or let's have peace'. (*Faites un Roi; sinon faites la Paix* was the title of the famous tract.) Other Socialists, like Gustave Hervé, infuriated the patriotic by the vehemence and vulgarity of their attacks on the Army, the flag, Joan of Arc, all the idols of the Nationalists and of ordinary patriotic Frenchmen and Frenchwomen. Jaurès would have liked to be free of such allies but he had to put up with them; he had to put up with a more dangerous ally, Joseph Caillaux.

Caillaux was able, but he was vulnerable. He had friends on the edge of low as well as in the centre of high finance. He was suspected of protecting his friends only too well, and of interfering with the regular administration of justice to do so.

The judicial system of the Republic differed little from that of the Empire or of the Monarchy. There was an elaborate hierarchy with nearly 4,000 'Magistrates' culminating in the appeal court, the Cour de Cassation, in Paris. The Judges were not recruited from the bar. They entered the magistracy by examination and rose or did not rise by industry—or favour. They were badly paid, especially in the lower branches, and needed to have private means or to marry rich wives. The old Catholic and Monarchist families were excluded from the Republican magistracy, and one added cause of the bitterness bred by the Affair was the conviction that the Judges of the regular courts belonged to 'them', the Judges of the courts martial to 'us'. The Judges had security of tenure, but what did that matter if their chance of a serious career depended on promotion, that is, on the politicians?

The comparatively low prestige of the regular courts contrasted oddly with the prestige of the Council of State. That was an administrative body, advising the Government, drafting bills for the Ministers. But it had also become the court in which the private citizen sought protection from the wrong-doing of the agents of the State. Its 'disputes' section had, since 1872, been, in all but name, an independent court, devoted to seeing that the State 'behaved like an honest man'. In 1889, it had successfully claimed original jurisdiction in all administrative cases unless it was specifically excluded by statute. Even then, it claimed appellate jurisdiction. The Judicial Section gained prestige from the Administrative Section and *vice versa*; the 'Councillors' had far more experience of the real world than had Judges entering the magistracy in their twenties; there were no scandals about promotion—that went by seniority. Entry to the Council was one of the greatest triumphs a bright young man could achieve. And all, councillors, 'maîtres de requêtes', 'auditeurs', were full of justified pride in the Council, or, as they called it, 'la maison'.

No such aura gilded the prestige of the ordinary courts, and it was shown that Caillaux had brought pressure to delay prosecution of a shady figure in the underworld of Paris finance. Then Caillaux had ignored the advice of an American politician, Boies Penrose (whom in many other ways he resembled): 'Never write a letter to a woman that you can't chill beer on.' Caillaux had written many indiscreet letters to a woman, now scorned, that the former Madame Caillaux had turned over to the editor of the *Figaro*, Gaston Calmette, who was campaigning for 'probity', the three years' service law, and the defeat of the infamous income tax whose chief spokesman was Caillaux. One letter would show, if published, that Caillaux's public zeal for the tax was not in accord with his private judgement. The current Madame Caillaux, whom further letters would embarrass, killed M. Calmette. And it is characteristic of the morality of 'the Republic of Pals', as Robert de Jouvenel called it, that the Prime Minister, a jovial Protestant, Gaston Doumergue, did not call for the resignation of his Finance Minister. But Caillaux went; his 'place was beside his wife'. The historically-minded recalled, with a shudder, the assassination of Victor Noir by Pierre Bonaparte in 1870. *Absit omen.*

The fears of the historically-minded seemed exaggerated in the spring and early summer of 1914. The plans for the visit of President Poincaré to Russia went forward. As in 1870, the French electors were profoundly pacific. The Chamber elected in 1910 had very reluctantly, fully conscious of the political dangers, voted a three years' service law. As its supporters feared, the electors were not impressed by their prudent patriotism. The Left, Radicals, Socialists and their minor allies won easily and Jaurès, horrified by the danger of war, was the ally and the guarantor of the policy of Caillaux. He, for the moment, had to stay out of office until his wife was acquitted (as, of course, she was), but he dominated the Radical half of the tacit alliance with the Socialists. Poincaré tried to dodge the verdict of the voters; in vain. All he could do was to entrust to the former Socialist fire-eater, now Poincaré's protégé at the bar, René Viviani, the task of arranging a compromise by which, it was probable, three years' service would be replaced by service for thirty-six months. Meantime, the conscripts were held for another year. The peacetime strength of the Army was at its highest level.

So was the splendour of Paris. All the world flocked there and the internationalization of French culture or the decline of French self-respect (it depended on the point of view) went further than ever.

'Tu boiras à longs traits tout le sang de l'Europe.'

So wrote that representative international and French figure, Guillaume Apollinaire. Chaliapin had followed in the wake of

Nijinsky. The aeroplane was beginning to be a normal part of life (it had already killed a Minister at a review). The taxi had, fortunately, almost replaced the fiacre. The industrialization of France had been slow but was rapidly increasing its momentum. The new industrial suburbs round Paris were replacing the old villages; Bobigny, as Ernest Dimnet noted, was no longer rural, had no use for the old country parish priest with his garden and his bees. It had no use for any other kind of priest. The worker, again and again deceived in extravagant hopes, was alienated from the State, often with good reason.

For the French worker under the 'Republic' was not better off, he was worse off, than the German worker under the Hohenzollerns (the Alsatians noticed this) or the British worker under the parliamentary monarchy. The high tariff policy of Méline was reflected in high prices and in the preservation of archaic and costly means of production. Somebody had to pay the cost of the artificial keeping-alive of so many small units; it was the new, industrial worker who reacted humanly, passionately, if stupidly. There were two economies in France—one a slow-moving, old-fashioned, unambitious France where there was an amiable, agreeable life. But this 'France la doulce' was parasitic on the other, the new, expanding France. It had its poets; it had even what passed for a philosopher, the sophist 'Alain', but it was a drag on the new, industrial France.

That France was handicapped not only by the refusal of the older France to accept the modern world; it was handicapped by the lack of industrial capital in one of the great money markets of the world.

XII

The new banking system of the Second Empire was tested by the financial needs of the Third Republic. The financing of the German indemnity and of the reconstruction of France called for a mobilization of French savings. The growth of the habit of investment in the *rentes*, and in railway securities under the Empire, was exploited by the new chain banks. The law on limited liability companies of

1867 facilitated the expansion of 'chain banking' which entered into
competition with the local banks (often founded on a local industry,
silk in Lyons with the Guérin family, milling at Grenoble with the
Banque Ferrodeau). But the chain banks had less in mind the financing of a local industry than the tapping of local savings. The Crédit
Lyonnais, from one point of view, was misnamed. It (and the Société
Générale), in entering a new region, sought profit as much in selling
securities, above all Government securities, as in normal banking
business. Where the chain banks aided local business, they preferred
to deal with merchants rather than manufacturers whose slow turn-
over did not add much to banking profits. The Schneider family had
to coax the Crédit Lyonnais to come to Le Creusot. It realized,
slowly, that the pay of the workers in the Schneider plants made
profits for shopkeepers who might be good customers of the bank.
In some regions where the great banks established themselves, the
attraction was simply the amount of liquid money to be drained
away. All over France, in quite small towns, branches were established to take advantage of the conversion of the peasant and small
trader and craftsman from that bad habit of mere hoarding that the
great spender and speculator, Balzac, had so deplored.

The savings thus tapped were often, too often, exported. The
great banks sold securities for the foreign governments who were, by
Government favour, given access to the French money market. The
Government used its power to give or deny access as a diplomatic
weapon. No English minister used the 'cavalry of St. George' more
lavishly or more rashly than the Ministers of the Third Republic
used the savings of the French peasant. Some of the governments
thus favoured were political allies, above all Russia, whose need for
the French money market was the main diplomatic weapon of the
Quai d'Orsay. Others were powers like Bulgaria and Turkey whose
favours, if paid for, were not accorded. The weaker the security
offered, the higher the commission charged by the banks. This export of French capital did French industry little good, for the needs
of backward countries could not be supplied by French industry.
Only the armament industries which armed the Balkan states (some
to be friends, one to be an enemy in the first World War) benefited.
The notorious risks of these loans were not compensated for by any

exceptionally high rate of interest; the French investors, if not the vending banks, would have been little worse off in immediate yield, and a great deal better off in security, if they had stuck to French Government obligations. In 1914, the French investor owned 1,000,000,000 francs (£40,000,000) in foreign securities, nearly all of them to be soon repudiated. It was a lesson that might have given much reason for bitter reflection to that village in the Lyons region where a branch bank had been opened in 1905 that in two years drained away all liquid savings, replacing them by Balkan and South American stocks of doubtful soundness. Perhaps the peasant hoarder of gold napoleons was right and Balzac wrong.

Yet France was, in a slightly archaic way, prosperous and prospering. An archaic tax structure forced the Government to borrow regularly to meet deficits, but the loans were always taken up. And an income tax law was at last on the point of being enacted. France was still paid the compliment of envy, for into her hospitable fields came Italians, Spaniards, Poles, Belgians, filling the gaps left by the lowest birth rate in Europe. The birth rate in Europe was falling in every country, but the German birth rate in 1914 was higher than the French birth rate of 1870. France and Germany had been equal in population in that year. Now Germany was more than fifty per cent more populous—and the disparity was growing. Germany could, with ease, bear a military burden that crushed France. There was, thought those Frenchmen who were preoccupied with the position of France as a great power, only one remedy: the Empire must be called in to replace the Frenchmen who were not being born.

XIII

The Empire was a going concern. Indo-China was pacified and a vigorous or ruthless Governor-General, Paul Doumer, had, by savage taxation, equipped the great colony with roads, railways, bridges, engineering works that made available to French planters and Tonkinese peasants millions of acres of neglected but fertile land. The old mandarin education was on its last legs; a new educated class,

educated in French, often in France, highly conscious of the relevance of the 'Rights of Man and the Citizen', was coming into
existence. So it was in North Africa. The job of making the authority
of the 'Sultan' of Morocco, that is, of France, effective all over the
vast, anarchical country was being put in hand with incomparable
dexterity by Hubert Lyautey. Algeria and Tunisia were completely
subdued and the fiction that Algeria was a 'part of France' was given
some plausibility by its economic assimilation, by the rapid growth
of French colonization, by the development of the not very abundant resources of the three departments. Much of the authority of
the Governor-General had been restored. Algeria was France—but
with an admitted difference. The great majority of the population
were French subjects, not French citizens, cut off from France—and
the modern world—by Islam. As a great French Arabist, Gautier,
was to point out, it was significant that after nearly a century of conquest and settlement, there were no half-castes. Arabs, in very small
numbers, could enter the French ruling class, but only by abandoning
Islam, which was not so much a religion as a way of life.

No such barriers prevented the entry of the Algerian Jews into
French life. They quickly assimilated the new culture, adopted
French family law, were the only group which was really bilingual.
By the famous or notorious Crémieux decree of 1870, they had been
made French citizens while the Arabs were still mere subjects. It was
noted that Crémieux was the leading French Jew. He looked after
his own, said the critics. So anti-Semitism was rife not only among
the Arabs, but among the colonists.

Many of the poorer colonists were not of French origin; they were
Spaniards, Italians, Maltese (Viviani was the son of an Italian settler).
The Jews were their competitors and Algiers (then an overwhelmingly 'French' city) was the centre of political anti-Semitism during
the Affair; its Mayor, Max Regis, one of the most violent anti-
Dreyfusard Deputies. For this small colonial group was represented
by Deputies and Senators who could both further the economic interests of the whole of Algeria and (what was not always the same
thing) their own.

A great deal of Algeria had been empty, barely occupied by nomadic tribes, a tangle of brush and scrub. To bring it into cultivation

needed patience, capital, security, western land tenures. Sometimes
rebellion, as in the Constantine district in 1871, gave an excuse
for confiscation, but usually the land was bought from the ignorant
and illiterate natives who had no more idea than so many American
Indians of what they were doing. The middlemen were usually the
bilingual Jews and the natives were not shifted off to reservations;
they remained as a landless proletariat in regions grown miraculously
fertile. It was hard for them to realize that the lands would never have
become fertile in their own incompetent hands. But the Arabs were
being effectually Frenchified by another means. Conscription was
applied to them. It was not a matter of a small body of volunteers,
the 'Turcos' of 1870; all Arab men passed through the Army,
learned the elements of French and a good deal of the strength and
weakness of their masters.

So it was in West Africa. The Senegalese provided admirable, loyal,
clean and often Christian infantry. Little could be made of the de-
graded inhabitants of the Congo, wrecked by disease and supersti-
tion, and mercilessly exploited by the great companies to whom
concessions had been so lavishly given. But in Black Africa, the
steamer, the railway; the new remedies against tropical diseases;
the French education given the 'élite'; the impact of military service;
the sucking of the colonies into the French imperial market; missionary labours; the suppression of the slave trade: all were transforming the great imperial domain. The Empire was a source of
strength and of pride.

The strength, it is true, was not much thought of by the Left voter.
He had no interest in Mangin's black infantry, little in Lyautey's
attempts to fuse French and Islamic culture. The Empire was run
chiefly by internal émigrés who found, in the colonies, careers from
which their religious or political views debarred them in France. Such
was the background of Lyautey and of a high proportion of his team.
The Left was ideologically hostile and practically indifferent to this
great French achievement. The Right was proud of the achievement,
but reluctant to think, in any long-term way, of where this forcible
imposition of western ideas would lead. They were reluctant, for
instance, to note the impact in Indo-China of the Japanese victory
over Russia, the still greater impact of the overthrow of the Manchus

in China; they neglected the importance, for France, of the triumph of the 'Young Turks', of the mounting tide of Egyptian nationalist protest against British rule. The Empire needed more thought than it was getting.

So did the Army. The days of the patriotism of the Left in the manner of Paul Déroulède—and of Georges Clemenceau—seemed to be over. The Army was a nuisance, not a vocation. It was not much use purging the High Command of reactionaries, if there were so few competent Republicans to replace them. It was one of the assets of the new Commander-in-Chief that, although a sound Republican, Joffre was on good terms with Catholic generals like Castelnau and Foch. But fewer and fewer of the brilliant pupils of the École Polytechnique entered the Army. Soon it would be rare to find an 'X' among the junior artillery officers, and if young men of great talents like Charles de Gaulle entered Saint-Cyr, more and more they came from Catholic and reactionary if no longer actively Royalist families. André had laboured in vain. And there were fewer and fewer reserve officers like Péguy (or like the average German reserve officer) to whom the rank and duty were an opportunity for public service.

It was a natural consequence that the leaders of the French Army should rely on the regular troops with the colours, the regular officers they could form, rather than on reservists, officers and men alike, dragged reluctantly from civilian life. Thinking this way, they neglected the reserves and the 'Territorial Army', and did not realize that their German opposite numbers ruled in a country with a different social structure and one where, despite the formal importance of the Socialists, patriotic docility was bred in the bone. It was a truth that, from another point of view, Jaurès ignored. In vain his quondam disciple the Alsatian, Charles Andler, told Jaurès a few truths about the impotence of the German Socialists to influence German policy, of their increasing infection with nationalist arrogance. Jaurès would not listen, could not listen. Was the Second International a rope of sand? He could not believe it (neither could Lenin).

The test was at hand. In the spring of 1914, a general *détente* seemed to have set in among the great powers. The various plans of the

Austrian General Staff for redressment of the balance in the Balkans, which the local wars had tipped in favour of Russia, came to nothing. Russian agents, more or less without the knowledge of their chiefs, encouraged the vaulting ambitions of the victorious and thwarted Serbians. And one of a conspiratorial band killed the heir to the Austrian throne, the Archduke Franz Ferdinand, in Sarajevo. The die was cast, not by a great power, but by the nationalist fanatics of a small power for which the 'liberation' of the Bosnians and Croats was well worth all the blood it was to cost.

For the rulers of the Austro-Hungarian Empire, also, the die was cast. This was the last chance to save the dynastic state. They may have been right or there may have been no last chance available. They decided that Serbia was to be crushed, not merely punished; they took, willingly, the risk that Russia would not permit the crushing; the Germans took the risk that their only reliable ally would involve them in a general war. Russia acted and France was necessarily dragged in as Germany had been. Wilhelm II was no more belligerent than his grandfather; his Chancellor, Bethmann-Hollweg, was no Bismarck. But once war was a real danger, once the elaborate military machines began to turn over, real power passed, in the post-Bismarckian tradition, to the High Command. Given the inevitability of war, it made superfluous and revealing mistakes. It demanded that, as a guarantee of neutrality, France should surrender the eastern fortresses; it refused to guarantee the French Empire. It demanded, in peace, the submission due to a victor after a totally victorious campaign. It might better have accepted as necessary the intervention of France on the side of her ally (its plans were based on this certainty).

It is possible that Britain would have intervened in any circumstance; a German victory gained in 1914, with Britain neutral, would have upset the balance of power more than any victory of Napoleon had done. Violation of Belgian neutrality was, again, part of the German war plan; it made British intervention not only certain but, from the British Government's point of view, easy. It would have been worth the price if, as the Germans confidently expected, the war had been short and easy. A score of mistakes in political manners and tactics had to be paid for when the war dragged on. The French and British peoples entered the war with, at any rate so far as the French were concerned, heavy if stout hearts, but easy consciences. That mattered as the war did drag on.

That it did drag on was to the surprise of the High Commands on both sides. The German and French General Staffs made exactly the same calculation; they provided 1,500 shells for each gun, at the expected rate of consumption enough for three months. The lesson of the Balkan wars was assumed to be that the alleged lessons of the Russo-Japanese war, the superiority of the defence, of the machine-gun, of the trench girdled with barbed-wire, were due to exceptional circumstances. All General Staffs thought in terms of 1870. Only the British had had a little realism knocked into them by their sad experiences in South Africa. Only civilians like Bloch and H. G. Wells and Walther Rathenau doubted the official doctrines.

The unexpected duration of the war upset equally the diplomats and the politicians. Given the State system of Europe, some great war was inevitable. It might not have come in 1914; that was possibly the best year for the Germans. 1916 would have been better for the French and Russians. What was to be called 'the Great War', then 'the World War', then 'the First World War' began as the second War of the Austrian Succession. It retained that character to the end, but as the war lasted, new wars were added to the original, new contests began. The rulers of Europe were less and less like captains in command of their ships, more and more like shipwrecked passengers clinging desperately to a new raft of the 'Méduse', joined by new belligerents as old ones were swept away. The illusions of 1914 were short-lived; all except one, the idea that this war was different, that it was the final struggle, 'la lutte finale', which would bring in the reign of peace linked with justice. If this was not so, what was the increasingly onerous and odious burden borne for? Year after year, ignorant armies clashed by night, borne up by a hope in a new world to come out of the obscure conflict.

The first weeks of the war that began in 1914 tested the courage and stability of the French people to a degree that was far more serious than in the corresponding period in 1870. There was no hysterical illusion of easy victory; no crowds filling the Paris streets with cries of 'À Berlin'. The formidable character of the enemy was taken for granted. But the alliance with Russia and Britain (the

Entente became a formal alliance in September) was a source of security. When the great Russian masses began to move, the Germans would be crushed. No such hopes were based on British military or naval aid. But the British reputation for tenacity, for political and diplomatic skill, for wealth, was highly reassuring. For once 'the cavalry of St. George' would charge on the French side.

The reassurance was needed. The war opened smoothly despite one disaster, the assassination of Jean Jaurès, murdered by a half-witted disciple of the Action Française. The crime was doubly alarming; it removed a great public figure and it might have stirred up a revolutionary ferment. There was in existence a 'B' list, containing the names of all the dangerous revolutionaries who might disturb mobilization. Among them was the violently Left Socialist deputy, Pierre Laval. But Caillaux's representative in the Government, Malvy, the Minister of the Interior, wisely disregarded the list. There were no arrests; no disturbances; the French worker, for the moment, forgave the French State. The mobilization went according to plan; there was none of the last-minute improvisation of 1870.

Nothing else went according to plan. The strategy of the French High Command, as set out in Plan XVII, was based on the belief that the two opposing armies would be roughly equal in strength. The French, based on the impregnable line of the eastern fortresses, could be superior at the striking point. The strategy was based on an error. The German Army was again greatly superior in numbers; it mobilized a mass of reserve divisions that enabled it to invade Belgium in force, turn the French flank and repel the French attack all at once. The attack, after a brief success in Alsace, the occupation of Mulhouse that recalled all too easily the occupation of Saarbrücken in 1870, failed with disastrous losses. The bayonet, the *furia francese*, was no use against the German machine-guns and heavy field artillery that easily outranged the admirable French '75's. French equivalents of the mobile German heavy artillery, the 105 and the 155, existed— but as prototypes only. In a series of bloody repulses, the French Army learned that Colonel de Grandmaison was wrong and that the pessimistic Colonel Pétain was right. Bullets kill; no tactical doctrine of the offensive at all costs could alter that.

Within ten days of the opening of the campaign, the French Army had suffered 300,000 casualties and a series of defeats far worse than Spicheren or Wörth. It was in full retreat, a retreat that the Germans naturally expected to turn into a rout. By the end of August, all France knew that it was being invaded by an easily victorious army, that the fate of the war might be quickly decided under the walls of the capital. It was worse than 1870; what was better was the political structure of the Republic and the moral and intellectual state of the Army. The Government rightly refused to be shut up in Paris as in 1870; it moved at once to Bordeaux. General Joffre did not lose his head nor did the battered troops under him lose their hearts. The British were persuaded to stay in line, not to clear out for home in what, the French thought, was their traditional manner. The Germans, loosely commanded in the style of 1870, attempted to by-pass Paris. Joffre struck at the exposed flank (some of the troops were rushed to the front in taxis). In danger, in their turn, of destruction, the Germans retreated at full speed. It is possible that if the British and French had been bolder, the German retreat might have been made a rout. But boldness was at a discount after Charleroi. The German Army was intact; it moved to the west; so did the British, the French, what was left of the Belgians.

In a series of desperate soldiers' battles, the new German attack was repulsed but, momentous and ominous fact, the German lines now ran from the Swiss border to the North Sea. Everywhere, the invaders held the hills and ridges; their temporary trench systems grew more and more elaborate, until the richest part of France, the only deeply industrialized area, lay behind a great fortress system. It was like the long walls of Athens; the Germans lay impregnable inside their lines, were vulnerable only when they quit them. But it took a long time for this to be understood. Against this fortress, the French, then the British, were thrown in repeated assaults. Always the lines held, always the defenders suffered far fewer casualties than the attackers. In vain the methods of attack were improved, more and more guns concentrated; the great break-through never came. The great cavalry masses waited their chance to emulate Murat, until even the most devoted horsemen learned that the days of cavalry were past.

These grim truths were not apparent in 1914–15. French diplomacy scored its first triumph. Italy boldly abandoned her allies. Then she changed sides, offering her services to the highest bidders, to Britain and France. This more than offset the adherence of the Turks to the enemies of Russia. But in the Dardanelles expedition to knock out Turkey, the French people and Government noted that, under British command on land and sea, a campaign failed disastrously. As a consequence of that failure, Bulgaria joined the Central Powers and an expedition was hastily dispatched to the Balkans to save what could be saved. This time, the French took command. There was no disaster—and no triumph.

By the end of 1915, the war had revealed its true character. Far from threatening Berlin, the Russians had suffered a series of overwhelming defeats. All of Poland was in German hands. So was a great part of France; but a great British army was being built up in France and it was fondly hoped that, in 1916, the invaders would be driven from the soil they polluted. The invaders struck first. They attacked Verdun and, for six months, the great battle raged. The Germans failed; 300,000 deaths were suffered on each side. It was a great French victory, however dearly bought, and it was five hundred years since the fate of France had depended on the deliverance of one city. There could be no surprise at the fact that General Pétain, the defender, got and in part earned some of the fame and reverence due to the Maid of Orleans. But if the defence of Verdun was a victory, it was a negative victory. 'The Germans are at Noyon', had been the slogan of the most famous critic of the Government, Georges Clemenceau. The Germans were still at Noyon. At a terrible price, the great new British armies failed to break through.

By now, the war had taken on something of the character of a great, natural disaster, something more like the plague at Athens than the Syracusan expedition. More and more rigorous conscription provided more and more cannon fodder. As Anatole France said, the Republic demanded and received from the French people far greater sacrifices of life and wealth than Louis XIV or Napoleon I had dared to ask. It was natural that there was war weariness, extraordinary that there was not more, that the national will did not break.

Naturally, the unity of the first months did not last. The Viviani Government fell after the first disasters as had the Government of Émile Ollivier. But, unlike the situation in 1870, the parliamentary system proved adaptable enough to make the necessary changes without revolution. The 'Sacred Union' lasted long enough to save France at the most critical moments. Then it began to wear thin.

The duration of the war presented all kinds of problems, not purely military. No country imposed conscription with such rigour as France and the economic life of the nation came almost to a stand-still. As the demand for shells, guns, motor vehicles grew, so did war industry—and the main French industrial region was in German hands. Each year, the soil of France yielded less, as was natural in a country where human labour had not had its place taken by machines. Slowly, very slowly, was the much disliked remedy of food rationing adopted; slowly, very slowly indeed, did the French submit to the outrage of frozen imported meat. The industrialization of hitherto rural parts of France proceeded under a forced draught. The use of women in factories and offices was a social revolution. The war had other revolutionary effects. Income tax had been instituted just as the war broke out, but it was impossible in war time to create a system that could make it effective. The Chamber was very reluc-tant to institute new taxes; the old system, even in 1914, was highly inelastic. The French Government met no war costs out of taxes; it did not even raise enough revenue to pay the peacetime costs of government. The result was, inevitably, inflation. The pensioner, the *rentier*, the civil servant paid in high prices; he did not understand why. He still lent lavishly, although the Government had to pay higher and higher interest rates. The credit of the State, restored by the Ministers of Louis XVIII and Charles X, stood firm.

But by the end of 1916, the edge of the national will to victory was blunted. The Joffre method had not driven the enemy out of France; Joffre was removed and replaced by Nivelle who promised a speedy victory. In England, Lloyd George replaced Asquith on a programme of an all-out effort. The secret news from Russia was bad. Italian vic-tories were dearly bought and sterile. The French home front was showing signs of weakening. Inflation, rash contracting by the Government, luck, some corruption produced new rich and new poor. The soldier, above all the soldier's family, suffered by comparison with the industrial workers. The French way of life that left dealing with hardship and misery to the State and the Church, did not easily encourage the proliferation of voluntary societies that relieved some of the strain in England. Elinor Glyn, working in France, was scandalized by what she thought the indifference of her aristocratic French friends to their plain duty. The contrast between the front and the rear was dramatic enough. A few miles to the north of Paris lay the tormented landscape where millions of men lived a new 'life of the martyrs'. In Paris, and in the provinces far from the invaders, life was safe and could be gay.

In the first months of the war, it had been easy to put party quarrels on one side. Monks, even Jesuits, exiled by the religious laws, flocked back to serve. Pacificist Socialists like Gustave Hervé changed overnight into patriotic fire-eaters. A few like Pierre Laval kept the faith. One of them was M. Malvy. He applied firmly, as Minister of the Interior, the old maxim of 'no enemies on the Left'. As the war lasted, pacificism revived and with it a movement for a realistic acceptance of the fact that Germany could not be conquered. Pacificism was not the same thing as defeatism (a new word for a new thing). The chief of the defeatists was M. Caillaux. He approved of M. Malvy's conduct, even of his subsidization of newspapers that the Germans, for their own good reasons, also subsidized.

Into this world of revived political ambitions, of war weariness, of reviving social conflict, two great events burst: the Russian Revolution and the intervention of the United States. And both came when the miserable collapse of the Nivelle offensive had destroyed all hope in the power of France to free her own soil. It could be freed, now, only by a general peace or by the impact on the German will to resist of American power.

The Russian Revolution was bound to impress the French people, deeply. The very word 'revolution' was magic. All through the summer of 1917, the reviving Socialist parties of Europe planned ways of ending the war. Had the German Government had any real political sense, it would have made peace. Any peace made in 1917 would have been, in its results, a victorious peace for Germany. By proclaiming an independent 'Kingdom of Poland', the Central

Powers had undertaken to redress the balance of power in eastern Europe in their own favour. The Russian Revolution made this policy feasible. The *status quo* in the west, even the *status quo* modified by a few concessions to France, by the formal restoration of Belgian independence, would have been a great victory for Germany, a great defeat for France—and still more for Britain. The chance was lost. So was the chance of taking advantage of the series of mutinies that swept through the French Army as the aftermath of the failure of the spring offensive spread despair and the news of the Russian Revolution spread hope. But the chance was not taken, and the new Commander-in-Chief, Pétain, earned and used his reputation as a soldiers' general. Discipline was restored. But the British Army exhausted its offensive power in the bloody assaults of Passchendaele, and the Italian Army was barely rescued from the *débâcle* of Caporetto. It was the darkest hour. The news from Petrograd made it darker. The Bolsheviks seized the capital and, whatever their limit of success, Russia was no longer a serious belligerent: Germany need not fight on two fronts. But, a neglected but in France, one great German calculation had gone wrong. The German Admiralty had calculated that unlimited submarine warfare would knock out Britain. The calculation was not foolish; it was almost right. But Britain survived and the price of the gamble—the effects of the intervention of the United States—had to be paid.

Yet France might not hold out long enough to preserve a battlefield for the United States. That she did was due to Georges Clemenceau. Ministry after Ministry had risen and fallen. ('Faites donner la Garde', as they had said under the Emperor.) Only Clemenceau was not involved in wartime failures, scandals, compromises. In his much-censored paper, *L'Homme Enchaîné*, he had preached the old Jacobin doctrine of war to the end. As chairman of the Army Committee of the Senate, he was in constant touch with the needs of the soldiers. And he was no respecter of persons. His policy, he announced, was simply 'to make war', and he must show France and the world that he meant it. There was, in fact, no alternative between the policy of Clemenceau and the policy of Caillaux, between war to the limit or peace on the best terms then possible. Abandoning the rules of the game, the Chamber accepted Clemenceau and he showed

his mettle by arresting Caillaux. It was as sacrilegious an act as the
arrest of the King on August 10, 1792. It was as necessary, if the war
was to be won. It was Jacobin justice. So was the arrest of Malvy, the
execution of his protégés, Bolo Pasha and other scum. It was the
spirit of '93, of 'la patrie en danger', all over again. For this revival of
an old order that now got only verbal imitation, this breach of the
rules of the 'Republic of Pals', Clemenceau was not forgiven, in life
or in death. He established his dictatorship just in time.

On March 21, 1918, the Germans struck and swept away the
British Fifth Army. Haig, the British commander, was resolute but
not hopeful; Pétain was resolute but reconciled to defeat; a new man
and a new spirit were needed. Clemenceau (and Milner) found him
in Ferdinand Foch. But the new Generalissimo had no infallible
recipe for victory. There were further disasters. But each month more
and more fresh, ill-trained, untired American troops poured in. In
June, the tide turned; in July, it began to run fast against the Germans
and, having left their impregnable fortress, they were not permitted
to get back to it. The last Austrian offensive in Italy failed; the Turkish
Empire was crumbling under the attacks of the British regular
Army. Franchet d'Esperey was preparing to attack in the Balkans. In
August the British attacked in Flanders, and from that moment the
Germans had no rest. The real ruler of Germany, General Ludendorff,
lost his head, while his nominal chief, Hindenburg, was still calcu-
lating what French territory should be annexed! Dispensing himself
from the duty of reading the bases of peace laid down by the American President, Woodrow Wilson, in his 'fourteen points', Ludendorff recommended or ordered an appeal for an armistice. The whole
edifice of German power crumbled; the Allies destroyed the Bulgarian Army and marched on the Danube. The Italians finally attacked the Austro-Hungarian Army, all that was left of the Austro-
Hungarian State.

There was the beginning of revolution in Germany: that is, of the
overthrow of the dynasty that owed its power to victory. Rigorous
terms were laid down by the victorious Foch; if the Germans accepted
them, they could not make war again. It did not matter, the Christian Marshal thought, that there would be no visible and bloody final
victory. The Germans accepted; fighting ended on November 11,

1918. Clemenceau and Foch were declared by Parliament to have 'deserved well of their country'. The German Army began to withdraw and the French followed, to Metz, to Strasbourg where the 'Marseillaise' had first been sung. France had lost nearly 1,500,000 lives—almost the total population of Alsace-Lorraine; and the victorious armies marched across a great scar of destruction, wrought by design as well as by military accident. It was victory; was it peace, and what kind of peace, if any?

VI

BETWEEN TWO WARS

I

THE contrast between appearance and reality was seldom better manifested than in the position of France in 1919. She was a victor power, and the most glorious of the victors. She had survived an ordeal such as few armies or nations have had to endure; the final victorious campaign had been conducted under the supreme command of a French general; and the Third Republic had not only asked and got from the French people sacrifices and services that no other ruler had dared demand, it had produced, from its much condemned political system, the great war leaders. Foch and Clemenceau, together, seemed the symbols of French military and political competence; the Marne and Verdun, the symbols of resilience and enduring heroism. The 'day of glory' had come on November 11 when the Second *Reich* surrendered.

The reality was very different; France had every reason to give heed to the counsel of La Fontaine:

> 'Défions-nous du sort, et prenons garde à nous
> Après le gain d'une bataille.'

France, if she had been the most heroic of the victors, was desperately weakened by her effort. Germany had been overthrown by the intervention of the United States. But for that intervention, Germany might have resisted both Britain and France. If the Third Republic had deserved credit for a policy that gave France Britain, Russia, and Italy as allies, it was German, not French, diplomacy that provoked American intervention. In this sense, French victory, however well deserved, was an accident, a sombre truth fully appreciated by Clemenceau. The French position would never be so good again. Now was the acceptable time, now was the day of salvation—or never. It was not only that Germany remained, intrinsically, what she had been since the victory of 1870–71 revealed her power. Her position was actually improved. For the collapse of the Austrian

245

Empire that Bismarck had feared was a danger to Germany only if a powerful Russia could exploit it. But there was no such Russia in existence. Easy talk of the disappearance of 'the three Empires' concealed the fact that the most powerful of them remained; the *Reich* was now a Republic. Did that matter? The French doubted it. The *Reich* was surrounded on her eastern and southern borders by new, weak, unstable states. She might easily add 'Austria', the German lands of the old empire, to her territory, thus more than compensating for any territorial losses she might suffer to France or to the new Poland. Only elaborate and difficult treaty provisions could prevent Germany from being the real victor in a war in which millions had died to prevent German domination. As Clemenceau knew and as the event soon proved, France's allies and the United States were blind to this truth. One great British object was achieved when Belgium (and the French Channel ports) were snatched from German hands; another when the German fleet was conveniently sunk. Germany, it was assumed, would not again commit the folly of antagonizing Britain. From that moment, the interests of France and Britain began rapidly to diverge. They were not to converge again until it was well past the eleventh hour.

The case of the United States was different. Again, Germany had surely learned her lesson and all that remained for American power to do was to create a world in which a war provoked by nationalist passion would not occur again because nationalist passion would be satisfied and because a new world order would discipline the old and the new nations. Clemenceau could understand much of British policy; he could barely understand the policy of Wilson and he had soon reason to wonder whether there *was* an American policy, apart from the personal passions, ideas, dreams of the President who, as the world was repeatedly told, did not represent the American people. Clemenceau had to gamble, on a deal with Britain, on concessions to the ideas of President Wilson. And he had to do it in face of a bewildered French public opinion.

The French, like every other people, had been taught to put all their hopes in victory. They had, like the Americans and the British, to learn that victory was not enough—and does not keep. The men who met in Paris were working against time; each day their power of decision grew less. As Marshal Foch pointed out, it was more important to find governments for eastern Europe than to find armies. A settlement, *any* settlement was better than none. 'The Big Four' heard 'time's wingèd chariot hurrying near'. Much had to be left to the future, to new solutions not yet capable of definition, to the healing effects of the mere end of slaughter. No one knew, for instance, what would emerge from the Russian cauldron. In desperate and futile efforts to keep open the eastern front, the Allies had backed various movements, leaders, and adventurers who at least were not, like the usurping Bolsheviks, open allies of the Germans. The Germans had collapsed; would their protégés imitate them? No one knew. The Supreme Council at Paris did not, could not deliberate in Olympian calm

'on the hills like Gods together, careless of mankind'.

They had to deal with human passions, exultations, agonies, not capable of reduction to rational discourse. And each of the victors saw the problems of peace almost exclusively from its own point of view. To Keynes, the French were trying to restore the Europe of 1870; it was dead. But Keynes was trying to restore the Europe of 1914, and it was equally dead. Wilson was trying to create a world that had never existed (in which he was perhaps the wisest of the lot). Lloyd George was trying to justify the rash promises he had made to the British people. Clemenceau was trying to secure the military safety of France. In these cross-purposes, none of the victors attained its ends.

M. Gaston Bergery, on the eve of the second World War, said that each of the principals of the tragedy of 1919, Britain, France, the United States, Germany, made enough mistakes to account for the second catastrophe. It is easy enough to list the French mistakes. There was, first of all, a failure to recognize the limited nature of the victory. The veteran Clemenceau was almost alone in his pessimistic wisdom. He knew that without British and American support, it was impossible effectively to restrain German power. Therefore, he gave up the tangible guarantees of victory and security wanted by the soldiers, the separation of the Rhineland from Germany, the permanent occupation of key fortresses, for an Anglo-American guarantee of the new borders. He could not believe that the American people would repudiate their President. They did, and the foolish rulers of Britain cheerfully took the chance to get out of their share in the guarantee. The average Frenchman thought he had been cheated; he had. Only by eternal vigilance could Germany be kept from upsetting the settlement.

It was an undisputed fact that Germany had invaded Belgium and France and had done immense damage there. It was obvious justice (even to many Germans) that reparations, in the limit of the possible, ought to be paid. But if 'reparations' were to mean only that, there would be nothing for Britain, that is for the foolish voters who had elected Mr. Lloyd George's Parliament. So, with the aid of the great South African casuist, General Smuts, 'reparations' was extended to mean every kind of claim the victors thought fit to make, down to payments to Australia and Portugal. To justify this doctrine of 'to the victors belong the spoils', the Germans were charged with making aggressive war. The controversy over 'war guilt' clouded the simple and sensible doctrine that Germany should and could repair the physical damage done to France and Belgium. Only by such a restriction of the debate could Germany have been convinced of the justice of the burden laid on her and France have been assured that some, at any rate, of her losses would be compensated for.

The French case, too, was muddled by the low level at which financial discussion was carried on in France. The French experts were a great deal less expert than the English and the Americans. Clemenceau's Finance Minister, Klotz, was, as his chief remarked, 'the only Jew who couldn't count'. Loucheur was a successful businessman who had no other competence and his wealth was not enough. The French people had been told that Germany would pay. They took a long time to learn that Germany neither would nor, on the scale of the pipe dreams of 1919, could.

This failure to face realities affected the currency. Many Frenchmen genuinely expected the Americans to go on supporting the franc in peace as in war. They were wrong. The moment foreign support was withdrawn, the franc began to fall. The wonder was that it did not fall further and faster. For all the elements of inflation were present. None of the costs of the war had been paid for by current taxation. In France alone, among the victorious great powers, peace did not lead to an immediate reduction in Government expenditure. The costs of reconstruction were as great as the costs of waging war. The United States could not be drawn on for the costs of reconstruction; Germany's contribution was remote, contingent, and sure to be inadequate. Yet the French investor had been successfully coaxed into taking bills of all denominations of the Bank of France as being as good as gold. They were not. By the end of 1919, the franc had lost half its pre-war value. Even a Minister as bold as Churchill could not seriously have proposed to double the value of the franc. One consequence would have been an intolerable burden of debt, for the war loans had been floated on more and more onerous terms. Interest was kept at 4% but the last loan was issued at 70·80%. Pouring out money on the great, necessary, but ruinous enterprise of re-building the devastated areas, not, until 1921, even raising enough revenue to pay 'normal' peacetime expenditure, the French Government could fall back only on open or concealed inflation. This, of course, meant rising prices and the indignant *rentier*, who was duly paid his interest, saw no relation between that fact and the steady fall in the purchasing power of the franc.

It was, it must be the fault of the Germans, of the Americans, of the English. It was, but it was also the fault of the French. The new income tax worked slowly, ineffectively, inequitably. There were mere speculative raids on the franc; there were excessive discountings of French prospects; but, all in all, the fall in the franc was in the nature of things. The French people, or their representatives, had decided that the war would be paid for by a slow and, at first, barely perceptible defrauding of the public creditors. The great achievement of the Restoration, the creation of public faith in public credit, was being undone.

It was being undone by a Parliament that, in many ways, was a 'chambre introuvable'. The Parliament elected in 1914 had prolonged its own life; not until the end of 1919 did it face the electors. It had, characteristically, shown that the Third Republic had only occasional use for great men. It had not chosen Clemenceau to succeed Poincaré. He was disliked by Catholics as being too 'lay', by Radicals for laying his hands on Caillaux, by Socialists as a warmonger, by Nationalists for betraying France to the Americans and the English. He was disliked for the savage wit he had too often displayed. So the National Assembly chose the elegant Paul Deschanel. The great man's Cabinet clustered round him to assure him of their loyalty. He, so the story runs, put his hand to his ear and asked, 'Did I hear a cock crow?' With that he stepped out of history to an obscure and poor old age. The Parliament that had rejected Clemenceau more innocently laid up trouble for France by altering the electoral law. A bastard system of proportional representation was provided for. A 'list' that got a majority of votes in any department got all the seats. The lists of the 'Bloc National' won a series of landslide victories. The prudent Radicals did not ally themselves with the Socialists, discredited with many as defeatist and threatened by the rise of Bolshevist groups in France. A great many Frenchmen were genuinely disgusted with the old political order; they remembered more easily that it had produced Caillaux than that it had produced Clemenceau.

The new Parliament thus recalled, very closely, the National Assembly of 1871. It was said, possibly correctly, that it was the first Parliament since 1871 to have a majority of practising Catholics in its membership. But there had been no wave of emotion and trust such as elected the Royalist majority of the National Assembly of 1871. The 'horizon blue' Chamber (so called from the colour of the uniform of the victorious Army) never represented the electoral mood, even briefly. France was still 'Left'. It was a pity that so many great problems had to be dealt with by a Parliament that was 'Right'.

It was not only that Parliament was unrepresentative. The new majority was far less competent than the majority of 1871. The long exclusion of the Right from political life had to be paid for. There was no Broglie, Buffet, Chesnelong, Decazes in the ranks of the new majority. The Right had to use the political personnel provided by the Left. It was, indeed, fondly hoped that the great war had produced a sobering and edifying effect on the masses. Had not the priests and monks shown their heroism? Were not most of the war heroes Catholics—Marshals like Foch, aviators like Guynemer? Some even thought that the imposed hierarchy of war could be carried into peace; that the veterans would accept the lead of their generals! It was as great an illusion as any held by the entourage of the Comte de Chambord. Only one of the great war leaders had a popular appeal; Philippe Pétain, not Ferdinand Foch, was the nearest approach to a general who was a hero to his soldiers. For Pétain had been thrifty of the lives of his men to the point of risking defeat; Foch lavish to the point of buying victory by holocausts. Such, at any rate, was the tradition.

It is possible that if the French Right had understood the desire of the long-tormented masses for some ideal adequate to their sufferings, they could have won them or some of them. But as Georges Bernanos was to stress, mere victory, mere military security, important as they were, were not enough. Only great, perhaps impossible, hopes could excite the people.

These hopes were being provided. The French Socialists had taken no part in the Clemenceau Ministry; they did not expect its success and were to some extent discredited by victory. The loss of Jaurès was bitterly felt; the new leader of the party, the elegant, cultivated, courageous Jewish lawyer, Léon Blum, was no adequate substitute. The leaders of the trade unions could not simply break off relations with the chief employer of so many of the workers. Jouhaux had to do business with Clemenceau and he got some important concessions, the adoption of the eight-hour day and the 'English week', that is, the prohibition of Sunday work (no longer was this a clerical trick) and the Saturday half-holiday.

But the French workers had hopes that soared far above details like this. There was an ominous riot in Paris on May Day, 1919. A Left zealot had shot and badly wounded the Prime Minister and the toxins of the Bolshevik Revolution were beginning to enter the French blood-stream. For the Bolsheviks had made a reality of the French workers' dream. Their seizure of power had far outlasted the Commune. They were being assailed by capitalist armies, among them the French. Where were the traditions of '93? Obviously with the Bolsheviks. So there was a great clamour of welcome at the news that sailors in the French Black Sea fleet, under the leadership of a warrant officer, André Marty, had mutinied. Marty was the son of a Catalan refugee who had taken part in the absurd southern parodies of the Commune in 1871. Memories and hopes all worked for the partisans of the new order in Russia. There the dreams of Blanqui had been made a reality. And, a sign of the times, even old libertarian Anarchists, who had resisted all the seductions of State Socialism, succumbed. There was a rush to join the new, victorious party. The capital of the Revolution was no longer Paris but Moscow. The French Socialists had enough men of probity and sense to fight this mass movement, but they lost the battle at the Congress of Tours in 1920. A majority of the French Socialists accepted Bolshevik discipline and took the assets of the old party, including the party paper, *Humanité*, 'founded by Jean Jaurès' as it proudly boasted, into the Russian camp. Jouhaux fought a more successful battle in the C.G.T. There were now two trade union federations, engaged in an internecine struggle in which the war gains in numbers, discipline and confidence were lost. Unsuccessful strikes reinforced the lesson. Either there would be no profound transformation of French life or it would be brought about by slavish imitation of the 'masters of them that know' in Moscow, men like Zinoviev and Bukharin who preached to a soft-necked generation.

It was not only the militant workers who believed that a profound transformation must come. There was a rush of converts to Catholicism, a rush that provoked the irony of André Gide; and, indeed, the conversion of Jacques Cocteau was amusing and that of Maurice Sachs scandalous. But there were more impressive converts than these; the Church knew a new and profitable birth of freedom. Ways of protest against the world that had produced the war and sterilized the victory took many forms. From Zurich, 'Dadaism' came to France with prophets like Tristan Tzara and André Breton ready to upset the bourgeoisie much more profoundly than had Théophile Gautier. The atmosphere of 'Le Bœuf sur le Toit' was less naïvely 'artistic' than that of its predecessor 'Le Lapin Agile'. Young poets, painters, exhibitionists, playboys joined the new movement, applauded its scandals and its outrages against bourgeois sentiments, morals and patriotism. Some of the playboys were simply playboys, some like Louis Aragon and Paul Eluard were, to use the symbol of another generation, 'waiting for Godot'. They, too, were to find him in Moscow.

The seekers were not only French. Nor were the teachers. The bewildered sought enlightenment from Gurdjieff in the forest of Fontainebleau, some remained faithful to the doctrines of Henri Bergson still dazzling in the public lectures of the Collège de France. Sophists from all the world, like Hermann Keyserling, came to peddle their wares in Paris, for if the consolations of philosophy were, materially speaking, more visible in New York, the Paris cachet was still envied and still marketable. France even exported her own sophists, giving the United States the boom philosophy of Émile Coué. To Paris, too, came seekers for more serious wisdom and the French were still ready to go to school to their most formidable neighbour.

In vain the Nationalist doctors had protested against the infatuation with Germanic thought. It had remained constant all through the triumphant years of the Third Republic. Kant was the official philosopher of the University but there were devotees of Schopenhauer (Flaubert was exceptionally eclectic in admiring both Schopenhauer and Herbert Spencer). The fame of Nietzsche grew but, above all, the fame of Hegel grew. These philosophical tastes were far from being unimportant in a country where the males of the ruling classes had all been subjected to some philosophical education. There were grumblers against this system, men who agreed with Littré that the main result was to give the young Frenchman a sense of knowing a lot in general without knowing anything in particular. Others, like Barrès, saw in the official philosophical teaching of the regime one of the causes of the separation of the French intellectuals from their national tradition. But the 'class of philosophy' was still the coping stone of French secondary education.

It had its limitations. The French philosophers, at that level, seemed to foreign critics curiously incurious and old-fashioned. They used talismanic words like 'the Cartesian spirit'; they knew of the philosophical revolution made by Kant; they were more and more influenced by the methodology of Hegel. But of the Viennese analytical school, of American instrumentalism, of Russell and Whitehead, of Moore, even of the Italian neo-Hegelians, they knew nothing. They were ready, that is to say, for an uncritical acceptance of Marxism, and German philosophy knew a domination that would have startled Albertus Magnus or Leibniz. Freud, like Marx, was a new force. He did not win so many and so uncritical disciples as in America or even England, but in France, as in England and America, he undermined the old order of rational ideas and traditional morals more effectively than did 'Dada' or Surrealism which he explained in too intelligible terms. He provided the vocabulary for new myths and re-made old ones. Oedipus was reborn if the 'complex of Philemon' was still in embryo.

If in the strictly intellectual sphere the dominant ideas were those that came from the Germanic world, the eyes of France were turned to two remote and deeply alien societies. No one could deny the impact of American power. And it was not merely the material power of the new society personified by Henry Ford that counted; there were the 'American way of life', 'jazz', an alleged freedom and equality between the sexes that was unknown to French tradition, Catholic and Voltairian alike. What that life meant was, so the French believed, demonstrated in all its necessary philistinism in the novels of Sinclair Lewis and the lesson was driven home by the American expatriates who poured into Paris, to attend the salon of Miss Gertrude Stein, a Philadelphian Mallarmé, to live freely and cheaply in Giverny or on the Left Bank, and to preach to gratified listeners the doctrine that in America:

> 'Things are in the saddle
> and rule mankind.'

The Soviet Union was seen in a more hopeful light. The very completeness of its rejection of bourgeois values appealed; it was doing what the French Left had so long talked of doing, re-making society, carrying on the programme of 'the Revolution'. True, there were odd things about the new order. Old-fashioned French politicians, only too anxious to keep to the Left, were astounded when told by the exigent Bolsheviks that they must cease to be Freemasons. The dictatorial tone of the legates of the new Church offended some; the sight of the new Rome shocked others. But the old principle of 'no enemies on the Left' still applied. Socialists drifted into the new party; congenitally foolish politicians like Marcel Cachin were welcomed as complacent figureheads. Such traditional intellectual ornaments of the Left as Anatole France and Romain Rolland gave their blessing, one with his accustomed frivolity, the other with his accustomed smugness. And for the first time, Marxism became a serious intellectual force. The Germanic bias of French philosophical education told; the feebleness of French economic teaching, the lack of respect for crude and inconvenient fact, told; the resentment at the sterility of post-war society and the retardation of the French economy told. The clue to what was wrong with France and what needed to be done was to be found in Marx. Popular potted versions of Marx had long known some success (but the French workers were much less serious political readers than the English workers). There were fanatical Marxists like Jules Guesde; there were learned Marxists like 'Bracke', the great Hellenist. But Jaurès, Sembat, Blum were far from being orthodox Marxists. Jaurès, indeed, was deeply if unconsciously an anti-Marxist. But times were changed. Marxism became a powerful orthodoxy, 'Marxism-Leninism' a guide to action. Sorel, reflecting the temper of the times, had written a 'plea for Lenin'. Such pleas were soon unnecessary.

The proof was seen in the reconsideration of the French Revolution. It was no longer a question of reaction betraying Robespierre at Thermidor. Was not Robespierre himself a traitor to the embattled workers? An old-fashioned Jacobin historian like Mathiez was almost as much out of date as Aulard. The great days that shook the world were not in Paris in 1789 or 1792 or even in 1871, but in Petrograd in 1917. There were old-fashioned Left politicians like M. Paul-Boncour who still cast themselves as Robespierre, as a generation before Floquet had cast himself as Danton, but their histrionics were the object of mockery now. French umbilical contemplation was replaced by reverent and soon servile imitation of the triumphant Bolshevik Party of the Soviet Union. The day of complete idolatry had not yet come but was at hand.

II

There was not much in the performance of the 'Bloc National' to provide an alternative doctrine. The simple-minded Deputies, elected by accident, were at a loss. Why had victory proved so barren and so expensive? The sad truth was hidden by special budget devices in which lavish expenditure was chalked up against future German receipts. The Government, by law, limited the advances of the Bank of France. But the franc kept falling; the Germans kept on not paying; the breach with England grew wider; the withdrawal of the United States from the world it had made, more visibly permanent and complete. There were moments of triumph. The westward sweep of the Red Army was halted outside Warsaw in a victory which the French, though not the Poles, attributed to the presence of General Weygand. A series of alliances, with Belgium, with Poland, with Rumania, with Czechoslovakia was a substitute, if a poor one, for the disowned Anglo-American guarantee. If the Second *Reich* was not paying, it was also in serious trouble. There were Communist conspiracies; there were army conspiracies: these showed that Germany was unrepentant, dangerous and divided. Perhaps it could be divided further? For in the new majority many clung to the illusion that German unity was fictitious, could be undone. Nationalists themselves, the French Right stubbornly refused to admit that German nationalism was as passionate and at least as deep as French nationalism. It was folly to hark back (with the *Action Française*) to the Treaty of Westphalia, folly, if less obvious folly, to hark back with Barrès to the days of the Confederation of the Rhine. Germany 'one and indivisible' had come to stay.

The shrewder French diplomats knew this. They discouraged the hopes put in the Rhineland separatists patronized by soldiers like Mangin. They did not even put much hope in one of the few tangible gains made by France in the peace settlement. The Saar coal basin had been detached from Prussia and Bavaria and made into an autonomous territory under French protection and inside the French customs system. The lucky Saarlanders escaped the burdens laid on the Germans and also the burdens, like conscription, that France laid on the liberated Alsatians. Their local autonomy and culture were left unmolested. After fifteen years, they could decide, by plebiscite, whether they wished this status to continue, whether they wished to join France or whether they wished to rejoin Germany. There were fond and foolish hopes in some French breasts. They reflected, irrelevantly, that but for the Hundred Days the Saar would have remained French as it has been for a generation. They reflected that Saarlouis bore the fleur-de-lis on its coat of arms, a memorial of the rule of Louis XIV. They ignored the century of German rule, the inevitable cultural attachments that ensued, the power of the Bishops of Speyer (Spires) and Trier (Trèves). The real gain for France was not a problematic victory in a plebiscite, but the ownership of the Saar coal-mines, transferred as compensation for the destruction of French mines by the Germans. The Saar coalfield was not a first-class prize, but it was a great deal better than nothing. The whole Lorraine iron-field was now in French hands; the Saar was a useful auxiliary to its functioning.

It was not the only French prize of war (the recovery of Alsace-Lorraine was regarded as simple justice). France got her share of the German colonies in Africa although the only valuable one, Tanganyika, went, except for a small area given to Belgium, to Britain which had conquered it. But Syria, which many Englishmen thought they had conquered and which some others thought the Arabs and Colonel Lawrence had conquered, went to France. This was the result of a bargain made in war time when the Allies were dividing up Turkey and when the chief gainer, on paper, was imperial Russia. Arrangements that had seemed sensible to British officials then seemed absurdly generous to France when the Russian threat disappeared with the Tsar. But the bargain was kept. France got the mandate for 'Syria', that is Syria proper and the Lebanon. But what all Arabs thought a part and, perhaps, the heart of Syria, Palestine, was given to Britain as a mandate, and one object of the mandatory power was to make in Palestine a 'national home' for Jews of the world. English Arab experts noted how unpopular was French rule in Syria; French experts noted how detested was British protection of the Jews in Palestine. Each hoped to benefit by the unpopularity of the other and the agents of the victors intrigued with a tenacity and bad faith of which M. Pierre Benoît's *La Châtelaine du Liban* gives only a slightly exaggerated picture.

'Syria' was not the only spot where French and British policies and personalities clashed. Mr. Lloyd George, for various reasons, was an uncritical backer of the Greeks in their war to take over the Ionian coast from the defeated and, it was assumed, helpless Turks. The effort proved a new Syracusan expedition. Mustafa Kemal whom Balfour, chief author of British Palestine policy, called, with characteristic infelicity, a 'bandit', re-created a militant Turkish state. The French saw the light and did a deal with the formidable neighbour on the northern border of Syria. The Greeks were swept into the sea, Mr. Lloyd George was swept out of office, and Anglo-French relations reached a new low level.

But there were more serious grounds of conflict than squabbles on the edge of empire. The European policies of the two victors were at complete cross-purposes. It was the British conviction that French reparations policy was unrealistic and a danger to European order; the British were right. It was the French conviction (also right) that the British view, that Germany was not, could not be dangerous, that the main European problem was the restoration of the old economic order that had profited Britain so greatly, was wrong and revealed an indifference to the just claim that Germany should undo the damage she had done. Bold British analogies which suggested that unemployment in Britain was the equivalent of the destruction of Albert or of the great scar that still ran across France were not well received. It was time to call a halt; to make the Germans pay, to take security that they would. The task fell to Raymond Poincaré.

The new Chamber had used up a series of professional politicians with none of whom was it really in sympathy. The President that the old Parliament had chosen over Clemenceau had rapidly proved to be mad, and Millerand had been chosen to succeed him. His Socialist and Dreyfusard past was almost forgiven. He was sound on Germany and he was sound on Russia. Had he not, when all the world could see that the Bolsheviks had come to stay, recognized Wrangel, most forlorn of white hopes, as the government of Russia? Millerand was sound but he was in the Elysée. It had to be Poincaré, the rigid, competent, courageous company lawyer, released from the fetters of presidential office, spokesman of the policy of disregarding British objections and seizing the German treasure house, the Ruhr. The new British Prime Minister, Bonar Law, tried to avert the breach; he offered a severely qualified renewal of the abortive guarantee of 1919. Poincaré refused, and his majority warmly approved, for the traditional Anglophobia of the Right was now in full command. French and Belgian troops crossed the Rhine; there was a token party of Italians present to show that the new Prime Minister, Signor Mussolini, was not to be left out of any division of the spoil. The British Government disapproved and the British public did more than disapprove; it strongly supported the Germans. For Britain had found victory even less of a refreshing draught than had France. The old order, the natural, British order of things had not been restored. It must be the fault of the unrealistic, vindictive, selfish French.

The German Government backed up the population of the Ruhr in passive resistance. Managers and men refused to work for the invaders, and in the effort to support the resistance in the Ruhr, the mark finally foundered. So, nearly, did the new German Republic. There were nationalist risings in which, for the first time, the name of Adolf Hitler was news. There were Communist risings which, naturally, intelligent people took more seriously. The struggle both exhausted Germany and disillusioned France. The trickle of coal from the Ruhr became much more than a trickle (and the quick British coal profits ceased). But the operation barely paid its way and the calling-up of reservists that had been necessary was terribly unpopular. The United States Government had to pretend that this was none of its business, but Wall Street knew better; the British Government, now headed by the undogmatic Stanley Baldwin, was worried. Poincaré knew that his operation had been only a limited success. Ramsay MacDonald succeeded Baldwin at the head of the first Labour Government. Peace in Europe, an end to old, meaningless quarrels was his programme, his only programme. All the interested parties had accepted the need for a deal, but it was not Poincaré who had to ratify French abandonment of the belief that Germany 'would pay for the war'. For the French electors had decisively repudiated Poincaré.

There was nothing surprising in his overthrow. The 'Bloc National' had suffered the fate that befell the administrations of Lloyd George and Woodrow Wilson, that had swept away parliamentary government in Italy. Had the electoral law of 1919 not worked so oddly, a Left-wing Chamber would have paid the price of responsibility in 1924. Again, the parallel with the National Assembly of 1871 was close. But the National Assembly was not only a far more competent body than the Chamber of 1919; its task in defeat was simpler than that of the 'horizon blue' Chamber in victory. In its four years of life, the Chamber had done wise as well as foolish things, but it had developed neither leaders nor doctrines. It had promised to make Germany pay; it had not only not done so, but on the eve of the elections it had, at last, accepted the necessity of making France pay; it had drastically raised taxes. In 1919, the electors, not a majority of them but many of them, had genuinely been frightened by the vision of the 'Bolshevik with the knife between his teeth' as the posters of the big-business lobbies showed him. The Bolsheviks had not only taken Russia out of the war at the cost of many, many thousands of French lives; they had defaulted on the Tsarist loans, inflicting far greater losses than Panama. But by 1924, bourgeois and peasant wrath could not be concentrated on the Bolsheviks. The French State, by allowing the franc to decline, was as great a sinner, almost, for it was still thought by the naïve that the franc could be restored to its old, gold rate if the Government really tried. And what was really a Left majority in 1919 was now too big a majority to be cheated by any electoral law in 1924. The loose alliance of the 'Cartel des Gauches' was sure to win. The old political cadres were to be restored to power, the Republic to be in the hands of the Republicans. Poincaré was out; it would soon be Millerand's turn.

It was. For the first demand of the victors was that the President should resign. He had not pretended to be neutral; he had adopted Poincaré's policy. He, too, was condemned. In vain he protested and talked of his legal rights. He could form no Ministry that the new Chamber would accept. He resigned and the presidential office was again cut down to size. The Chamber would rule. The good old days were back.

It was clearer that the electors had voted against the policies of the Bloc National than that they had voted for the policies of the 'Cartel des Gauches'. Many had hopefully voted for a return to 1914; many had voted for 'the Left', as usual; many had voted for a reduction in taxation which the Left candidates had cheerfully promised; many had voted for a new era in which even Germans would be included.

But the problems that had been too much for the Parliament of 1919 soon proved too much for the Parliament of 1924. It was easy to restore martyrs ranging from Caillaux to Marty to freedom and civil rights. It was more difficult to act on the slogan of Pierre Renaudel, 'All the jobs and quick about it'. But it was possible to give the Left some symbolical satisfactions like the burying of Jaurès in the Pantheon, like the national canonization of Anatole France. It also seemed easy to satisfy the militant anti-clericals who had much to complain of.

Émile Combes, during the war, had expressed dire fears that the spirit of the 'sacred union', the return of the exiled priests to serve France, would weaken the rigorous application of the lay laws. It had. Monks, friars, even Jesuits were back in France and were tolerated. If there was one doctrine that the new spirits of the age had no use for in politics, art, philosophy, it was the old-fashioned anti-clericalism of M. Homais. But these changes in doctrine had not yet penetrated the minds of the thinkers of the Café du Commerce in Gonfle-Bonfigue. So it was proposed to withdraw the Ambassador from the Vatican where one had been sent during the war; it was proposed to keep a vigilant eye on the religious orders, to refuse all legal authorization for their existence. And it was proposed to put an end to the crying scandal of the failure to apply the laws of the Republic in Alsace-Lorraine.

The recovery of the lost provinces had been the most tangible material and physical gain of the Treaty of Versailles. The crime of 1871 was expunged. But disillusionment soon set in, on both sides of the Vosges. Alsace and France had both changed a great deal in nearly fifty years. Most Alsatians were now products of the German educational system. Alsace had been bilingual in 1870; it was nearly monolingual in 1918. The 'dialect' might be bad German; it was; but it was a German dialect. It was not a mere dying *patois*. And across the Rhine was a culture and an economy with which Alsace had been increasingly integrated. There had been a serious emigration, especially of the bourgeoisie, into France; they had been replaced in Alsace, and still more in Lorraine, by German immigrants. Then, it had become more and more evident that Alsace would not be returned to France except after a great European war. From 1900 on, especially after anti-militarism triumphed in France, it was a forlorn hope to think of France's undoing the Treaty of Frankfort. Both Alsatians and Frenchmen showed, by their acceptance of this situation, that Aesop was right: 'There is no name with whatever emphasis of passionate love repeated, of which the echo is not faint at last.' It was an open question whether it was not the duty of a Francophile Alsatian of the upper classes to accept German rule so that he might serve the interests of Franco-Alsatian culture and tradition. This was the theme of Barrès's novel that scandalized the simple. To enter German service was one way to serve Alsace. René Bazin might write a more naïve novel on the opposite side, but Les Oberlé was to Au Service de l'Allemagne as Bazin was to Barrès.

Of course, all the old links did not break. In towns like Colmar, the jail got the name of the Hôtel-de-France. Hansi still made fun of the German officials who collaborated with him as was their wont. The brutality of the German officers in Saverne (Zabern) created a scandal in Germany as well as in France on the eve of the war. Alsace had been too thoroughly Frenchified, especially by the Revolution, to make a docile German province. There was nostalgia in plenty for the old union of Alsace and France. It was after reading an article by one of the most eminent exiled Alsatians, Pastor Marc Boegner, that Albert Schweitzer decided to offer his services to the Paris Missionary Society; it was to get away from the prosperous, stifling Germanized life of Mulhouse that the young Jean Schlumberger escaped to Paris to join the infant Nouvelle Revue Française. During the war, Joffre promised that all Alsatian rights would be preserved, while the rightfully distrustful Germans, by their severity, undid what good an increasingly liberal policy had done them. There was a brief moment of honeymoon delirium in 1918 but the realities of marriage, or remarriage, proved chilling.

At first, the French Government showed a sense of realities. There was no immediate assimilation of the three recovered departments to France. Millerand, as High Commissioner, showed tact as well as skill. The University of Strasbourg, one of the chief instruments of the cultural Germanization of the province, was promised special treatment. Very eminent Alsatian scholars came back from Paris to reinforce the Alsatian teachers, while the numerous German

professors were summarily expelled. Above all, the Concordat was
not tampered with. Priests, ministers, rabbis were paid by the State;
all schools were 'confessional'. But toleration of this kind was not
enough. Alsace had to rebuild communications with France. The
Germans had naturally seen that all transport was orientated towards
Germany. Even in 1870, the Vosges had been a formidable barrier.
France set about building roads, tunnels, canals, but the improvement
of communications would take time. Under the Germans, the
'Reichsland' had had far more autonomy than any French department was allowed. Now there were three departments with, after
the ending of the High Commissariat, no common centre for their
common interests. Strasbourg sank from being a regional capital to
being a mere 'chef lieu'. Even the University began to suffer from
the pressure for uniformity. Not all of its teachers or students were
convinced that it gained by this assimilation to the French pattern.
And the local administration was more and more flooded by new-
comers, often speaking no German, convinced that the departments
of the Upper and Lower Rhine were like the Upper and Lower
Charente. If not, why not in the one indivisible Republic?

The new Ministry soon found out. It was headed by an eminent
'universitaire', almost the only eminent 'universitaire' in politics
that the Radical party could now boast of. M. Édouard Herriot had
been and was a reforming Mayor of Lyons. He knew something of
British local government. He was convinced that he could get along
well with the new British Prime Minister, Ramsay MacDonald,
and, indeed, they had many things in common. But Herriot was a
Normalien with some of the prejudices of his type. He decided (he had
to) to impose the full rigour of the lay laws in Alsace and, with a
revealing lack of tact, he announced this in a letter to M. Léon Blum,
the leader of the Socialist party, himself of Alsatian Jewish origin.
And Alsace was the only part of France where anti-Semitism was
deep and widespread. Within a few weeks, Alsace was in an uproar
and there seemed some danger that the recovered province would be
as hostile to France as it had long been to Germany. The preachers of
the full lay doctrine were mostly 'universitaires'. Some were Alsatians like M. Charles Andler who believed or, at any rate, said that
nothing was in question but the greed of Alsatian priests who wanted

their salaries. He did not ask himself why Alsatian peasants and even workers sided with the priests. He forgot that, in Alsace, the priests had been the agents of resistance to Germanization. He even ignored the possibility that not all the results of French laicity were universally admired.

The Cartel might have carried out its anti-clerical policy if it had had a successful financial policy to offer. All it had was rhetoric. Not all of the rhetoric was irrelevant. The Bloc National had most certainly not made Germany pay. It had, in effect, robbed the public creditors. If France had had a more effective tax system, much trouble would have been avoided. But the sad fact remained that the costs of reconstruction which still continued could be met only by borrowing, that the constant deficits had meant continued pressure on the franc. It was of little use, in the long run, to shake out mere speculators by counter-raids, although Poincaré had done that. The main cause of the weakness of the franc was the budget deficit, and that deficit could be cured only by economy and high taxation which, given the primitive character of French public finance, even with the new income tax, was bound to fall harshly on the poor. But the poor were also great holders of Government securities; many of them had been holders of Russian securities; many were prudent men who had not turned their gold over to the Bank of France in 1914 and had less intention than ever of doing so. If the Herriot Government had dared to tell the French people, in 1924, that the franc could never be restored to the old parity; that Germany, no matter what was done, could repay only part of the damage she had wrought, that France would have to pay and pay in high taxes, the Cartel might have survived. But the Cartel was tied by doctrines and by electoral promises.

There was a great deal in the Socialist criticism that France needed a profound structural change, especially in the field of public finance. But the Socialists had not converted their Radical allies to that point of view. The Radicals had no doctrine of public finance; politics had, for them, a mainly verbal 'ideological' content. Great economic issues were not the matter of politics; politics was the field in which the mere voter consoled himself for his impotence in great issues of peace, war and economics. Such was the doctrine of 'Alain', a stimulating secondary-school teacher of philosophy whose not very ingenious sophisms were much admired. His prestige was of the kind that 'predicts the ruin of the State'. At any rate, it predicted the ruin of the Cartel. All expedients were tried, even the use of the magic name of Caillaux. But the magic had evaporated from the name of the great 'technician'. The parliamentarians found out how little power they had. They had alienated the Catholics and the Catholics had ideological as well as sound financial reasons for not lending money to the increasingly bewildered Finance Ministers whose re-assuring oratory simply drove the franc further down the slippery slope where the German mark had gone. The voter, the Left voter, even the lay voter had had enough. Poincaré was called in. The Left panaceas were scrapped. Confidence, at all costs, was to be restored. If that meant abandoning the enforcement of the lay laws in France, that could not be helped; if it meant leaving the *status quo* in Alsace intact, that could not be helped; if it meant enduring the leadership of the dry, unsympathetic, imperfectly ideological corporation lawyer who had been driven out of office so triumphantly in 1924, that could not be helped, at least until the franc was stabilized.

This was done, in effect, long before it was done legally. The franc was finally defined in terms of gold at a fifth of its pre-war value. Four-fifths of French savings in Government securities were sacri-ficed. Thus France paid for reconstruction. Good patriots were em-bittered, with reason, but most *rentiers* were glad to save anything. The Left parties were shocked and embittered. The small but grow-ing Communist party rejoiced. The Socialists learned that, at the last moment, their Radical allies would refuse to join in a desperate assault on the 'wall of money'. All parties learned, or thought they learned, that the one thing that could upset the political apple cart was a threat to the franc.

The collapse of the Cartel was so ludicrous that its real achieve-ments were overlooked. Although the bases of the settlement of the German reparations question had been laid before Herriot came into office, it was while he was in office that the Dawes plan went through. With the benevolent neutrality of Washington, Germany was lent enough money to stabilize her currency and then to begin to pay reparations. Germany did begin to repair some of the damage she had done. Ramsay MacDonald and Édouard Herriot in the Geneva protocol of 1924 proposed a scheme of mutual guarantees that did, in part, replace the guarantee repudiated in 1919. The new Conservative Government in England refused to ratify the protocol, but it was now convinced that it must do something to stabilize the political situation in western Europe. The French Left, too, had found a diplomatic symbol to offset the Right financial symbol of Poincaré: Aristide Briand was permanent Foreign Minister. And he symbolized what the French people wanted more than anything else, peace.

While he was Foreign Minister, so Briand asserted, there would be no war. It was not only in France that he was believed. He was a great and much admired public figure in England, America, even Germany. His greatest triumph was the Locarno agreement with his partners, Stresemann and Austen Chamberlain. There, it was thought, the war was finally liquidated. Germany was to be admitted to the League of Nations in return for accepting the western territorial settlement as a free bargain, not as part of a 'Diktat'. France was to guarantee Germany and Germany France against invasion, and Britain was to guarantee both. For the moment, the gain was Germany's; soon it would be France's, for it was impossible to believe that Germany would upset the *status quo* in face of British intervention. And the most important part of the *status quo* was the demilitarized state of the Rhineland. As long as the Germans could not fortify or even occupy the Rhineland with armed forces, any war would begin by being fought in Germany. Since only Germany had any interest in starting a war and since she had no interest in starting a war in these conditions, peace was secure. It would be safe to anticipate the evacuation of the Rhineland by the Allied armies; this would soothe German *amour propre* without endangering French security. Negotiations to put the agreements into effect did not always move perfectly smoothly. There were those who wondered whether Stresemann was as devoted to peace as Briand, but the 'spirit of Locarno' was too precious to be allowed to wither under such criticism. Old-fashioned French Nationalists, old-fashioned French soldiers might lament that real security was being bargained away for mere paper guarantees. But who could doubt the good faith of Britain? Was that not guarantee enough? Into this world of illusion came a reinforcing wave of illusion from the new world.

What had begun as an innocent exchange of pledges between France and the United States became the 'Kellogg Pact' by which all important States renounced war as an instrument of national policy. The United States, which had abolished the evils of drink by the eighteenth amendment, invited the world to abolish war by taking the pledge. The world, not quite daring to believe or doubt, obeyed.

To the French, there seemed good reason for confidence. At last Germany was paying some reparations (reparations financed out of American loans to Germany). The immense task of reconstruction was completed. In 1919, it had been easy to despair of ever restoring northern France to its pristine prosperity. But the job had been done. Peasant obstinacy had prevented a rebuilding of the wrecked farms and villages on more modern lines or in more suitable locations. Even the town dwellers insisted on restoring the nineteenth-century errors and horrors of town planning. But Lens and Bapaume rose again; only the great cemeteries and war memorials reminded tourists of the so recent horrors. Only at Verdun in the great ossuary, the greatest military charnel house in history, was the memory of the past kept alive in the form of the famous and delusive slogan: 'Ils ne passeront pas.' If the greater part of French capital expenditure went simply to restoring what had existed in 1914, the need for replacing the wreckage of war had resulted in the modernization of much French industrial equipment. The dispersion of industry that had been imposed by the needs of war production was not undone, the more that the rapid development of France's great resources in 'white coal' (hydro-electric power) did much to limit her dependence on imported fuel and made hitherto poor areas in the south and in the Massif Central economically important. Alsace was effectually joined to the rest of France. The great port of Marseilles had definitely outdistanced Genoa; a tunnel driven through a mountain made the great lagoon of the Étang de Berre available to relieve the congestion in the port. The shift in passenger traffic from emigration (cut to a trickle by the United States) to tourist trade gave the French Atlantic ports, above all the rebuilt passenger port of Cherbourg, a new importance.

For more than ever, tourist services were France's greatest invisible export. Not only had Paris retained or augmented all her old prestige, but the Riviera triumphed easily over upstart rivals like the

Lido. The summer season paid even better than the traditional winter season, and Eden Roc and the Rock Pool both helped the French balance of payments. So did the attractions of Paris. Pessimists noted that some of the old French attractions had been replaced by imports. In the adopted city of Offenbach, the greatest success of the light musical stage was an innocuous American importation, *Rose Marie*. If the theatre was still one of the glories of Paris, it was the theatre not the plays, the directors, the producers, the Atelier, the Vieux Colombier, Jacques Copeau, the 'Quinze' and Michel Saint-Denis, who impressed the sophisticated. In the firmament of the world theatre it had long been true that France did not shine with her old splendour. Brieux and Becque, even Cocteau, were pale beside Shaw, Strindberg, Pirandello, O'Neil, Brecht. Bernstein and Sacha Guitry were not an adequate offset. The renascence of the Paris stage was to be the glory of another republic. But in the meantime, there was the film. In Lumière, France could claim to have produced one of its parents, and in René Clair's *Chapeau de Paille* the modern equivalent of Meilhac and Halévy. In music, 'Les Six' maintained the prestige won by Debussy and Fauré. Ravel in 'Bolero' provided marginal middle-brows with an equivalent of Dvorak's most popular efforts. In France, the French—and their guests—could rejoice in

'le vierge, le vivace et le bel aujourdhui'.

The feeling, perhaps the illusion of well-being was not confined to the mother-country. 'France Overseas' shared in it. In the war, the Empire had contributed lavishly in men and raw materials; Senegalese, Moroccans, Algerians, even Tonkinese had died in thousands 'for France', or so the French complacently believed. The rigorous methods of vigorous Governors, Doumer, Van Vollenhoven and others, had begun to pay off. Indo-China and French West Africa, even the newly acquired Cameroons, were showing gratifying rewards for the efforts of their rulers. Dakar and Hanoi were ornaments of Empire that would have gladdened the hearts of Faidherbe or Jules Ferry.

But the showpiece was Morocco. When war came in 1914, the French protectorate, not yet three years old, was effective only on the coast and in a few towns like Fez. Hubert Lyautey knew how fragile was the authority he exercised in the name of the Sultan. With nearly all his troops drained off to France, he had to cajole and bluff, he could not coerce. So he bargained with the Berber chiefs of the High Atlas, with such potentates as El Glaoui, the Pasha of Marrakesh. Slowly, the authority of the 'Maghzen', that is of France, was extended over all of the territory allotted to France. Lyautey did all that was possible to conceal the realities behind the fiction of the Sultan's power. The Sultan, a young man, was brought up to respect his masters who professed merely to be his allies. Lyautey did not repeat the mistake made in Indo-China where the authority of the Emperors of Annam and the Kings of Cambodia and Laos had been made ludicrous by the reckless way in which French Governors deposed and appointed the sacred monarchs. It was Lyautey's fixed principle to give real authority and, still more, the appearance of real authority to the indigenous powers of the 'Sherifian Empire'.

Unlike Tunis and Algeria, Morocco was rich and easily exploit-able. Into its empty lands poured French colonists who made fertile farms where the Moors had seen only bad grazing. The village of Casablanca, by bold engineering works, was turned into a great port. The whole world was called on to admire 'Lyautey Africanus'. No one sang his praises more warmly than Kipling. But the political structure was unstable. Spain had been given a portion of the Sherif-ian Empire to administer and in the Riff, in 1921, the Spaniards suffered the greatest defeat a colonial power had suffered in Africa since the Italians were destroyed by the Abyssinians in 1896. Like Adowa, Anual set great forces in motion. The Spaniards, under their new dictator, Primo de Rivera, slowly evacuated their garrisons from the Riff. The victorious Kaid, Abd-el-Krim, over-estimated his power and invaded French Morocco. In what was a great tribute to the Kaid's fame and power, Marshal Pétain was hastily sent to resist him and the too bold chieftain went into exile like a new Abd-el-Kader.

The Riff war ended Lyautey's pro-consulate. The soldier was re-placed by a series of civilian Residents who forgot how much the great Marshal had ruled by tact, by diplomacy, by indirection. French power, it was thought, was established for good. There was no need to wear a mask. Morocco was but a larger Tunis, perhaps even simply a backward Algeria. There, at any rate, French authority was assumed to be secure. To the outward eye, the three Algerian departments were increasingly French. The new Arab bourgeoisie was French in education and often in tastes. The rapid growth in population flattered French rule and the unemployed peasants of Kabylia more and more often emigrated to France where they learned French, were infected by ideas that made them discontented when they returned home, with money carefully saved and often with a new taste for alcohol and carrying the seeds of tuberculosis.

But the only permanently troublesome part of the Empire was the mandated territory of Syria. It was broken up into four sections; united in one; divided into Syria and the Lebanon; it was still sullen. A vigorous policy of public works, carried out chiefly by forced labour, improved the economic assets of the territory but made the mandatory power even more unpopular. The triumphant 'Cartel des Gauches' in 1924 replaced the openly Catholic and, it was thought, secretly Royalist General Weygand, by the one reliable Republican general, the friend of the martyred Caillaux, Sarrail. It was his third chance, but the military idol of the Masonic lodges was again unlucky. He found himself forced to kidnap some rebellious chiefs and to bombard Damascus, actions not much in keeping with a favourite of the 'League of the Rights of Man and of the Citizen'. Sarrail was removed; this time for good, and Syria sank into a sullen peace.

III

In France, a state of political euphoria prevailed. The Radicals had broken with Poincaré as soon as the franc was safe, but the old political games seemed hardly worth playing. Millerand had been succeeded, not by the official candidate of the Left, the mathematical politician, Painlevé, but by Doumergue, a politician whose jolliness belied his Calvinist origins. It was this Protestant President of the Republic who, inducted by proxy as a Canon of St. John Lateran (a benefice traditionally held by the head of the French State), symbolized that triumph of the 'Ralliement' for which Leo XIII had laboured. All but the most fanatical priest-eating politicians of the Midi or the most jealous functionaries of the rival church, 'the University', were tired of the Church and State quarrel. The returned orders were unmolested; Dominicans and Jesuits walked the streets openly. The Pope, canonizing Joan of Arc and Theresa of Lisieux, paid homage to the traditional French fertility in sanctity. The much debated question of the maintenance of the churches and cathedrals, left in the air at the time of the Separation, was quietly settled on lines that showed that Pius XI was not as intransigent as Pius X. He gave proof that he differed in other ways.

On the eve of the war of 1914, the theologians of the Holy See reported on the doctrines of the Action Française. They condemned them, not unnaturally, for there were few less naturally Christian souls in France than Charles Maurras and few political doctrines less tainted with Christian ethics. But Pius X loved Maurras for the enemies he had made and the Pope kept the censure secret. In the ferment of ideas that followed the end of the war, the Action Française was at a loss. No one could seriously believe, now, in the solution of the restoration of the House of France. The Republic had survived the war. It was the traditionalist monarchies that had perished. And when 'reaction' scored its first triumph in the Fascist Revolution in Italy, parodied by the new dictatorship in Spain, it took all Maurras's dialectical talents to squeeze Mussolini and Primo de Rivera inside his doctrine. Many of the young still followed his lead, but the great days of the movement were over. Nor were the relations of its chiefs with the new Pretender, the Duc de Guise, good. The faithful might believe all that they read in the daily jeremiads of the newspaper, but as a political force, the movement was in the doldrums.

It had now to withstand the blow of a papal condemnation that not only put the works of Maurras but the newspaper itself, for the future as well as for the past, on the Index. The most eminent of French Jesuits, Cardinal Billot, who had resisted the papal policy, was forced to resign the purple and, all over France, hundreds of simple and devoted souls were refused the sacraments because they clung to the Maurrasian heresy. The quarrel reminded the literate of the endless and unedifying quarrel over the Bull *Unigenitus* and, naturally, men and women who had defied the Pope, for whatever reason, got sympathy from anti-clerical journals like *Le Canard Enchaîné*. After all, had not Daudet, in addition to resisting the Pope, secured the Prix Goncourt for the long novel of his rich, hypochondriac, half-Jewish friend, Marcel Proust? To have spotted the merits of *À l'Ombre des Jeunes Filles en Fleurs* covered many sins.

Not for the Pope; he was unshakable. All French bishops, whatever they thought, submitted. Lavigerie was justified—and avenged —at last. The 'Ralliement' was complete; Church and State were separate but no longer enemies. It was a world in which that guardian of the Radical conscience, M. Albert Bayet, and that priest of the old high-and-dry literary and philosophical criticism of *Le Temps*, M. Paul Souday, were not at home.

But if the relations between the two traditional rival powers were peaceful, it was perhaps because the two powers had each its own problems and some common problems. The Pope could order obedience to the Republic, but in departments like the Ardèche, where the existence of a large, tenacious and long-memoried Protestant minority kept Catholics and Protestants alike full of politico-religious zeal, the truce was effective only on the surface. Elsewhere, most of the junior clergy had been converted to a vague Christian Socialism; the seminarists were disciples of Marc Sangnier or readers of the little Christian Democratic party's organ, *L'Aube*, more ready to follow M. Champetier de Ribes or M. Georges Bidault than Maurras. But the more intelligent seminarists, like the more intelligent priests and bishops, knew how far the de-Christianization of France had gone. It was no longer even true that the town workers were at least baptized, married, and buried in or from a church. The vague, intermittent, ritualistic Catholicism that Péguy had known in Orléans was almost dead. In Orléans, in Limoges, above all, in the Paris suburbs, Catholics were a small minority and outside the living community of the political church to which so many of the workers belonged.

For the Communist party was steadily growing. And it was a party of a kind France had never known. It was one of the unadmitted grievances of the old-fashioned Radical, the old-fashioned Socialist, that the Church with its Sisters of Charity, its Conferences of Saint

Vincent de Paul, its teaching and nursing orders, its Catholic boy scouts, its holiday camps, its 'patronages', the support given to all these activities by great Catholic industrialists like the Michelin family, had an unfair advantage over the secular parties that offered nothing but political banquets and an occasional procession, that left the provision for all the non-political emergencies of life to the State—or to the Church.

One successful activity of the Church presented its own and a new problem. Catholic employers and zealous 'social priests' had founded or encouraged the founding of 'Christian' trade unions. These had long been feeble creatures, busy in minor good works or regarded, with much justice, by the regular unions, as 'yellow', as company unions. But they had come of age. Wise priests, if not wise employers, had seen that they could have no real life if they were not independent, like the German Catholic unions, and that meant that they must be free to act against Catholic employers and against the advice of bishops and priests. They were especially strong in the north, where they enrolled substantial numbers of textile workers and even of miners, and in the Parisian region where they competed with some success with unions of Socialist tendency for the allegiance of clerical workers, especially women. They developed in their members a new class consciousness, even if it was a Catholic class consciousness, and angered 'social Catholics' of the old school for whom Leo XIII's *Rerum Novarum* had had a very different meaning. And these fears were magnified when it was found, as it was found more than once, that Catholic and Communist unions acted together in specific disputes. Many a Catholic employer denounced the 'demagogy' of union leaders and of their clerical allies, but the Communists, if not the Catholics, had nothing to fear from such collaboration.

The Communists could compete with the Church on its own ground better than it could compete with them. They had created a complete range of social organizations, surpassing the Catholic in completeness, in discipline and in zeal. The child of Communist parents could grow up in a social world dominated by the Party as no Catholic child, even in La Vendée or the Haute-Loire, could grow up in a world dominated by the Church. A boy entering the Jeunesses

Communistes was, in a sense, doing what a Catholic boy did on entering not a religious society for laymen but a religious order like the Jesuits. And the old charge, that the Jesuits gave to their superiors a blind obedience, 'sicut cadaver', was true of the converts to the Party. All over the industrial areas, the Party grew, and with it its web of auxiliary societies. Although France had welcomed the Swiss architect, Le Corbusier, the French State had not done much to encourage the new styles. There was a symbol to be seen in the new modernistic churches that Cardinal Verdier sowed in the Paris 'red suburbs' and the modernistic buildings of Drancy and Villeurbanne put up by Communist municipalities.

But it was not only in the industrial areas that the Communists made progress. There was plenty of discontent in the countryside. Six hundred thousand farm workers had perished in the war and had not been replaced, at least not by Frenchmen. Prosperous landowners could buy machinery and thus fill the gaps but a poor widow or old peasant father could not. A great deal of land went out of cultivation or went over to pasture. The great fall in land values that had depressed the economy of the Third Republic had reached rock bottom around 1890. But mere ownership was never again so attractive as it had been under the Second Empire. And in the inflationary boom, land values did not rise in anything like due proportion to the devaluation of the franc. A tenant farmer on a long lease, an owner with a heavy mortgage benefited, but the solvent peasant of 1914, with the traditional stocking full of gold 'Napoleons', was replaced, often enough, around 1930, by a peasant with depreciated francs or securities and land that had lost a half of its value. Moreover, the peasant, now linked more than ever with the towns by the motor-buses, was conscious of the difference between his way of life and that of the town workers. He might cling to the little plot he had inherited; his son did not. Women had, for a generation before 1914, been drifting away to the towns; the war, by sucking them by the hundreds of thousands into the war factories, had emptied the countryside. In poor departments, like the Ariège, rural life seemed slowly dying. In regions like western Burgundy and the Allier, where forest workers and sharecroppers had plenty of real grievances, the Communists found recruiting easy. Even in independent and fairly prosperous departments, like the Corrèze, more and more peasants voted Communist, even if it was only a way of voting 'Left'.

Sometimes, the 'Communism' of a rural department represented the triumph of the energy of an especially talented leader like Renaud Jean in the Lot-et-Garonne. The return to single-member constituencies ('scrutin de liste') before the election of 1928 gave a false appearance of a check to Communism; thus Renaud Jean was reduced to his newly acquired fief of Marmande. But parallel with the exclusion of the Socialists from the industrial regions round Paris (which had driven Léon Blum to take refuge in the remote constituency of Narbonne), there was a steady Communist infiltration into the countryside. Radical notables saw their power undermined in regions where the Socialists had never been strong and a highly conservative village Mayor, the local and noble squire of a village in the Catholic Haute-Loire, saw, with resigned clarity, that although he would be Mayor as long as he lived, his successor would be a Communist blacksmith. It was ominous that the Socialist party was less and less a party of workers in the great new industries, and more and more a party of white-collar workers and civil servants (including school teachers in that class). It was also ominous that small peasant proprietors were being seduced with the promise that measures of land nationalization would not be applied, against their will, to them. Only 'kulaks' were in danger and 'kulaks' were always other people.

One force aiding the growth of the Communist party, and the increase in the number of its sympathizers, was the semi-foreign character of much of the urban population. Even before 1914, there had been a flow of immigration into France from all the neighbouring countries. After 1918, with the prodigious losses (not only the dead but the crippled and unborn) to be replaced, France became the chief recipient of European migration, the more that the United States had 'closed the gates of mercy' on a great part of mankind, long used to taking the inscription on the Statue of Liberty seriously. By 1930, there were 3,000,000 foreigners in France and millions more of recent immigrant origin. Among these Italians, Poles, Spaniards, Belgians, Kabyles, Communism made many, many easy converts.

Communist propaganda was soon to receive reinforcement from capitalist sources. With the collapse of the New York market, in October 1929, came a new set of 'days that shook the world'. Innocently, the United States had been providing the capital for German and Austrian recovery. Already the drain on liquid capital caused by the extravagant boom on New York had caused stress in Vienna and Berlin. The collapse made a hole in the dyke through which flowed disaster for all the world.

At first, France seemed immune. She had known a long inflationary boom that contrasted agreeably with British stagnation. The fall of the franc had improved her competitive position in world markets and that, in turn, had made the franc a favoured currency. Poincaré had built up a great gold reserve, and prudence or backwardness had kept the French banks out of the maelstrom of speculation into which the high authorities of New York and London had sailed so gaily. The Paris banks preferred the safer profits of financing the loans which the French Republic made to its new allies, Poland, Rumania, Czechoslovakia, or to aiding in the purchase by Schneider-Creusot of a controlling interest in the great Skoda armament works. France was no longer in a position to lend as lavishly as before 1914. This caution seemed to pay. A new arrangement for the financing of German reparations, the Young plan, made, like its predecessor, under unofficial American auspices, left to the Germans the determination of when reparations transfers endangered the mark. In 1931 the Germans declared that the time was now. New York and London, both of which had a great deal to lose in Germany, pleaded with Paris. A few months before, the acidulous Labour Chancellor of the Exchequer, Philip Snowden, had insulted the French Finance Minister. Now he had to plead, desperately, for help to save the pound. The French authorities were in no mood to listen to any further sermons on public finance from Mr. Snowden or Sir Otto Niemeyer. But the Bank of France and the Federal Reserve Bank of New York rallied round; they made lavish advances to the Bank of England to save it from the results of its own folly or greed. In vain; Britain went off gold. The old order, apparently restored after 1918, was dead.

But the most respected leaders of French opinion, the 'experts' of the great banks, drew another lesson from the British collapse.

France must contract out of the ever-deepening crisis and, as the Labour experience, following on the breakdown of the 'Cartel des Gauches', had shown, 'Socialism kills currencies'. Shop windows were plastered with assignats of the Revolution as a lesson to those who might have forgotten the panic summer of 1926. The Left might not believe all this; but enough of their electors did to make it politically suicidal to abandon gold.

The country, however, was moving Left if only on the condition that nothing must be done to weaken the franc. The jovial Doumergue had been succeeded by the grimmer Doumer, and when he was assassinated by a crazed White Russian the National Assembly hastily elected the President of the Senate, Albert Lebrun, as President of the Republic. As was now usual, the victor was the choice of the Right and Centre and, although a former Minister of the pre-war Republic, and a graduate of the École Polytechnique, the new President was openly said to go to mass, not ostentatiously but regularly. This was not the only conversion to moderation. The once revolutionary M. Pierre Laval, after an increasingly profitable career at the bar and in business, had become a very orthodox Prime Minister. He had many of the talents, many of the views, many of the tastes of Briand who had died, broken-hearted, at his defeat for the Presidency. M. Laval was most certainly a man of peace and, while gratifying the Right by the soundness of his financial views (natural enough in a man who had become so rich, so fast, so quietly), he had kept in touch, by tactical necessity and by genuine sympathy, with many old friends on the Left.

But, as was usual at the beginning of a new Parliament, it was necessary to give the Left a run for its money. The first starter was M. Herriot, who fell in 1932, gloriously, in the forlorn hope of trying to persuade a French Parliament to pay interest on its debts to the United States when the President of the United States was pressing France to give up its claims on Germany. No American Congress could afford to see any connection between the two sets of claims, no French Parliament could afford to fail to see their indissoluble connection. What absolute monarchs or the representatives of oligarchies could have done, the representatives of the great democracies could not. Herriot fell; France imitated Germany and the whole fabric of debts and reparations collapsed. It was not all that collapsed. Hitler came into power in Germany on a programme that could only mean war; Roosevelt came into power in America to carry through what turned out to be a highly isolationist policy. The first impact on France came from the American abandonment of gold. From that time on, there was no hope of France's staying on gold. She was the only great power on gold, and the 'gold bloc' that she headed was too weak in productive power to influence the much more potent nations that were 'managing' their currency, Britain, the United States, Germany. From the spring of 1933, French financial and economic policy was directed with a greater and greater strain to maintaining an impossible value for the franc. In that hopeless task, more and more of the authority of the French State was wasted.

One reason for this long, disastrous and doomed rearguard action was the confusion between the situation in 1924 and the situation in 1933. In 1924, the French economy was booming; only the State was insolvent, and that insolvency was due to an easily curable budgetary deficit. In 1933, France, although she had escaped the worst disasters that had befallen more progressive nations like Britain, Germany, and the United States, was at last suffering from the world depression from which the other leading nations were, at last, beginning to recover. The artificially high price of the franc cut down the market for French exports which, mainly luxuries as they were, must have suffered from the general slump. An adverse balance of payments meant continual pressure on the franc, and the only answer of successive French Governments was to cut down imports and, at any cost, balance the budget. So to the high French tariffs were added quotas that made business a lottery and a matter of favour. Unemployment was kept at a low figure, in part because an economy based in large part on peasant-farming like the French was less vulnerable than a highly industrialized economy like the British; also, by not only barring all immigration, but by expelling hundreds of thousands of foreign workers, France exported her unemployment problem to countries suffering badly from unemployment problems of their own.

It was in this dreary task that the Left majority employed itself. To M. Édouard Herriot succeeded M. Édouard Daladier. Like M.

Herriot he was a Normalien. As was usual, he had risen by attacking the conservatism of his chief, and as, unlike M. Herriot, he was silent, some said sullen, he got a reputation for strength of character and sagacity that was soon to be tested. The seizing-up of the French economy inevitably encouraged the parties of violence. For many young Frenchmen like Pierre Hervé in 1932, to enter the active service of the Communist party was to take the only reasonable step in a world in which Fascism was triumphing everywhere, while capitalism was represented by Britain, the United States, and the last agonies of the Weimar Republic. What if one of the most effective knives thrust into the body of the Weimar Republic was Communist? A lunatic like Hitler was not dangerous, was no match for the veteran leaders of the largest Communist party in the world outside Russia. Few then could know that entering the Party was like being branded with the fleur-de-lis as was a convict of the old regime. For the brand of the hammer and sickle burned into the heart and mind of the neophytes. If they tried to escape, they found it more and more difficult to breathe outside the iron lung of the Party. If they did escape, they often had a nostalgia for the safe and ordered Bastille they had left—or for its psychological equivalent.

On the Right, the depression accentuated the discontent of the landowners, the *rentiers*, the small businessmen, affected by dear money and falling demand. The golden days, for some, were before 1914, for others, before 1931; they were gone. Catholics who resented the papal campaign against the Action Française, Royalists who resented the Pretender's flirtations with 'liberalism' and 'socialism', the discontented of all schools who had long admired Mussolini and had begun to have a sneaking respect for Hitler, saw in the flounderings of the parliamentary politicians a condemnation of the regime. Anti-Semites resented the role of Léon Blum as a Socialist leader who condemned and took no responsibilities, and a great many veterans, contemplating France fourteen years after 1918, asked, like General Bonaparte in 1799, what had the politicians done with victory?

There were the materials for an explosion; the match was supplied by a very unimportant minor adventurer on the edge of Parisian low finance. It was an age of great financial scandals. Compared with Ivar Kreuger or some of the sharks of the American bull market,

Serge Stavisky was a minnow. Of Russian Jewish origin (his ancestry had an important part to play in the legend that grew up around him), he dabbled in company promoting, in all forms of gambling, was well but not favourably known to the Ministry of Finance, and had several charges hanging over him in the courts. But no charges were pressed home and it was thought to be obvious that Stavisky had a protector or protectors. So other speculators of the same type had had in the drab financial history of the Third Republic. An excessively optimistic issue of bonds, secured on the meagre assets of the municipal pawnshop of Bayonne, was the immediate cause of Stavisky's downfall. With him came down the Radical Mayor of Bayonne, a Deputy, and soon after fell a Minister of the Republic, M. Dalimier. The *Action Française*, by exposing the links between this 'Métèque' and Deputies and Ministers, suddenly recovered most of its old readers and acquired many new ones. It played the role of *La Libre Parole* in the collapse of Panama. The parallel was completed when Stavisky was found, conveniently slain by his own hand. To the shortsighted, the affair was over.

In reality, it was only beginning. MM. Garat and Dalimier were not the first Deputies and Ministers to be involved in the courts, associated with crooks. There had been a series of scandals, none of them great, all of them depressing. Confronted with the picture of parliamentary politics painted by such opposed but, in this instance, co-operative journals as the *Action Française* and *Humanité*, confronted with the repeated official excuses that these scandals were as nothing compared with Panama or with the career of Ouvrard under Napoleon I, millions of Frenchmen, bewildered by the economic crisis, more and more alarmed by the news from Germany, bemused by the examples of Moscow and Rome, turned from Parliament in disgust. Corrupt, complacent, ineffective, incapable of continuous action, victim of a crook whose very pettiness was an insult, how could the regime last? Who would defend it?

> 'For things like these what decent man
> Would keep his lover waiting,
> Keep his lover waiting?'

The Prime Minister of the fleeting moment was peculiarly unfitted

to answer such a question. M. Camille Chautemps was a hereditary
Minister, what the French crudely call a 'fils à papa'. He had talent,
ambition, sound Republican principles. He was a perfect specimen
of what Robert de Jouvenel had called the 'Republic of Pals'. He
was high in the inner circles of Freemasonry and he had the misfortune to have for a brother-in-law the head of the Paris *parquet*, also a
high-ranking Mason and the official whose office had so conspicuously failed to deal with the late M. Stavisky.

Like Guizot, M. Chautemps relied too confidently on the parliamentary majority that was guaranteed him by his alliance with M.
Léon Blum and the Socialists. But as Jaurès had not been able to
save Combes and André, M. Blum was not able to save M. Chautemps. For Paris was now the scene of daily and nightly rioting. The
'Camelots du Roi', the storm-troopers of the Action Française, were
constantly in ingenious action against the police; they were joined by
various less famous combatant bodies. The Communists naturally
joined in this attack on the regime. M. Chautemps stood firm; there
was to be no parliamentary inquiry into the Stavisky affair. Not only
M. Chautemps said so, but M. Herriot said so. The whole Left
majority and nearly all the governing personnel of the majority
were thus committed. But even M. Chautemps seemed to sense
that this majority was not enough, or perhaps he thought that
the time had com for a dexterous retirement. He resigned and was
replaced by M. Daladier. M. Daladier reduced the crisis, for a moment, to farce. M. Pressard, the negligent brother-in-law, was given
high judicial office; M. Chiappe, the dictatorial Prefect of Police, was
removed; the head of the Sûreté which had not done enough to impede Stavisky, was made head of the Comédie Française, the 'maison
de Molière'. Only Molière could have done justice to the situation.
But the end of farce was at hand.

On February 6, 1934, the new Government at last dared to meet
the Chamber. The session was stormy within, but the real storm was
outside. For to the 'Camelots du Roi', to the 'Francistes', to the
Communists operating on the edges, was added the most formidable
of the ex-servicemen's organizations, the 'Croix de Feu'. Originally
this was an organization of what the Germans called 'front-line'
soldiers. But these had been diluted by all sorts of auxiliaries, until it

was little more a true veterans' organization than the contemporary American Legion. Its chief was a serious, good-looking, not very intelligent professional officer, Colonel de la Rocque, in whom some saw the saviour of France. But the real importance of de la Rocque and of the Croix de Feu was their incarnation of the angry despair with which so many Frenchmen contemplated the regime. It was the Croix de Feu which made the mob that marched across the Pont de la Concorde impressive. The police on duty fired; there were deaths and wounded; the riots spread; if there was any plot to seize the Chamber (it is very unlikely) it had failed. But there was blood on the hands of the Daladier Government. 'Never touch a machine-gun if your hands aren't clean', was the comment of an intelligent Left deputy, M. Gaston Bergery. M. Daladier's hands were clean, but there were enough dirty hands in the Chamber to offset this fact. The Government collapsed. A Paris mob had reversed a parliamentary majority.

The regime was in peril; it fell back on a 'National Government'. The new Prime Minister was Doumergue. But the great strength of the new Government was not the Prime Minister but the new Minister of War, the senior Marshal of France since the death of Foch. It was Philippe Pétain who gave the Government prestige and possibly saved the parliamentary Republic. There was a Government of all the talents, but there was also the first sign of a movement that was to know, for a time, a brilliant fortune. The Communist leaders had stuck to their principle of war to the knife against all parties, especially the Socialists. But the Paris workers, even the Communists, had more sense than their leaders. They had no mind to imitate the Berlin Communists who had helped Hitler into power. The most popular leader of the Paris Communists, Jacques Doriot, was already in revolt against the imbecile leadership from Moscow that had led the workers to so many defeats. Against the demonstrations of the Right, there were demonstrations of the Left. The birth of the 'People's Front', of the 'Front Populaire', was beginning.

The Prime Minister began preaching to the country, using the new medium of the radio. He was no longer the jovial character he had been in the Elysée. He preached, now, like his Calvinist ancestors. Not all that he said was silly; but his manner recalled Grévy at his most pompous. The average parliamentarian, remembering the Prime Minister's past, was not impressed. His remedy for the weakness of the executive (in which he and others rightly saw the real cause of the immunity of people like Stavisky), the dissolution of Parliament, was regarded as deeply anti-Republican. Above all, popular discontent was moving away from the crimes of the crooks to the dangers to the Republic. For in the world of Hitler, Mussolini, Sanjurjo, Pilsudski it was easy to be fearful. Except in the United States, the drive, initiative, hope seemed to be on the Right. The Croix de Feu was now a mass body; it had its rivals like the Jeunesses Patriotes of Taittinger as well as old organizations like the Action Française. There were Bucard's Francistes with their palpable copying of Hitler; there were the well-financed if absurd mercenaries of M. Coty, the eminent perfumer. There were rumours of secret Right conspiracies like the famous 'hooded men', the Cagoulards. And there were unexplained mysteries enough in the backwash of the Stavisky affair, like the death of the magistrate Prince; enough odd outrages to make any theory plausible. The Communists at last were seeing the light. Even in Moscow, it was realized that a war to the death with the Socialists was suicidal in face of the growing power of Hitler.

The Fête Nationale of 1935 was the scene of a great reconciliation that recalled (as it was meant to) the Feast of the Federations of 1790. All the Left parties took part in the great procession from the Place de la Bastille to the Place de la République. It was far more impressive than the traditional military review of the 14th of July or of the procession of the Croix de Feu to the tomb of the Unknown Soldier under the Arc de Triomphe. A Roman might have cried *absit omen* as the great tricolour flag that floated over a collection of Socialist, Communist, and Radical politicians, split into two, blue and white on one side, red on the other. But for the moment, all was hope; the Republic was safe.

So was not France. There was no denying any longer that Hitler was in command. The Saar plebiscite had been an overwhelming triumph for the Third *Reich*. Socialists and Catholics voted, almost to a man, to return to Germany, any Germany. Germany was obviously re-arming. And Italy was asking a high price for staying in the Franco-British camp, if there was a Franco-British camp. For Britain, tactfully choosing the anniversary of Waterloo, had made a treaty with Nazi Germany that limited naval armaments but, by implication, left Germany free to arm to the teeth on land. All French eyes ought to have been turned to the east, but they were turned inwards, to the deepening financial and economic crisis. The peasant was hit at last by a collapse in agricultural prices that no Government juggling could conceal. Every traditional device was tried, including another appeal to the incomparable technical skill of M. Caillaux. But the one remedy, a devaluation of the franc, following the profitable Belgian example, was still taboo. Prices must be screwed down; the budget balanced; the franc 'saved'. The darkening of the economic sky hid the far more serious darkening of the diplomatic sky. Signor Mussolini was now determined to go ahead and liquidate the Abyssinian Empire. This seemed an eminently reasonable if risky operation to the new French Prime Minister, M. Pierre Laval.

The defenders of the franc were playing their last card. Laval was no technician but he was the most astute of politicians, cunning and confident in his cunning to an extent astonishing even in an Auvergnat. He found, to his disgust, that the British Government had suddenly developed a novel interest in the sanctity of treaties and in the sanctity of boundaries. To this absurd belief, they were willing to sacrifice the goodwill of the ruler of Italy and drive him into the German camp. M. Laval could not believe that the British Government really meant all the cant it talked. He was right, but the British people did not know this. The League of Nations was led to condemn Italy; mild sanctions were imposed; the British Foreign Secretary, Sir Samuel Hoare, and M. Laval drafted a compromise that would have preserved some kind of Abyssinian State. British public opinion would have none of it and Mussolini gave warning that real sanctions, sanctions that would impede the conquest of Abyssinia, meant war. So Abyssinia was conquered, quickly and easily, to the surprise of those who remembered Adowa. The western allies were divided for good.

Herr Hitler, disregarding the timid counsels of his generals, decided to test the courage of the French and the intelligence of the

English; both failed to meet the test. German troops entered the Rhineland, ending the only effective guarantee of peace. French generals passed the buck to the politicians, who passed it back again. To resist would have meant partial mobilization and look at how the Ruhr mobilization ruined the Bloc National! In England, it was simply acknowledged that 'Cologne is in Germany'. The most professionally intelligent were as silly as the most ignorant. Few were those who read in this decision the news:

'Venit summa dies et ineluctabile tempus.'

They were denounced as militarists and warmongers. Germany, it was said, would now settle down. In France, all thoughts were on the elections. M. Laval had been got rid of; the elections had to be made by someone less suspect. An attack on M. Blum by thugs of the Action Française reminded people of the recent dangers to the Republic. But the triumph of the 'Rassemblement Populaire' was due, far more than to anything else, to the snapping of the French patience with the drastic and ineffective remedies of deflation. It was, if the voters knew what they were voting for, a decision to devalue the franc. And it was a decision to replace the bogus Left majorities that had ended up by supporting M. Laval, with a real Left majority in which Radicals, Socialists, Communists would agree on a common policy, the defence of the Republic, of peace, of the poor against the Fascist leagues, Hitler, the interests of the 'two hundred families that ruled France'.

It was not an impossible or an extravagant programme. The best, perhaps the only, chance of safely resisting Hitler had been lost in March. The Belgians had seen the light. If the French would not defend their position in the Rhineland they were dangerous allies. So Belgium withdrew from her French alliance. It was an unfortunate decision, for the main French military effort had been put into building an elaborate chain of fortifications in Alsace called, after the War Minister who pushed the project through, the 'Maginot Line'. But the Maginot Line ended well short of the Belgian border and with Belgium and France no longer allies, the defensive systems of the two countries were no longer co-ordinated.

Whatever danger the Republic had been in was over; the French people were not converts to Fascist doctrines or practices; the defence of the poor required a strong and vigilant Government, neither doctrinaire nor timid. It required, too, a sharing of responsibility by all parties to the alliance. It was not enough that, for the first time, the Socialists were ready, as the biggest party in the victorious alliance, to lead the Government. It was necessary that the Communists should share, in office, the risks and responsibilities of action. They refused; they reserved to themselves the 'beau rôle' of combining the advantages of opposition and government. The trade union movement was reunited in conditions that gave the Communists grounds for thinking that they, not M. Jouhaux and his friends, would benefit most. All the claims of the workers could be pushed with zeal; the task of finding resources to meet them would be the job of M. Léon Blum, not of the handsome, confident, winning ex-miner who was the formal head of the French Communist party. No one knew, outside a very small Communist group, who gave orders to Maurice Thorez. Meantime, he was a more dramatic and popular figure than M. Léon Blum, the elegant lawyer, dramatic critic, debater who was the new Prime Minister.

From the first, Blum was swept along on a current he could not control. By refusing to devalue the franc at once, he merely ensured that his Government would not reap the profits that the unideological Belgians had secured. The profits were needed if the Government was to move freely. For it was hampered in other ways. The triumph of the 'Front Populaire' had released forces long held in check. The great demonstration of popular passion was the occupation of the great Paris factories, notably the big Renault plant, where the autocratic owner, Louis Renault, had shown a deep ignorance of the temper of his workers. No government, certainly no government of the 'Front Populaire', could have expelled the workers by force. The Government and the employers were forced to submit. The Matignon agreements (so called from the name of the Prime Minister's official residence) marked the momentary triumph of the workers. There was to be a forty-hour week; paid holidays; improved social services; but the Poincaré franc was still sacred. The air was full of hope. The class barriers that cut the French worker and still more the peasant off from higher education were to come down. French education, long starved, was to be lavishly sub-sidized; the work of Renan as well as of Pasteur was to be continued.

Now the backwardness of French economics had to be paid for. France was not suffering from unemployment but from under-production. For this the forty-hour week was no answer. France was impoverished by the deflationary policies of the previous Parliament, but the new policies did not directly enrich her. There was some justice in Caillaux's gibe; this was 'a new deal for Lilliput'. The French economy was not insulated from the outside world and, by a currency agreement with the United States and Britain, the franc was at last devalued, at a rate that brought prices in France into something like equilibrium with those of the outside world. Of course, the new value of the franc was declared to be permanent. Had the conversion come earlier, this promise might have been kept, but the devaluation came too late. Then a great external event profoundly embarrassed the French Government. Civil war broke out in Spain.

It was a sign of the times that it was impossible to get any measure of agreement as to what was happening in a country within a not very long journey from Paris. To the supporters of the Blum Government, all was simple. Another government of a 'People's Front', duly elected to make the new Spanish Republic a liberating force, had been attacked by a conspiracy of generals, Jesuits, Monarchists, aided by heathen Moors and then by Italian Fascists and German Nazis. On the other side, a proud, Christian people, momentarily misled by mischievous propaganda, had revolted against a feeble Government, incapable of preserving order and in momentary danger of passing completely under the control of the Russian Government. To one group, the danger to France of a 'Fascist' triumph was obvious and terrible; to another group the danger to France from a Communist Spain was immediate and terrifying.

Soon there came out of Spain news, only too authentic, of horrible crimes committed by the partisans on both sides. Spanish civil war was taking its accustomed course. But the French, like the English, like the rest of the world, refused to see, in the Spanish Civil War, mainly or merely a Spanish Civil War. (It was over a generation since Spain had had a civil war.) Spain was a symbol; a symbol of the unending and hitherto totally successful aggression of 'Fascism'. For the lesson of armed revolution seemed to have been better learned on the Right than on the Left. The survival of the Spanish Republic was an emotional more than a material necessity. Volunteers poured into Spain on both sides. But the 'volunteers' from Italy and Germany were, like the small groups of Russian technicians, agents of their Governments. The French (and British) volunteers of the International Brigades were the modern representatives of the Philhellenes of a century before. Of course, France sent people quite unlike M. André Malraux. There, in Spain, as a ruthless agent of Russian policy, was the former 'hero of the Black Sea', André Marty, displaying all the confident savagery of a 'representative on mission' of 1793. There were crooks and adventurers but, when all is said and done, the devotion of much of the Left to the cause of the Spanish 'Loyalists' was genuine. (The term was significant of the weakness of the Left all over Europe, of its need for legitimacy.)

The Blum Government could not afford to gratify that passion, for it was absolutely necessary to stay close to Britain, and the British Government was committed to a policy of non-intervention. That this policy helped the 'Nationalists' more than the 'Loyalists' is true; that it decisively affected the course of the war is far from certain; that it broke the heart of the Blum Government cannot be doubted. For the hopes and faith of the summer of 1936 were dying. The Blum 'new deal' did not solve the French economic problem, the stagnation of production was in humiliating contrast with the rapid and ominous expansion of Germany's economic and military power. The great Paris exhibition of 1937 underlined the contrast. For when it opened, the exhibition was very far indeed from being finished, and while French workmen dawdled over the French pavilions, the Russian and German pavilions were finished and ominously alike.

The Russian pavilion was also the object of malicious curiosity for, day by day, more and more of the Russian leaders whose pictures had adorned the pavilion were denounced by the Soviet Government as traitors. It was difficult to decide which was the more terrible alternative, that the Russian Government was telling the truth or lying. Either way it was probably a matter for rejoicing that the alliance made with the Soviet Union, by M. Laval, had not been followed up by implementing military conventions.

Yet, the Soviet alliance was so obviously a necessity! More countries than Belgium had read the handwriting on the wall that the acceptance of the occupation of the Rhineland signified. Already, Pilsudski's Poland had decided that France was an unreliable ally. The assassination, in 1934, of King Alexander of Yugoslavia in Marseilles had deprived France of her most loyal Balkan ally. Rumania was going Fascist. Only Czechoslovakia was indisputably loyal. Italian impudence grew. The conquerors of Abyssinia demanded Tunis, Nice, Corsica, Savoy, Jibuti as the price of forbearance.

Compared with Mussolini, Hitler was tactful. He demanded only the withdrawal of France from her alliances in central and eastern Europe. Some Frenchmen thought that there was a good deal to be said for that policy. The die was cast; the position established at Versailles had been lost. Why pay attention to English protests? Was not England the chief underminer of the Versailles settlement? Was it not better to deal with a frank enemy than with a shifty ally? The British Government did nothing to make these arguments, insinuated by many skilled, tactful and, in some cases, honest propagandists, less plausible. Pierre Laval, in exile from power, repeated them and suggested, too, that the Duce could be won over. And the élan of the 'Front Populaire' was broken for ever.

The Blum Government, like every other Left Government, was in retreat before the powers of high finance or, to put it more candidly, before the fact that no French Government was now strong enough to impose any bold policy in any field, above all in the field of public finance. Parliament had acquired the incurable habit of overthrowing Governments, making a consistent policy impossible, then abdicating its powers into the hands of a Minister or Ministers who would carry out the necessary if politically dangerous retreats. The French Left always learned, roughly two years after the general elections, that for the rest of the life of that Parliament, power would rest with the Right. The voter was cheated; it is not quite so certain that he was deceived, that he was ready for the risks of a bold Left policy. Blum announced a 'pause'. But the Senate refused M. Blum the 'full powers' he asked for. The end was in sight. From that point until the outbreak of war, the old pattern was repeated. Ministries came and went. M. Blum served in subordinate capacities; then there was a Radical Government with no Socialists in it. It was headed by M. Chautemps who found it convenient to be out of office when Hitler occupied Austria. War was seen to be inevitable by all but the most blind or the most servile. In vain M. Blum tried to form a Government in which both Communists and the Right would serve. He failed and, with his failure, the hollow pretence of the continuation of the 'Front Populaire' ended. The effects of the failure went deep.

The shock especially benefited the Communists. It could be argued that they, by their playing of a lone hand, had been one of the chief architects of defeat. But they had avoided direct responsibility for the defeat of the great, hopeful experiment of 1936. Its failure seemed to show that, basically, the Communists had been right, that the profound alterations in French society, in which so many millions had believed, were impossible under the current conditions of French political life. The lesson seemed plain; Left majorities in 1924, 1932, 1936 had uniformly resulted in right-of-centre Governments in 1926, 1934, 1938. The Soviet Government was seen, innocently, as the only defender of the Spanish Republic, of peace, of freedom, openly attacked in Berlin and Rome, shabbily betrayed in London and Paris. The United States was too far away, too strange, too little known in France (no country in western Europe had less knowledge of America) to serve as a comforting example. Franklin D. Roosevelt suffered as a world figure by being associated with Chamberlain and Chautemps.

True, the news out of Russia continued to be troubling. In the 'thirties, in France as elsewhere, eminent literary figures had made their pilgrimage to Moscow in the flesh or in the spirit. Shaw, the Webbs, O'Casey, Dreiser had been answered according to their folly. In France, the conversion of the most admired, fastidious, elegant representative of bourgeois culture, André Gide, was a great event. So was his disillusionment with the servility and adulation that he found in Soviet society. But many who imitated Gide had not his candour or fundamental scepticism.

French cultural traditions pleaded for complete, absolute solutions. For generations, it was the mark of the enlightened man to despise the bourgeois. The most talented sons of the condemned society were the most acrid critics of the order that had produced them. Who could admire or wish to die for the bourgeois order described by François Mauriac or defended by the smug apologists of 'the trusts'? Selfish, timid, conformist, condemned by history, this class provoked the old war-cry, 'Écrasez l'infâme'. And the Communists showed skill in persuading some naïve Catholics that the infamous thing was now not the Church, but the class society in which it was dangerously embedded. To others, the Russian Revolution was the triumph of the great movement launched in 1789. It was imperfect, bloody; but, repeating Barnave, many intellectuals asked, 'and was this blood so pure?' They swallowed all; trials, confessions, the remaking of history, the new scholastic or rabbinical reason that called for a new Rabelais, the casuistry that called for a new Pascal. Many joined the Party; after Tzara, Stalin. Others hung round its edges like so many wistful agnostics of the past century praying, 'Aid thou mine unbelief'. Pride, intelligence, surviving bourgeois scruples about objective truth, reasonable doubts about the worth of some of the most zealous converts, kept many of the ablest and most honest of the young from abandoning to the Communist party what Lenin had demanded of the old Bolsheviks, 'the whole of their lives'. But the faith of the faithful was envied, that faith to be described by the martyred Gabriel Péri, faith in 'a future full of song'. That faith and that obedience was beyond them; they could only stand:

'tendebantque manus ripae ulterioris amore'.

They were moved less by love of the Soviet Union than by love for and faith in the French workers. Born in bourgeois society, serving it in often frustrating forms, finding 'que la vie est quotidienne' in Le Havre as it had been for Laforgue in Berlin or Baden-Baden, they idealized 'the People'. They did not ask themselves, any more than that bourgeois prophet, Georges Sorel, had done, whether the French workers, divided, ill-disciplined, bemused by the idea of 'Revolution', with a capital letter, in a manner deplored by Lenin, sharing in the backwardness, in the current technical world, of French bourgeois society, incurably petty bourgeois in so many of their tastes, were really ready for the task to which 'History' had called them. The People, the new St. Augustine, the child of so much love, could not be lost and all judgements, all programmes, must be subjected to the test, Did they suit the passions, the prejudices of the industrial workers? So, like the characters of Sartre's novel, they re-visited the Rue Royale or other streets in the smart districts, as foreigners, as invaders.

The bourgeoisie, which bought the novels and saw the plays its rebellious sons produced, was angered by the defeats of 1936. The nationalization of the railways, even of the Bank of France, were not triumphs for the enemies of society. They were a necessary conces-sion, a necessary abandonment of ballast. But for many of the possess-ing classes, the social question was not acute. France was still 'France la doulce', tormented by agitators. It was easy to imitate M. Jacques Chardonne, to recall 'the happiness of Barbézieux', and neglect the fact that that happiness was not universally shared in Barbézieux and was unknown in Bobigny. It was easy, too, to write off the experiment of the 'Front Populaire' as a total and inevitable failure, the natural result of trusting unpractical men, mere talkers, 'princes of the Clouds' as Maurras had put it—and to attach excessive impor-tance to the pardon given by the Pope to Maurras and Daudet after they had gone to Canossa.

But the plans of the 'Front Populaire' were not all worthy of Cloud-Cuckoo Land; the dreamers were, in some things, better realists than the practical men. For Léon Blum had seen that the principles of '89 could not be kept in cold storage in Algiers and in Hanoi, that neither the rich planters, 'the colons', nor the poor white settlers could continue to monopolize, overseas, the full rights of the city. He had seen that the problems of the Empire were at a stage at which mere economic progress, even had its results been evenly divided, was not enough, that France must come to terms with nascent nationalism in Syria, in North Africa, in Indo-China where the proximity of China and the continuance of the Chinese Revolution threatened French authority.

A mutiny in Indo-China in 1931 had been a sign no bigger than a man's hand. The Socialists had noticed it; no one else had. No one else now cared to think out the problems of the Empire. It was, indeed, the eleventh hour. With Austria swallowed, Hitler turned to

Czechoslovakia. This was the test case. Here was France's last ally. But the responsibility of dealing with the problem was transferred to the confident English Prime Minister. At Munich, the first stages in the dismemberment of the Republic, founded so confidently twenty years before, were completed. There was an outburst of relief and gratitude in France of which the new Prime Minister, M. Daladier, was capable of being ashamed. Pacificist sentiment, natural enough in a country that had suffered so much and had, so soon, found victory so barren, flourished, especially among those quondam preachers of Republican patriotism, the elementary-school masters. Even the belligerent patriotism of many of the workers seemed more an aspect of their loyalty to the Communist party rather than to France. Many of the old traditional patriotic groups were almost as devoted to the star of Mussolini as to the old, unquestioning devotion to the simple, narrowly conceived interests of France.

On the material side, the situation was not brilliant. For nearly twenty years peace had been assumed to be secure. The military policy of the General Staff was impregnated with the cautious, defensive, thrifty doctrines of Marshal Pétain. Fewer and fewer young men of ability entered the Army as regular officers. The only original military thinker produced by the French Army during this period, Colonel de Gaulle, would have been kept from all promotion but for the intervention of M. Daladier, who was the nearly permanent War Minister. The Air Force, once dominant, was short of aeroplanes and commanded by unintelligent, routine-minded officers. Only the Navy, under Admiral Darlan, was fit for the ordeal that was coming.

Above all, the political preparation for crisis was lacking. The Daladier Government, after Munich, rightly attacked the forty-hour week. This was a luxury France could not afford any longer. But it was a symbol of the brief hopes and triumphs of 1936. The unions tried to resist by a strike; they were easily defeated. But nothing was done to make the Government's victory appear as a victory for France, not as a victory of the French employers over the French workers. Hitler took over what was left of Czechoslovakia. The Spanish Republic died; Britain still took the initiative in negotiating with Germany, in guaranteeing Poland, in negotiating with the Soviet Union. As long as Russia continued to preach the union of the 'democracies' against the Fascist powers, the failure to win over the workers was thought not to matter. The second devaluation of the franc had underlined the instability of the economy. The bourgeoisie were not given many reasons to be content, except that the workers had been taught their place. If the double devaluation relieved some peasants, it bred fresh distrust in others.

That war was coming few could doubt. It was feared for itself, not because it might bring defeat. Against the hastily created Reichswehr would be ranged, so it was thought, the mass of the Red Army and the power of the French Army commanded and trained by the victorious generals of the great war, based on the impregnable Maginot Line, reinforced by a British Army being rapidly increased in numbers, by a Navy overwhelmingly strong, by an Air Force that would supply defects from which, it was rightly feared, the French Air Force suffered. Even if Italy, so easily victorious over the semi-savage Abyssinians, joined Germany, the preponderance of power was all on one side, that of the pacific 'democracies' of which the Soviet Union was one. The loss of the Bohemian bastion was serious; but the Polish Army was numerous, brave, and was being strengthened by British and French money and arms. 'Nothing was lacking', as General Weygand was to say in one of those defensible but unforgettable phrases that predict disaster.

If war came it would be a war not fought rashly, in the reckless and self-destructive fashion of 1914. The Commander-in-Chief, General Gamelin, had learned his business under Joffre and so had learned the lessons of Morhange and Charleroi. War would be unpopular, wasteful, but not dangerous. For both the British and French Governments were far more clear about the kind of war that they would not fight, than about the kind of war they would fight. Moreover they hoped, up to the last minute, to avoid war. Surely Hitler would not rush on destruction, surely he would halt to digest his spoils? Out of what was, for the man in the street, a clear sky, came the thunderbolt of the agreement between the Soviet Union and the Third *Reich*. Hitler was relieved of the nightmare of a war on two fronts, that is of his main reason for fearing war. Unless the two western allies gave way and abandoned Poland as they had abandoned Czechoslovakia, war was certain. There were in London and

Paris, but especially in Paris, men ready to abandon Poland, but no British Government could repeat Munich and the hesitant Government of M. Daladier was dragged after the suddenly resolute Government of Mr. Chamberlain. On September 3, 1939, France followed Britain into war with Germany.

Slowly, the French Army advanced on the edges of the Siegfried Line, leaving the Reichswehr free to annihilate Poland in a campaign whose true character the complacent French High Command failed to study and whose lessons were ignored. There were good weapons but too few of them; there were independent officers but they were frowned on. Under a cover of superficial culture and military sophistication, there was concealed from the French people (but not from the German High Command) a deadly spirit of routine and of intellectual complacency. The army of the Marne and of Verdun, it was thought, had nothing to fear. On its impregnable defensive position the Germans would break their teeth—if they were foolish enough to attack.

The Germans did not attack. Both sides limited themselves to a war of light skirmishing and Britain and France slowly, with no great sense of urgency, began to accumulate supplies and to prepare for action in some remote time, building, in the meanwhile, trench systems and strong-points that prolonged the impregnable Maginot Line. It was what exigent American critics, determined to be spectators only, contemptuously called 'the phoney war'. But the repeal of the Neutrality Act opened the immense resources of American industry to Britain and France. They could have all the weapons they could pay for and, in addition, a great deal of genuine if not immediately utilizable sympathy. This was to be an eighteenth-century war, economical of life, lavish of money, perhaps to be ended by some happy compromise or a palace revolution in Berlin or Moscow. That the kind of war that was to be fought would not be decided by the pacific and still somnolent democracies was not anticipated. If the morale of the French Army was declining, it was because it had nothing to do and there were fears that the Germans would sit it out behind *their* impregnable lines, that the main difficulty of the Allies would be to find a battlefield when they were ready to give the final blow. Meantime it was inadvisable to overstrain an economy half paralysed by a general mobilization, suffered rather than welcomed by an increasingly sullen people.

As the war drew visibly nearer, the French Government was, so it thought, free from one of the anxieties that had superfluously worried the Government of 1914. This time there could be no doubt of the devotion of the workers to the cause that, however reluctantly, the French Republic was about to defend. For the party of the workers had adopted as its own all the heroes of the French past, from Vercingetorix and St. Joan to the *grognards* of Napoleon and the *poilus* of Verdun. This would more than offset the pacificism of such bodies as the elementary-school teachers or of so many of the Socialist spokesmen. Against Fascism, the French workers would stand firm.

It was decided otherwise. The news of the Ribbentrop-Molotov pact struck the French Communist leaders dumb or, rather, it left them still mouthing the patriotic slogans that had been the Party warcry even after the 'Workers' Fatherland' had made its compact with the Devil.

The Government of M. Daladier, foolishly, suppressed the Communist Press whose last issues had still promised the loyalty of the workers to the good cause. The leaders of the French workers were thus saved the difficult and humiliating job of explaining their retreat from the war, their treasonable docility. Maurice Thorez, called up for military service, was smuggled off to Russia. It was a successful flight to Varennes, and Moscow became the Coblenz of the new emigration. Not all Communist leaders followed this ignominious course. Some stuck by their country and condemned the change of front. These, unless (like M. Joliot-Curie) they were so eminent and useful that they had to be spared, were never forgiven.

The Soviet invasion of Poland ended all equivocation. The French Communist party now advocated the appeasement of Hitler, the acceptance of the new Tilsit. As the 'phoney' war dragged on, the mask was dropped. The clandestine Communist Press, the clandestine Communist organizations were employed to break the patriotic will of the French worker, to convince him that his enemies were at home, not in Germany. Not since the wars of religion had traitors worked with such good conscience. Their work was not ineffective and their chances of success were increased by the stupidity of the Government and the worse than stupidity of many 'conservative' forces. There were plenty of rank-and-file Communists whose consciences, good sense, common decency made them nauseated with the new Party line. Nothing was done to win them over. Their old pacificist enemies on the Left were delighted to score over them; their old class enemies on the Right were glad to insist that the true character of the social movement of the 'Front Populaire' had been revealed. The new managers of *Le Temps* had no patience, now, with those attacks on the absolute rights of property that had marked 1936 and 1937. The hesitant and conscience-stricken were not allowed quietly to abandon the Party. They were to be pursued like Jansenists in the eighteenth century, to be forced to renounce, publicly, their recent past or to accept, sullenly, the arguments and the authority of the most effective French allies of Hitler, the Communist leaders. Their 'honour rooted in dishonour stood', but no easy way out of their dilemma was made open to them. Nor was the conduct of the war such as to force on them a total reconsideration of their position. France and Britian had let Poland be crushed with hardly a minimal effort to help their ally. The Russian invasion of Finland, if it swept away the last pretences about the character of the Soviet policy, gave a welcome opportunity to many elements in France to make the war against Hitler also a war against Stalin, a policy that had much moral and intellectual justification but was political folly.

Although the sudden end of the Finnish war saved France and Britain from this suicidal policy, serious damage had been done, The workers were sullen and more and more alienated. The 'Confédération Générale du Travail', purged of its treasonable Communist leadership, was an anaemic shadow of the militant organization of 1936. Even if the labour policy of the Government had been more ingenious and more vigorously pursued, the fact remained that a large part of the most active trade union leaders, in all ranks of the trade unions, had been Communists. They were now silent, or imprisoned, or working secretly to weaken the Government that was waging 'the imperialist war'. But there was no great revolutionary movement. The decline in trade union zeal that the failure of the general strike of 1938 had revealed, continued. (The metal workers' union that had had 600,000 members in 1937, had 30,000 in May 1940.) The French worker was sullen, disorientated, exiled.

Meantime, there was no action to stir the hearts or imagination of the people. It was asserted, over and over again, that France and Britain would win because they were stronger, that the victory would be won not by feats of arms but by economic pressure, by the slow accumulation of superior resources. It was not a kind of war to appeal to the French temperament nor one for which the French economy and social system were well designed. There was pressure to do *something* and the decision was taken to cut off the iron ore supplies that the Germans brought down the covered way of Norwegian coastal waters.

The authority of the Prime Minister, M. Daladier, was contested, by advocates of a more vigorous policy whose spokesman was M. Paul Reynaud, and by the spokesmen of a deal, of a liquidation of a war that seemed to have less and less purpose. The prudent refusal of Mussolini to join his German ally at the outbreak of war in 1939 had fanned hope in the breasts of politicians like M. Pierre Laval who prided himself on his special links with the Duce and saw himself as the new Talleyrand who would end the adventure.

But the adventure was changing character. The German's response to the threat to the iron ore supply (or to the chance that the foolhardy policy of cutting it off gave them) was a lightning invasion of Denmark and Norway that not only soon succeeded, but which, to many Frenchmen, revealed the serious limitations of that British sea power on which such hopes had been placed. Like the Dardanelles campaign it was a failure—and not even a glorious failure. Daladier gave way to Reynaud and the new Prime Minister pondered the question of removing the torpid and complacent Commander-in-Chief, General Gamelin.

But the Führer struck. On May 10, the Germans swept into Holland and Belgium. The French and British Armies, sucked north by the attack, were in a day or two driven out of Holland, and, on May 17, at Sedan, the Germans burst through the weakest spot in the French line and what had not been achieved in 1914 or 1918 was achieved in 1940. The British and Belgian Armies and nearly all the French armour were cut off from the main French forces and from the garrisons of the Maginot Line. King Leopold III of the Belgians surrendered his army and himself. Gamelin was replaced by Weygand but even more quickly than in 1870, the formal, professional war was over. Pinned up in Dunkirk, the British Army (and masses of French troops) were evacuated in one of those heroic and necessary retreats that British tradition rejoices in, but which Continental allies see in so different a light. The British would come back, but when?

All the internal strains had to be paid for. The Communist leadership rejoiced in the defeat of the class enemy, the French bourgeoisie. The German workers, it was mendaciously asserted, would deal with Hitler, and under the kindly patronage of the Soviet Union, the French workers would end the foreign and win the domestic war. How much of this nonsense was believed it is impossible to say. Twenty years of lies had no doubt befuddled many minds. All that the Communist programme offered, in form, was the chance of another and more disastrous Commune. What it offered in fact was the placation of Hitler by his quasi-ally, Stalin.

The treasonable nonsense on the Left encouraged further illusions on the Right. The traditional Anglophobia of the Right was given free play. So were the illusions about Italy. Some saw in the Duce what the Communists professed to see in Stalin, the mediator who would save France from the results of her follies and her sins.

And all the while, the refugees poured in their millions along the roads, cumbering the route of the retreating armies, sharing in a mutual demoralization. The political leaders were swept away like flotsam. In vain, the new British Prime Minister, Mr. Churchill, strove to give to the French Ministers some of his own courage, energy and authority. They were no more capable of responding to the crisis than Neville Chamberlain had been. Even the most militant of them, like M. Reynaud, lacked authority. That lay, if anywhere, in the symbolic figure of Marshal Pétain, recalled from the Madrid Embassy to give to the tottering regime a simulacrum of authority. The Marshal, a pessimist in 1918, was a pessimist and, what was more dangerous, a moralist in 1940. France was both defeated and guilty—or rather the politicians were guilty. Like the new and despairing Commander-in-Chief, Weygand, Pétain had no hope of victory and had a genuine fear of civil war. If the Communists were not liars, the danger of a suicidal revolt was real and the decision to prevent a new Commune was not unpatriotic. It was foolish, since it was based on a belief, real or affected, in the reality of Communist threats.

As the Government trailed away from Paris to Tours (as in 1870), to Bordeaux (as in 1870 and 1914), the Anglo-French alliance began to fall apart. By a decision, totally justified however harsh, the new British Prime Minister refused to commit his last trump card, the fighter squadrons of the R.A.F., to a fruitless battle in France. That would have been magnificent but not war. The decision was approved by the officer, newly made a general, whom Reynaud had called back to aid him in his desperate plight. Then, for the first time, the eye of Winston Churchill fell on Charles de Gaulle.

Round the Marshal crowded all the faint-hearted, all the tepid, all the born intriguers. M. Camille Chautemps, accepting more responsibility than had been his wont, worked for surrender. Pierre Laval waited for his day. Mussolini at last took the jackal's plunge. Paris passed peacefully into German hands. The militant workers were sullen and silent.

Projects of resistance overseas were debated. The Government (including the President of the Republic) prepared to move to North Africa. There, sheltered by British and French sea power, the reconquest of France could be planned. From across the Atlantic came brave words, all that the head of a suddenly alarmed people dared offer. Some Deputies started for Morocco. But the forces of surrender were too strong. An armistice was asked for and disdainfully granted by the exultant Führer. The decision was entirely his; there was no power of resistance in metropolitan France any longer. And it was Hitler's calculation that some show of magnanimity would pay him, would dissolve the last remnants of combative will of the rulers of the French State and the French Army.

There was not much will left to dissolve. What avail had sea power been in the Norwegian campaign? How long could Britain, even worse prepared for war than France, hold out? What weight could be given to American encouragement coming from a people clinging, in desperation, to its threatened immunity? The very ferocity of the German rulers helped them. It was no light matter to incur, for

France, the fate of Poland. And over all these calculations, humane, fearful, base, patriotic, Marshal Pétain cast the aegis of his authority. There was none other in France. The Marshal took command on June 17. On June 18, anniversary of Waterloo, he was answered from London by the almost unknown General de Gaulle. 'This war is a world war. All the mistakes, all the delays, all the hardships, do not prevent there being in the world all the means necessary one day to destroy our enemies. . . . Whatever happens, the flame of French resistance must not be put out, will not be put out.' The great word was given, but few heard it and fewer believed it. And many of the few who heard and obeyed had little or no faith in victory; they only knew where honour lay and decided, like the officers before Waterloo, to fight 'without fear and without hope'.

More than the war was to be liquidated. The two Chambers, united in a 'National Assembly', met at Vichy. On July 10, the Assembly transferred its powers (including the constituent power) to Marshal Pétain. Some respect was paid to form. The Chambers did not dissolve themselves, neither Deputies nor Senators lost their status nor their salaries. They behaved like the Senate of Napoleon I with Pétain as the new Louis XVIII and Pierre Laval as the new Talleyrand. On July 11, Marshal Pétain abolished the office of President of the Republic and named himself 'Head of the French State'. Against this abdication by the National Assembly, eight Deputies and Senators had found the courage to protest. But, for the moment, there was no doubt that the French people, shocked into something like a coma, had condemned the Third Republic as completely as it had condemned the Bourgeois Monarchy. Indeed, even that regime did not die as ingloriously.

The motto of Mary Queen of Scots could well have been the motto of the Third Republic. 'In my end is my beginning.' Born of military defeat at Sedan in 1870, it died of military defeat at Sedan in 1940. It died almost as quickly and at least as ignominiously as the Second Empire. It had survived, victoriously, one great and catastrophic war and it had not enough energy, courage, confidence to survive another. In part it failed because the French people, faced with the fact of catastrophic defeat, had not only, for the moment, no faith in victory, but no belief that victory, if it was still possible, was worth having at the immense price that would have to be paid for it. The generations that ruled in 1940 had known victory, had learned how little, in itself, it meant except the avoidance of defeat. (They were to learn the price of not avoiding it). Was France again to know the torments of 1914–18 to no better end than the peace of 1919–39? What fate condemned the nation, twice in one generation, to such ordeals? So a French scholar put the question in the hour of defeat.

> 'Nec fuit indignum superis, bis sanguine nostro
> Emathiam et latos Haemi pinguescere campos
> . . . Satis jam pridem sanguine nostro
> Laomedonteae luimus periuria Troiae.'

The sins of the nation, such as they were, were to be terribly expiated. So were weaknesses that were the price of the earlier victory, above all the terrible bloodletting of the first war. But if the French people failed to rally as they had done after the first Sedan, after the first defeats of 1914, it was in great part because the French State had abdicated authority, had evaded decision, had organized its political life to penalize and, indeed, prevent greatness. The Third Republic that had, in one mood, preferred Deschanel to Clemenceau, in another Doumer to Briand, that had erected evasion of responsibility into a system of government, was incapable of calling out the reserves of faith and courage that, the event proved, still existed. The generals despaired as easily as in 1870, but there was now no Gambetta in reserve. Desperately wounded on the battlefield, the Third Republic committed suicide, condemned itself as no previous regime had done. It had lasted longer than any other of the regimes that the Revolutionary crisis had bred, lasted because it had no doctrine. Now it had no living principles. Again and again, since the happy days of 1789, the French people had been told that the promise of the deputies assembled in the Tennis Court, to give France a constitution, was fulfilled. That promise was again shown to be false, the hopes it bred again betrayed. A people which, in one hundred and fifty years, had astonished the world in every field of achievement, which had known every form of glory, in war, in sanctity, in all the arts and sciences, had yet failed to find institutions that united the French people and gave them a political way of life worthy of their genius, their courage, their legitimate hopes. Possibly the historian is wise to content himself with echoing the philosopher and not being either disappointed or surprised. 'The world is the best of all possible worlds, and everything in it is a necessary evil.'

INDEX

305